RICHMOND BARRACKS 1916
We Were There
77 Women of the Easter Rising

\E FHINE G/`
'RARIES

RICHMOND BARRACKS 1916
We Were There
77 Women of the Easter Rising

Mary McAuliffe and Liz Gillis

DUBLIN CITY COUNCIL 2016

Decade of Commemorations Publications Series

First Published 2016 by
Dublin City Council
c/o Dublin City Library and Archive
138–144 Pearse Street
Dublin 2

www.dublincity.ie/decadeofcommemorations

Comhairle Cathrach
Bhaile Átha Cliath
Dublin City Council

Text © the contributors 2016
Concept © Dublin City Public Libraries and Archives

Designed by Source Design
Cover Design by Eibhlín Ní Chléirigh

Printed by The Printed Image

ISBN – 978-1-907002-32-8

77 Women of the Easter Rising

1. Kathleen 'Katie' Barrett (*née Connolly*)
2. Bridget 'Brigid' Brady (*later Murphy*)
3. Kathleen Browne
4. Martha Browne
5. Eileen Byrne
6. Katie Byrne
7. Mary 'May' Byrne (*later Doyle*)
8. Winifred 'Winnie' Carney (*later McBride*)
9. Máire (*Mary/May/Meg/Maura*) Carron
10. Annie Cooney (*later O'Brien*)
11. Elizabeth 'Lily' Cooney (*later Curran*)
12. Eileen Cooney (*later Harbourne*)
13. Marcella Cosgrove
14. Bridget Davis (*later O'Duffy*)
15. Ellen 'Nellie' Ennis (*later Costigan*)
16. Madeleine ffrench-Mullen
17. Kathleen 'Kitty' Fleming
18. Brigid 'Bríd/Bridget' Foley (*later Martin*)
19. Mary 'May' Gahan (*later O'Carroll*)
20. Helen 'Nellie' Gifford (*later Donnelly*)
21. Bridget 'Bridie' Goff
22. Julia (*Sheila/Sighle*) Grenan
23. Roseanna 'Rosie' Hackett
24. Bridget Hegarty (*later Harmon*)
25. Anne 'Annie' Higgins/O'Higgins
26. Ellen 'Nell' Humphreys (*née O'Rahilly*)
27. Margaret 'Maggie' Joyce
28. Catherine 'Katie' Kelly
29. Josephine Kelly (*later Greene*)
30. Martha Kelly (*later Murphy*)
31. Margaret 'Loo' Kennedy
32. Bridy Kenny
33. Catherine 'Katie' Liston
34. Mary Liston
35. Elizabeth 'Bessie' Lynch (*later Kelly*)
36. Kathleen Lynn
37. Brigid Lyons (*later Lyons Thornton*)
38. Agnes MacNamee/McNamee
39. Kathleen 'Katie' Maher
40. Constance Markievicz (*née Gore-Booth*)
41. Bríd S. Martin
42. Kathleen 'Kate' Martin
43. Julia McCauley
44. Josephine 'Josie' McGowan
45. Margaret 'Maggie' McLoughlin
46. Rose McNamara
47. Florence 'Flossie' Meade (*later Griffin*)
48. Caroline 'Carrie' Mitchell (*later McLoughlin*)
49. Helena Molony
50. Pauline Morkan (*later Keating*)
51. Elizabeth 'Lizzie' Mulhall
52. Roseanna 'Rose' Mullally (*later Farrelly*)
53. Kathleen Murphy
54. Bridget Murtagh (*later O'Daly*)
55. Annie Norgrove (*later Grange*)
56. Emily Norgrove (*later Hanratty*)
57. Lily O'Brennan
58. Nora O'Daly (*née Gillies*)
59. Margaret 'Cissie' O'Flaherty (*later Timmons*)
60. Sheila O'Hanlon (*later Lynch*)
61. Emily O'Keeffe/O'Keefe (*later Hendley*)
62. Josephine 'Josie' O'Keeffe/O'Keefe (*later McNamara*)
63. May O'Moore (*later Wisely*)
64. Louisa O'Sullivan (*later Pollard*)
65. Mary O'Sullivan (*later O'Carroll*)
66. Mary Partridge (*née Hamilton*)
67. May 'Mary'/'May' Perolz (*later Flanagan*)
68. Countess Mary Josephine Plunkett (*née Cranny*)
69. Maria Quigley (*later Clince*)
70. Priscilla 'Sheila' Quigley (*later Kavanagh*)
71. Barbara Retz/Reitz
72. Catherine 'Kathleen' Ryan (*later Treston*)
73. Ellen Mary 'Nell' Ryan
74. Mary Kate 'Kit' Ryan ((*later O'Kelly/Ó'Ceallaigh*))
75. Kathleen 'Catherine' Seery (*later Redmond*)
76. Jane 'Jinny' Shanahan
77. Josephine (Spicer) Spencer

Contents

FOREWORD

—

The walls of any military barracks resonate with the stories of those who have marched through its squares and none more so than Richmond Barracks in Inchicore, Dublin. The courts-martial of the leaders of the 1916 Rising took place here and because of its size, the Barracks was also used as a holding place for all the insurgents arrested after the surrender on 29 April 1916. Among those arrested were seventy-seven women, incarcerated in the married quarters of Richmond Barracks on the night of 30 April 1916 before being moved to nearby Kilmainham Gaol. Each one of these seventy-seven women was arrested for her involvement in the fighting of Easter week 1916. Now this book tells the stories of each of these women, from their initial politicisation before 1916 through to their role in the Rising and their lives post-Rising and post-Independence. *Richmond Barracks 1916: We Were There – 77 Women of the Easter Rising* is a welcome addition to the growing body of research and writing on the women of the 1916 Rising, uncovering and remembering their role in this pivotal event in Ireland's history. Their contribution may have been forgotten for too long, but now we can read about their commitment and courage as they stood alongside their male comrades in the cause of Irish freedom.

Is mór mar a chuireann *Richmond Barracks 1916: We Were There – 77 Women of the Easter Rising* leis an taighde agus scríbhneoireacht ar mhná Éirí Amach 1916, taighde agus scríbhneoireacht atá ag fás an t-am ar fad agus atá ag tabhairt chun cuimhne ról na mban san imeacht ríthábhactach seo i stair na hÉireann. Ligeadh i ndearmad ar feadh rófhada an méid a rinne siad, ach anois is féidir linn léamh faoina dtiomantas agus faoina misneach agus iad sa bhearna bhaoil in aice lena gcomrádaithe fir ar son shaoirse na hÉireann.

Críona Ní Dhálaigh
Ardmhéara Bhaile Átha Cliath
Lord Mayor of Dublin

RICHMOND BARRACKS

———

Arguably one of the most exciting and anticipated events of the 2016 celebrations is the opening of Richmond Barracks at Inchicore, Dublin 8. A place of huge significance to our national story, though nearly lost in the collective memory, the Barracks was elevated to one of the State's 'permanent reminder' 1916 projects because its buildings were a key site for many significant events in Ireland's history and are of particular importance to the period around 1916.

The leaders of the 1916 Rising were interned here and court-martialled in the Barracks before being transferred to Kilmainham Gaol. Over 3,000 insurgents, including seventy-seven women, were held in the Barracks in the immediate aftermath of the Easter Rising. It was also from here that soldiers, including the poet Francis Ledwidge, were sent to fight in the First World War. After Independence the Barracks became Keogh Square where many families lived and a school, St. Michael's CBS, was established here in 1929.

For many years the Inchicore Kilmainham Heritage Group has 'held a candle' for the buildings still remaining at Richmond Barracks. Working together as part of the locally based Richmond Barracks Advisory Committee with Dublin City Council we have realised this significant heritage project scheduled to be unveiled on 2 May 2016.

The redeveloped Richmond Barracks will tell the story of those who have lived and worked for Ireland over the past two hundred years. Visitors will be invited to step back in time to experience the varied and interesting history of Richmond Barracks through personal stories – what were conditions like for the rebels imprisoned in here in 1916? What was it like to raise a family in Keogh Square? What was it like to go to school in St. Michael's CBS? An immersive audio-visual experience set within the barrack gymnasium will evoke the anticipation, anguish and intensity which would have filled this space following the Rising. Surrounding graphics will provide the context of the Rising and feature stories of some of those involved, including seventy-seven women who were imprisoned in the married quarters of the Barracks.

Surrounded by gardens, the redeveloped Richmond Barracks will have tea rooms, exhibitions, archives for local and national history and classrooms from the 1929 school building and will become a venue and resource for community, educational and artistic purposes in this important part of Dublin city.

Éadaoin Ní Chléirigh
Chair, Richmond Barracks Advisory Committee

INTRODUCTION

The 77 Women of Richmond Barracks

There could be worse ways of commemorating Ireland's revolution than restoring these forgotten women, and the lost ideals that inspired them, to prominence.[1]

THE GENESIS OF THIS BOOK LAY with the desire of the authors, and the long held intention of the locally based Richmond Barracks Advisory Committee, to focus on the women of the 1916 Rising. In particular, it is the histories of the women arrested and held in the Barracks after the Rising which form a central strand of commemoration in the Richmond Barracks heritage centre.

Richmond Barracks, in Inchicore, Dublin 8, was purpose built in 1810 – 14 to deal with the threat of a Napoleonic invasion, as well as the ever present danger of internal violence or revolution in Ireland – it being little over a decade after the upheavals of the rebellion of 1798. In order to counter these perceived threats the then Lord Lieutenant of Ireland, Charles Lennox, 4th Duke of Richmond, oversaw the construction of new defence systems in Ireland, including the Martello towers dotted around the coast to watch for invading French fleets. This was accompanied by a complete overhaul of the military barracks system, which 'saw the closure of many small barracks... and the creation of newer, larger ones'.[2] In Dublin two new barracks were built, a cavalry barracks at Portobello and an infantry barracks at Goldenbridge, both on the south side of the city. The new barracks at Goldenbridge were named after the Duke of Richmond, and it was the construction of the Grand Canal nearby which was instrumental in the decision to site these barracks at Goldenbridge. The barracks enclosure occupied 23 statute acres, with two entrance gates (north and south gates, each with a guard room). Within the enclosure there were two parade grounds, 'the officers square to the east and the soldiers parade square to the west', divided by a two story block with an archway at its centre for access.[3]

Between 1864 and 1867, three additional buildings were constructed to accommodate a gymnasium and two recreation rooms. The building served as a British military barracks for over 108 years and detachments of Irish soldiers left from Richmond Barracks for service in conflicts which included the Crimean War, Boer War and World War 1. After the outbreak of war in 1914, the Barracks served as a depot providing accommodation for regiments such as 5th Royal Inniskilling Fusiliers (in which poet Francis Ledwidge served on the Western Front, as part of the 10th [Irish] Division), and the 4th, 8th, 11th and 13th Hussar Lancers, while the Royal Irish Regiment was stationed there in 1916. In all, the Barracks could house upwards of 1,600 soldiers. Because of its size and location on the outskirts of the city centre, its large parade grounds and open squares, it was considered a perfect place to hold the large numbers of prisoners arrested in the aftermath of the Rising.

Richmond Barracks has a central place in the story of the 1916 Rising. It was here that the majority of those involved in the Rising, men and women, were held after the surrender. It was in the Barracks gymnasium that detectives of 'G' Division from Dublin Castle identified those whom they knew to be leaders and prominent figures in the Volunteer movement. It was here also that the courts-martial of nearly 100 men and one woman took place. After being court-martialled they were taken to Kilmainham Gaol to await the verdict of the court. In the weeks following the Rising hundreds more Volunteers from all over the country were arrested and brought to Richmond Barracks and then shipped to England and Wales for internment. For most it was their first experience of imprisonment and left an indelible mark on their memory. The women, who had been stationed at Marrowbone Lane Distillery, were among the first female combatants to make the journey to Richmond Barracks after they surrendered on 30 April 1916. Rose McNamara provided a vivid description of that journey. The women, lined up inside two rows of Volunteers:

> marched down between two lines of our brave men. We waited until all the arms were taken away. The men gave each of us their small arms to do as we liked with, thinking we were going to go home, but we were not going to leave the men we were with all the week to their fate; we decided to go along with them and be with them to the end whatever our fate might be. Some of the girls had as many as three revolvers; some had more.[4]

The 'girls' were 'singing all the time amidst the insults, of the soldiers and the people along the route' as they walked to Richmond Barracks.[5] When they arrived at the Barracks, the women were 'separated from the men and led away to the far side... for the night where we got tea, etc.[6]' Annie Cooney, a member of the Inghinidhe branch who had served in Marrowbone Lane, remembers her night in the Barracks:

> We marched right into the big square, where we were halted. There we were separated from the men who were put into a separate building. We were all – 22 of us – brought into a large building up the stairs and we were first put into a rather small room, where we were divided up for the night, eleven of us in each of two rooms. A British military sergeant had charge of us and brought us tea in a bucket and same hard biscuits which we called dog biscuits. We ate and drank, what we got, as we were hungry. The sergeant apologised for the sort of food he had to give us.[7]

The women were actually housed in the married quarters in the Barracks before they were transferred to Kilmainham Gaol early the next day, 1 May. As Richmond Barracks served as a sorting centre, they did not have to remain there very long. Pauline Morkan, a member of the Central branch, Cumann na mBan, mentioned that they were well treated in Richmond initially; 'some of the soldiers gave us a few army biscuits which we thought were awful. They all behaved very nicely to us'.[8] The men were not to be given the same courtesy. Joe Good, a member of the Irish Volunteers, remembered standing in the boiling sun for hours, without a drop of water, with several men on the point of collapse.[9] Up in the married quarters, McNamara and her 'girls' were also worried about the fact that they still had the guns they had taken from their male comrades at Marrowbone Lane and had brought with them to Richmond Barracks. Fearing they would be searched they managed to secrete them up the fireplace in the room in which they were locked.

Later that day women from the other outposts began to arrive, including Kathleen Lynn and the Irish Citizen Army women who had fought in City Hall and those who had served in the Four Courts and Church Street area. The married quarters in Richmond must have come as a relief to those who had fought in City Hall. After they surrendered on Tuesday 25 April, they were taken to Ship Street Barracks, which were filthy. Despite protesting about being held in such conditions, they remained there for nearly a week. The women and men from the GPO garrison, who had spent Saturday night 'up to the green front of the Rotunda Hospital, where [they] were all commanded to get on to the grass. [They] were placed under armed guard, and remained there – men and women – higgledy-piggledy, all night'[10], were brought in. Rosie Hackett wrote of the hostile crowd the garrison from the Royal College of Surgeons had marched through en route to Richmond via Dublin Castle. Through the shouts and jeers of the crowd, William Partridge (a member of the Citizen Army whose wife would soon be arrested and held in Richmond Barracks), kept telling them to keep their heads erect.[11] Frank Robbins also mentioned the abuse the insurgents suffered as the Staffordshire Regiment marched them through Inchicore to Richmond Barracks, where 'the cries of encouragement to the young Englishmen in that regiment, the shouts of "Good Old Staffords" "Shoot the Traitors" and "Bayonet the Bastards"', rose from the crowds.[12] Later, Brigid Foley, Countess Plunkett and Mary Partridge, who were arrested at their homes, and Nell Ryan and Kathleen Browne, who were arrested in Wexford and imprisoned in Waterford Gaol for a number of days, were also taken to the Barracks.

By the time Brigid Lyons reached Richmond Barracks, having spent a night under arrest in the Four Courts, eating crackers and chocolate and sleeping 'in the judges' ermine', the treatment of women had deteriorated.[13] She was 'thrown' into a room with the 'two Sullivan girls... Flossie Mead and Carrie Mitchell... Winnie Carney', while the 'sentries outside threw us a few dog biscuits through the fanlight'.[14] As the prisoners arrived at the Barracks they came under scrutiny from the Dublin Metropolitan Police (DMP) and the British troops. The G-men from the DMP began to sort them into those they considered the leaders who would be subject to court-martial, those who should be kept in prison and those who should be deported or released. Many of the women who arrived on the first and second day after surrender were interviewed one by one. Later, about 7p.m. on the second evening, they were taken to the barrack square where they met Countess Markievicz and some of the other women. They were then lined up, looking very bedraggled, and marched to Kilmainham Gaol with the 'crowds outside along the route [giving them] a mixed reception, cheering, jeering, booing [sic] and making remarks, mostly uncomplimentary'.[15] Pauline Morkan also mentioned this hostile crowd and how Markievicz told the women to '"keep your heads up, girls" and a few other phrases like that' as they marched from Richmond Barracks to Kilmainham Gaol.[16]

As all seventy-seven women were detained in Richmond Barracks en route to or from other prisons, the authors felt that these seventy-seven women would be a lens through which the experience of the female participants could be commemorated. The names of all seventy-seven women are known from the release lists which appeared in newspapers subsequent to the Rising. Among them were some of the better known women of 1916: Countess Markievicz, Kathleen Lynn, Helena Molony, Madeleine ffrench-Mullen, Lily O'Brennan and Rosie Hackett. However, the majority of the seventy-seven women are unknown, their names have rarely, if ever, appeared in studies of the Easter Rising, even those studies focused on women. It was this unique opportunity to research the lives, activism and contribution to the Easter Rising and the Irish Revolution of these unknown women which provided the motivation to focus on their stories.

By recovering the histories of the seventy-seven women there was an opportunity to provide a forensic snapshot of female activism and participation at a particularly transformative time in modern Irish history. These seventy-seven women do not, and could not, represent the totality of female experience in the period 1900 – 1916 in Ireland, or indeed the totality of female experience during the Easter Rising. There were many women who were members of Cumann na mBan but who did not participate in the Rising or indeed agree with the Rising at all. There were women whose politics were unionist in orientation who disagreed with any nationalist ideologies. There were women who supported the constitutional route to Home Rule and supported John Redmond and his National Volunteers. There were women, whose husbands, sons, fathers and brothers were fighting in the British Army in France or elsewhere, who saw the Rising as a betrayal. Some of these women and the female participants encountered each other, often violently, during the week of the Rising. Annie Cooney, Inghinidhe branch of Cumann na mBan, recalled that as she and her comrades were marching away from Marrowbone Lane Distillery with the 4th Battalion, Irish Volunteers after the surrender, the 'separation women' were 'shouting out abuse and obscene language at us'.[17] Both male and female rebels remember vividly the shouts of abuse from the women identified as 'separation women' as they marched towards Richmond Barracks. Additionally, there were other women who had a different experience of the Rising, women who were looters, women who were victims of the violence and were wounded or killed and women who were passive onlookers.

In fact the seventy-seven women are representative of a minority within a minority, as they are representative of a cohort of activist, politicised women. The vast majority of women in Irish society at the time were not engaged in the political sphere in any significant way. Despite the influence of half a century or more of feminist activism, the participation of women in cultural, constitutional and advanced nationalism, as well as trade union activism, most women led a private, domestic life. It is this discourse of domesticity that was dominant; a woman's life was dictated by her respectability, marriageability and passivity – the dictat that a woman's place was in the home rang very true. Despite this pervading attitude, these seventy-seven women are representative of an important minority, a group of women politicised through feminism, nationalism and trade unionism, who were determined to have their say and their place in the shaping of the future of their country. Viewing this cohort of politicised women, through a forensic study of the chosen seventy-seven, allows a more nuanced understanding of why these women and many more like them became involved in violent revolution.

There have been a number of major studies of Irish women and the Irish Revolution over the past four decades, beginning with Margaret Ward's ground breaking *Unmanageable Revolutionaries: Women and Irish Nationalism* in 1983. This book introduced readers and historians, many for the first time, to the many female-led and driven political, suffrage and militant nationalist organisations which operated in Ireland between 1880 and 1920; the Ladies Land League (1881), Inghinidhe na hÉireann (1900), the Irish Women's Franchise League (1908) and Cumann na mBan (1914) among others. Ward wrote that she intended her work to be a 'stimulus for other feminist historians, so that in the future a much fuller account of the history of Irish women will be available to us all' and so it proved to be.[18] Since then Ward added to her own work with the publication of *In Their Own Voice: Women and Irish Nationalism* (1989) which brought the words and thoughts of the women themselves into focus. Among further publications dealing with women's participation in the public realms of feminism, nationalism and trade unionism in this period are Rosemary Cullen Owens' *Smashing Times: A History of the Irish Women's Suffrage Movement 1889 – 1922* (1984), Mary Jones' *Those Obstreperous Lassies: A History of the IWWU* (1988), Ruth Taillon's *When History was Made: The Women of 1916* (1999), Sinéad McCoole's *No Ordinary Women: Irish Female Activists in the Revolutionary Years* (2003), Louise Ryan and Margaret Ward (eds) *Irish Women and Nationalism: Soldiers, New Women and Wicked Hags* (2004), Rosemary Cullen Owens' *A Social History of Women in Ireland, 1870 – 1970* (2007), Cal MacCarthy's *Cumann na mBan and the Irish Revolution* (2007), Ann Matthews' *Renegades: Irish Republican Women 1900 – 1922* (2010) and, more recently, Senia Pašeta's *Irish Nationalist Women 1900 – 1918* (2013).

There has also been, in recent years, a real effort by most historians writing on the revolutionary period generally, to include the experience and contribution of revolutionary women. Ferghal McGarry's *The Rising, Ireland: Easter 1916* (2010) includes significant sections on women as does John Borgonovo's *The Dynamics of*

War and Revolution, Cork City, 1916 – 1918 (2013) and Roy Foster's *Vivid Faces: The Revolutionary generation in Ireland, 1890 – 1923* (2014).

This study of the history of the Easter Rising through the lives and activism of seventy-seven female participants uncovers the extraordinary complexity of the histories of these women. Many of them came not just from Dublin, but from all over the country, and they were also disparate in terms of their class, background, education, and motivation. In the context of the often times male-centred commemorations, this work shines a light on the contributions of women to revolutionary activism. What becomes obvious are the interlinked campaigns for national freedom, female suffrage and citizenship, workers' rights and especially the battle for the rights of women workers. In particular, as many of the seventy-seven were working class Dublin women, the research highlights the contributions and the legacies for future generations of this often forgotten and overlooked section of society. While the names of the seventy-seven women have been known since the days of their imprisonment in Richmond Barracks, the details of their lives and their contributions have not. Women such as Kathleen Barrett, Bessie Lynch, Josephine Green, Annie Higgins, Florence Meade, May O'Moore, and Barbara Retz are rarely if ever mentioned in the history books, yet they deserve their place. In recent years, as more archives and primary source materials have become available to historians, our understanding of the contribution of women to 1916 has expanded. In particular the Bureau of Military History (BMH) witness statements and the Military Service Pensions Collection (MSPC) have been a boon to the researcher of women and the revolutionary decade. By the time the BMH had finished its job of recording witness statements in 1957 it had accumulated '1,773 witness statements... 36,000 pages of evidence and over 150,000 documents'.[19] With the MSPC, in 1940 a Dáil committee was told that there had been 21,121 applications to date under the Military Services Pensions Act (1924, which excluded women), with 3,850 successful awards. It is estimated that there were well over 80,000 further applications under Military Services Pensions Act (1934) under which women were allowed to apply.[20]

As historian Marie Coleman has noted the 'value of MPSC is especially noticeable with regard to the smaller organisations like Cumann na mBan, Fianna Éireann and the Irish Citizen Army'.[21] In addition the BMH allows historians 'provide a more nuanced picture of the role of women' in one of the main organisations with which women fought in 1916, the Irish Citizen Army. There are extant witness statements from six leading members of the Citizen Army, Nellie Gifford, Helena Molony, Kathleen Lynn, Maeve Cavanagh, Marie Perolz and Rosie Hackett.[22] Of these women, only Maeve Cavanagh was not arrested after the Rising. In addition to these witness statements several of the women who were in the Irish Citizen Army also applied for military pensions, including Hackett, Molony, Gifford, as well as the Norgrove sisters, Jinny Shanahan, Kathleen Barrett, Brigid Goff and several others. Cumann na mBan women also gave witness statements and applied for pensions, sometimes the same person did both so it is possible to compare both sources. One of these, for example, is Brigid Foley who gave a long, detailed witness statement on her revolutionary activism and despite stating that she wouldn't apply for a pension 'on principle', she did actually apply a year after giving her witness statement. The details on her witness statement and her application are similar, with the prior witness statement possibly being a basis for the application. However, her referees all agreed with her pension application and what she said she did. Other women never gave witness statements or applied for pensions. Julia Grenan and Elizabeth O'Farrell, who both rejected the legitimacy of the Free State, refused to engage in either process. Annie Higgins died before she could apply, as did Josie McGowan, Kathleen Treston and Marcella Cosgrove and several others.

Of course both the BMH and the Military pension applications were written decades after the events being related and therefore a cautious approach to the material is necessary. However, in so far as is allowed by the available sources, the testimonies of the BMH witnesses in particular, are more reliable than historians previously accepted. While some like Helena Molony[23] definitely had an axe to grind, either politically or personally, most retell their stories in a relatively neutral narrative of events and activities, and their part in these. It must, however, be accepted that the passage of time and life experiences between the events of 1916 and the 1940s/1950s influenced the retelling of the personal narratives. Both the BMH and the MSPC files are a mediated form of history, a telling of history through state-directed projects, influenced by politics, personal ambition, grudges and biases and flawed remembering. Encouragingly points of similarity often do emerge in the retelling of the same events by different witnesses. Taking all this into account, and combining the BMH and MSPC records with contemporaneous accounts (newspapers, memos, political writings, diaries, police reports, census records etc.) as well as later memoirs, biographies and the many political archives of Rising combatants and witnesses available, a valuable, if somewhat subjective, view of the seventy-seven women and their contributions to the Easter Rising emerges.

Belonging: the 77 women

The majority of the seventy-seven women who were arrested and taken to Richmond Barracks belonged to two organisations, Cumann na mBan and the Irish Citizen Army. In Dublin, the women of Cumann na mBan who participated in the Rising came from four branches: the Central, Inghinidhe na hÉireann, Colmcille and Fairview branches. Three of the branches (Central, Colmcille and Fairview) were based on the north side of the city, while the Inghinidhe branch was based on the south side. The first and largest branch was the Árd Craobh, or Central branch, set up in April 1914. Nationally this was Cumann na mBan's most important branch as many of the executive members belonged to it. The executive and the branch had lost some of it early members due to the split occasioned by John Redmond's call for the Irish Volunteers to support the war effort in September 1914, but weathered that storm and, as Jennie Wyse Power later remarked, the split 'cleared the road for the work of Cumann na mBan'.[24] Certainly clarity of purpose in the type of training and work they were to undertake informed the post-split Cumann na mBan. Classes were set up where first aid, drill, rifle practice, and signalling were taught, often by a comrade from the Irish Volunteers. Fundraising was also very important with many of the branches running concerts, dances, ceilis, flag days, door to door collections, collections at sporting events to raise money, often times for purchase of arms for the Irish Volunteers. The President of the Central branch in the months preceding the Rising was Kathleen Clarke and its membership included Jennie Wyse Power, her daughter Nancy, Áine Ceannt, Áine O'Rahilly, Nancy O'Rahilly, Annie Higgins, Eily O'Hanrahan, Rose McGuinness, Louise Gavan-Duffy, Elizabeth Bloxham and Máire Nic Shiubhlaigh amongst others.

Had the Rising gone to plan, the Central branch of Cumann na mBan, attached to the 1st Battalion of the Dublin Brigade of the Irish Volunteers, would have been stationed mainly in the GPO and the Four Courts area. Because of the confusion of the countermanding order, issued by Eoin MacNeill on Easter Saturday cancelling all route marches and planned mobilisations, members of the Central branch who had mobilised on Easter Sunday had gone home. Some remobilised again on Monday but didn't receive any orders directing them to the battalions to which they were to be attached, so the women made their way as best they could to the various outposts.

Because most of Central branch women found their way to the GPO and the Four Courts areas they were among the many women who evaded arrest after the Rising. Therefore, only twelve members of the Central branch were arrested. The smaller Colmcille branch, based on the north side in Blackhall Place, was only three weeks old on Easter Monday and its thirty members mobilised in the Fianna Hall on Merchants Quay.[25] Like so many of the Cumann na mBan branches, they received no definite instructions and most of the Colmcille women returned home. They met again on Tuesday and, still with no direct orders, decided that women could 'do what seemed the most urgent at the time by bringing all the ammunition... down to the barricades'.[26] Among the members who made their way into the action were Brigid McKeon, Josephine Flood, Eilís Ní Riain, Margaret Martin, Lily Murnane and Dora Harford. Most of the Colmcille members spent the week in the Four Courts and Church Street area. Most also evaded capture and only two members, Kathleen Martin and Bríd S. Martin, were arrested.

The other two branches of Cumann na mBan whose members participated in the Rising in Dublin were the Inghinidhe branch and the Fairview branch. Inghinidhe na hÉireann was a militant, feminist, separatist organisation set up in Dublin in 1900 by a group of nationalist women, most famously among them, Maud Gonne.[27] By 1914 some women who remained in Inghinidhe were incorporated as their own branch of Cumann na mBan. This branch was the only branch of Cumann na mBan on the south side of the city and so was attached to both those Battalions of the Irish Volunteers who operated in that part of the city. The Inghinidhe branch was motivated, well organised, tight knit and worked closely with the 3rd and 4th Battalions of the Volunteers, an indication why it was the branch which mobilised most effectively on Easter Monday. The Inghinidhe branch was divided into two groups, one of which was attached to the 3rd Battalion, and one attached to the 4th. On the morning of Easter Monday, the group attached to the 4th Battalion, commanded by Commandant Éamonn Ceannt, mobilised at Cleaver's Hall, Donore Avenue, South Circular Road, and marched to the Marrowbone Lane Distillery, one of the outposts which was essential in protecting Ceannt's Headquarters in the South Dublin Union (SDU). The women in this group, including Rose McNamara, Marcella Cosgrove, the Cooney sisters, Josie Kelly, the O'Keeffe sisters, Katie Kelly, Bridie Kenny, Josephine Spicer and others, spent the week with the Marrowbone Lane garrison. The other Inghinidhe group was to join the 3rd Battalion, which was under the command of Éamon de Valera at Boland's Mill, but were informed by a courier sent from Boland's Mill that they were not needed. Some of them then joined other garrisons, while others spent the week serving as couriers to and from Boland's Mill. In all, twenty-nine Inghinidhe women were arrested after the surrender.

The final branch, in Fairview, on Dublin's north side, was one of the first set up after the formation of Cumann na mBan in 1914. Nora O'Daly was present at the first meeting of the Fairview branch and she said that their principal study was first aid. They also did courses in 'rifle cleaning and sighting, drill and various other things which might prove useful in assisting the men of the battn. [sic] 2 (Irish Volunteers) to which our Cumann was attached'.[28] When O'Daly and the Fairview women arrived at Fr. Mathew Park on Easter Sunday for the planned route march, they were disappointed to find it had been cancelled. On Easter Monday individual members of the branch received mobilisation orders and passed the information on to others. They made their way to various outposts: O'Daly and her friends, Brigid Murtagh and May O'Moore, went to St. Stephen's Green; Gertie Colly, Esther Wisely and Matilda 'Tilly' Simpson went to the GPO, where they met their Commanding Officer, Molly Reynolds and another member, Statia Toomey. Some women also made their way to join the 2nd Battalion of the Irish Volunteers who, under the command of Thomas MacDonagh, had occupied Jacob's Biscuit Factory. MacDonagh, although a supporter of female suffrage, was reluctant to let women join the garrison and issued no orders for Cumann na mBan. However, Cumann na mBan women, like Abbey actress Máire Nic Shiubhlaigh, did join him and served there for the week. When the surrender notice was communicated to the garrison MacDonagh ordered all those not in uniform, including the women, to leave. Nic Shiubhlaigh, in her memoir *The Splendid Years*, remembered that MacDonagh was most anxious that the 'girls' get out before they were arrested. Like their comrades in the GPO they obeyed the order to leave, as a result none of the Jacob's Factory women were arrested.[29] Elsewhere, however, five members of the Fairview branch were arrested after the surrender.

The women of the Irish Citizen Army[30] fought mainly in two outposts during the 1916 Rising: City Hall and St. Stephen's Green/Royal College of Surgeons. These women were all members of the women's section of the Citizen Army and had spent the weeks before the Rising preparing for the fight. Among the advanced nationalist women who were Citizen Army members were Countess Markievicz, Helena Molony, Madeleine ffrench-Mullen, Marie Perolz and Kathleen Lynn. In addition to these middle class (and one aristocrat) women, most of the other female activists in Liberty Hall were working class women such as Rosie Hackett, Jinny Shanahan, Bridget Brady, Bridget Goff, Martha Kelly and others who had joined the women's section of the Citizen Army in 1913 and 1914. Eighteen women from the Citizen Army were arrested during and after the Rising.

These are the women who, along with a small number of individual women also arrested, make up the seventy-seven woman cohort who form the central study of this book.

Notes

1   Ferghal McGarry, 'Helena Molony: A Revolutionary Life' in *History Ireland*, Issue 4
        (July – August 2013), Volume 21

2   Liam O'Meara, *From Richmond Barracks to Keogh Square* (Dublin: Riposte Books, 2014), p. 33

3   Ibid., p. 41

4   BMH WS 482 (Rose McNamara), p. 8

5   Ibid.

6   Ibid.

7   BMH WS 805 (Annie Cooney / O'Brien), pp. 10 – 11

8   BMH WS 432 (Pauline Morkan / Keating), p. 5

9   Joe Good, *Inside the GPO; A first-hand account* (Dublin: O'Brien Press, 2015), pp. 132 – 133

10   BMH WS 370 (Fintan Murphy), p. 11

11   BMH WS 546 (Rosie Hackett), p. 9

12   BMH WS 585 (Frank Robbins), p. 83

13   BMH WS 259 (Brigid Lyons / Thornton), p. 7

14   Ibid., pp. 7-8

15   Ibid.

16   BMH WS 432 (Pauline Morkan / Keating), p. 5

17   BMH WS 805 (Annie Cooney / O'Brien), p. 10

18   Margaret Ward, *Unmanageable Revolutionaries: Women and Irish Nationalism* (Dingle: Brandon
        Press, 1983), p. 3

19   Ferghal McGarry, *The Rising, Ireland: Easter 1916* (Oxford: Oxford University Press, 2010),
        p. 5

20   Eunan O'Halpin, 'The Military Service Pensions Project and Irish History: a personal
        perspective' in *Guide to the Military Service (1916 – 1923) Pensions Collection*
        (Óglaigh na hÉireann, 2012), p. 145

21   Marie Coleman, 'The Irish Citizen Army and the Military Service Pensions Collection' in
        Mary McAuliffe (ed.) *Rosie: Essays in Honour of Roseanna 'Rosie' Hackett (1893 – 1976):
        Revolutionary and Trade Unionist* (Dublin: Arlen House, 2015), p. 92

22   Ibid.

23   Molony was particularly exercised by the depiction of Countess Markievicz by Sean O'Faolain
        in his biography of the Countess. See Eve Morrison, 'The Bureau of Military History and
        Female Republican Activism, 1913 – 1923' in Maryann Gialanella Valiulis (ed.) *Gender and
        Power in Irish History* (Dublin: Irish Academic Press, 2009), pp. 59 – 83

24   Cumann na mBan, *Leabhar na mBan* (Dublin, 1919), p. 5

25   Cal McCarthy, *Cumann na mBan and the Irish Revolution* (Cork: The Collins Press, 2014,
        revised edition), p.59

26   Ibid.

27   Inghinidhe na hÉireann will be discussed in more detail in the next chapter.

28   Nora O'Daly, 'The Women of Easter Week: Cumann na mBan in St. Stephen's Green and the
        College of Surgeons' in *An tÓglach*, April 3rd 1926, p. 3

29   Máire Nic Shiubhlaigh and Edward Kenny. *The Splendid Years: recollections of Máire Nic
        Shiubhlaigh* (Dublin: Duffy and Co. , 1955)

30   The women and their experience in the Irish Citizen Army will be discussed in the next chapter.

CHAPTER ONE

—

The Route to the Rising:
Women and Politics, 1900 – 1916

*The whole garrison then surrendered. Miss McNamara ordered that
we were to surrender with the men, and we all did with one exception.
We marched behind the men from the Distillery to Ross Road.*[1]

THE END POINT OF ROSE MCNAMARA's involvement in the Rising came when she and twenty-one other women of the Inghinidhe branch of Cumann na mBan surrendered with the Marrowbone Lane garrison on Sunday, 30 April 1916. McNamara had spent the week in charge of the Inghinidhe women and now she marched at their head as they went to Richmond Barracks. An hour earlier she and her 'girls' had been told to go home by Éamonn Ceannt, but a need to attend to a wounded Volunteer delayed their departure. Now as they lined up between the two lines of Volunteers who were surrendering, the group marched away while McNamara and her 'girls' sang 'amidst the insults, of the soldiers and the people along the route'.[2] McNamara had explained to the British officer in charge that the women 'were part of the rebel contingent and were surrendering with the rest'.[3] For these politicised, militant women their insistence on their role as combatants in the Rising was definite, as had been their insistence on joining the fight when it began. For many this had not been easy, they were turned away or told go home in several places but they persisted. Because of this insistence, over 280 women were 'out' in the Rising in Dublin, Galway, Enniscorthy, Co. Wexford and Ashbourne, Co. Meath in 1916. Almost all of these women had been involved in politics since mid-1915 and some for many years before that.

At the beginning of 1916 a vocal, radicalised cohort of women was present in Dublin and other, mainly urban, centres around Ireland. Three movements – feminism, socialism and nationalism – energised and engaged a new generation of female activists from 1900. By 1916 there was real interaction between female nationalists and feminists. Historian Mary Cullen has noted that despite tensions between these ideologies and the women who espoused them, 'an implicit feminist awareness appears to have informed almost all of the developments even when the objectives were not explicitly feminist'.[4] Feminism and the labour movement were also intertwined; many of the more radical nationalist feminists were also socialists. The road to female involvement in militant nationalism and participation in the Easter Rising can be explored by understanding the growing engagement of women of all classes in one or more of these three ideologies and their associated organisations as well as their political, cultural and social networks prior to 1916. Roy Foster has written about a new generation of young radical revolutionaries, the 'vivid faces' who rejected much of the cautious constitutional nationalism of their parents' generation in the first decade of the twentieth century. He describes this generation as 'bent on self-transformation' and united, for all its internal disagreements, in the making of a revolution.[5] Among this revolutionary generation he focuses on the elite middle classes, those women (and men) who were engaged, among other issues, with feminism, socialism and nationalism. These were women who, as well as participating in the public realm of politics and culture, were often living deeply unconventional lifestyles. At a time when the dominant discourse for women was that of domesticity, marriage and motherhood, they lived 'public lives, frequently appearing in the press on political platforms... they were exceptional in their willingness to live against the grain in Irish society'.[6] Among them were women who participated in the Easter Rising including Countess Markievicz, Helena Molony, Madeleine ffrench-Mullen and her partner Kathleen Lynn, Nellie Gifford and Marie Perolz. However, this middle class, educated, politicised cohort which Foster concentrates on, were a small minority of the women who were participants in the Rising of 1916. Alongside these leadership groups were younger, working class women (and men) influenced by ideas of nation, gender and class freedom whose contributions and activism also helped bring about the startling transformation of Ireland that began in 1916.

At the turn of the twentieth century, Irish women who had experienced a 'political awakening'[7] in the previous four decades were beginning to join more radical organisations. Female suffrage organisations had been, as Senia Pašeta has argued, a 'crucial agent in the politicisation of Irish women'.[8] By 1900, a younger generation of women, benefitting from the achievements of moderate suffrage activists of the later nineteenth century, were beginning to engage with more radical politics. Many of these younger women were part of the non-political Gaelic League, one of the few organisations which allowed men and women to join. Founded in 1893 to promote the Irish language and culture, women were involved as members and as organisers from the outset and the League was a starting point from which many women became politicised. Many of the seventy-seven women of Richmond Barracks joined the League as younger women, including Kathleen Barrett, Florence Meade and Winifred Carney. Nell Humphreys, the Cooney sisters, the O'Keeffe sisters, Nora O'Daly and Kathleen Browne were also members. As Jennie Wyse Power, later a founder member of Cumann na mBan, said of the League:

> The echoes of the Parnell affair had not yet died when a new movement was inaugurated by the founding of the Gaelic League. This novel cultural body rejected the false sex and class distinctions which were the result of English influence. And to the Gaelic League is due the credit of having established the first Irish national society which accepted women as members on the same terms as men. [9]

This was overstating any actual or imagined radical nature of the League. The Irish Ireland movement was replete with contradictions in its concept of the place of women in the nation. Hanna Sheehy Skeffington said that 'it was primarily in her capacity as mother and housekeeper' that women were welcome in the League, but as D.A. MacPherson has pointed out, 'work such as fundraising, organising camogie matches, promoting Irish manufactured goods... or forming Irish language colleges was presented as a particularly feminine type of public activism'.[10]

Kathleen Browne, arrested in Wexford in 1916, was an early member of the League, joining in early 1900. She soon immersed herself in the language revival and spent many of her holidays in the Ring Gaeltacht. The first branch of the Gaelic League in Wexford was formed in Enniscorthy in 1900 and she attended a convention held there in September 1901 to form a 'Co. committee to consolidate and control the activities of the movement', becoming a member of this committee.[11] The crux of her belief in cultural nationalism was the need to revive the country's own tongue, and, more particularly, for those in south Wexford, the importance of proficiency of the local dialect Yola (meaning 'old'). As well as being devoted to the language, history and culture of the country and county, she liked to be photographed in 'Celtic' costume, viewing this as a representation of the idealised 'true' Irish woman. Her costumes consisted of a dress with typical Celtic spiral designs and a cloak or *brat*, which represented an idea of how ancient Irish people dressed. She was photographed in costume with an Irish wolfhound. As well as dressing the part, Kathleen was an organiser with the League, becoming the secretary for the county branch, and organiser of feiseanna throughout the county. Another member was Marie Perolz who joined the League in 1898 and participated in the parades to commemorate the centenary of the 1798 Rebellion. Brigid Foley and her siblings were all members of the Keating branch of the Gaelic League in Dublin. Foley's brother Risteárd, 'Fiachra Éilgeach', was a Gaelic scholar who wrote for the League newspaper, *An Claidheamh Soluis* and was a founder member of the branch with J.J. 'Sceilg' O'Kelly. The members considered that, as Sceilg later said, it was 'the Keating branch that made the Nationalist movement a going concern in the full sense'.[12] There is no doubt that the Gaelic League contributed to 'the nationalisation of a generation of Irish women, but it did not single-handedly politicise them'.[13]

There was not one single organisation or ideology that politicised Irishwomen in the early decades of the twentieth century, instead it is necessary to understand the cross fertilisation which occurred as a result of exposure to and involvement in several different strands of activism and idealism. One of the earlier radical organisations in which women became involved was Inghinidhe na hÉireann, set up in 1900 by Maud Gonne and a number of like-minded radical thinkers. Historians of Irish women's involvement in politics argue that Inghinidhe was one of the most important political organisations founded in early twentieth-century Ireland. Margaret Ward has noted 'had Inghinidhe not existed, a whole generation of women would have never developed the self-confidence which eventually enabled them to hold their own in organisations composed of both sexes'.[14] A prominent member, Helena Molony, who joined in 1903 stated that Inghinidhe:

> formed itself into a permanent Society, of Irishwomen pledged to fight for the complete separation of Ireland from England, and the re-establishment of her ancient culture. The means decided upon for the achievement of this object was the formation of evening classes for children, for Irish Language, Irish History – Social as well as Political – the restoration of Irish customs to every-day life, Irish games, Dancing and Music.[15]

Along with the objectives outlined by Molony, as a separatist organisation Inghinidhe was also dedicated to the complete independence of Ireland. Although initially set up to provide women with a platform from which to work for the cause of Irish nationalism, Inghinidhe soon included feminist ideals as well. Using different cultural and educational fora to get their nationalist / feminist messages across, most famously in their *tableau vivant* productions, the Inghinidhe literary and theatrical activities often included strong female role models from Irish history and mythology such as

St. Brigid, Queen Maeve of Connacht, Gráinne Mhaol and Anne Devlin, and they drew on inspirational and militant females from European history like Joan of Arc.

Inghinidhe searched for ways to express female politicisation, even politicising motherhood. From 1907 onwards under the stewardship of Molony, Inghinidhe moved in a more radical direction, emphasising their ideals of advanced nationalism, feminism and socialism. In 1908 the group launched the first nationalist / feminist newspaper *Bean na h-Éireann*; indeed its masthead proclaimed its support for 'complete separatism, the rising cause of feminism and the interest of Irishwomen generally'.[16] Molony, as editor, was determined that *Bean na h-Éireann* would be 'a women's paper advocating militancy, separatism and feminism'.[17] In 1908 an article entitled 'An Irish Women's Duty' called on mothers to use the fact that as a mother they have the 'sacred charge of forming young minds... as housekeepers they have the expenditure of Ireland's income... [and] as citizens they have their share... in the formation of public opinion'.[18] A number of Inghinidhe women were also involved in the formation of Sinn Féin in 1905, the first nationalist organisation where women could hold executive offices alongside men. Women who were involved in Sinn Féin and who held office prior to the Rising included Jennie Wyse Power, Kathleen Browne, Countess Markievicz and Lizzie Mulhall (who was also an elected Poor Law guardian and member of Dublin Corporation). As well as Molony, activist women involved in Inghinidhe included Countess Markievicz, Marie Perolz, Madeleine ffrench-Mullen and Julia Grenan. Markievicz, Molony and Perolz, politicised through cultural nationalism, would be 'to the forefront of the next phase of women's political activism'.[19]

Although it was an explicitly nationalist and separatist organisation, Inghinidhe na hÉireann also advocated feminism. In 1908 a more explicitly feminist group was formed, the Irish Women's Franchise League (IWFL) which was set up by Hanna and Francis Sheehy Skeffington and Margaret and James Cousins. The IWFL represented a new generation of suffrage activists, a generation who had lost patience with the more moderate tactics of the older suffrage organisations. Influenced by the militancy of the British Women's Social and Political Union (WSPU), they were determined to push their ideology, which according to their slogan was 'Suffrage before all else'. More radical and outspoken than previous suffrage groups, initially its main aim was to achieve female suffrage within the context of the campaign for Home Rule. Criticised by nationalist organisations like Inghinidhe, who felt that female suffrage should not take precedence over nationalism, the IWFL and other suffrage groups nevertheless grew in strength and influence in the decade up to 1916. Countering arguments from some nationalist women who felt that an Irishwoman should not campaign for the vote from an alien government, Hanna Sheehy Skeffington wrote that 'until the Parliamentarian and the Sinn Féin woman alike possess the vote, the keystone of citizenship, she will count but little in either party'.[20] Sheehy Skeffington was not at all pleased that women like Markievicz, Molony and others 'whose natural sympathies should have been with us and pitted against English politicians' were more inclined to put the cause of nationalism first.[21]

Despite this, the women of Inghinidhe, Sinn Féin and the IWFL often found common cause with the many issues, especially social issues, in which they were engaged. As historian Mary Cullen has outlined, the fortnightly suffrage newspaper the *Irish Citizen*, edited by Francis Sheehy Skeffington and James Cousins, while concentrating on the campaign for the female franchise, also carried articles of broader interest to the feminist and labour movements. Among the issues discussed were conditions and pay for working women, the need for trade unions for working class women, issues of domestic and sexual violence against women, feminism and militancy, war and pacifism, the need for women police, lawyers and jurors.[22] However, the failure of the IWFL and other suffrage groups to get women's right to vote included in the 1912 Home Rule Bill created an unbridgeable gulf between most IWFL supporters and the Irish Parliamentary Party. Many women soon became more involved with Sinn Féin and later with more advanced nationalist organisations.

A cause which provided a uniting platform for advanced nationalist and feminist women was the cause of labour. Women active in both Inghinidhe and in the IWFL were becoming more engaged with socialism and active in the labour movement. The Inghinidhe women had been concerned with child poverty from its inception and by 1910 the group decided to 'inaugurate a scheme by which a certain number of poor children will be supplied with free food'.[23] Together with individual members of the IWFL they set up the Ladies' Dinner Committee (LDC) to provide meals for poor children.[24] This work introduced many of the advanced nationalist and feminist women to the cause of labour and especially the problems faced by working class women. But the links with socialist activism had long been present. For example, Francis Sheehy Skeffington and Kathleen Shannon, both founding members of the IWFL, were secretaries of the Socialist Party of Ireland. James Connolly, the trade unionist and socialist, was a supporter of the feminist cause and promoted the activities of many women involved in socialism and feminism. He was particularly close to women like Molony, Markievicz, Perolz and Kathleen Lynn, all of whom were by 1911, active in nationalism, feminism and socialism. The other main trade union leader James Larkin, who set up the Irish Transport and General Workers' Union (ITGWU) in Dublin in 1909, had included adult suffrage and equal voting rights in his initial programme. However, in common with the male nationalist organisations, women were not 'wholeheartedly welcome' in the ITGWU.[25] Instead, Larkin encouraged the formation of a sister organisation to look after the rights of women workers. The Irish Women Workers' Union (IWWU) was founded in 1911 under the stewardship of his sister Delia and was supported by Sheehy Skeffington, Molony and Markievicz.

The Dublin Lockout of 1913 would prove the first real test of the ITGWU and the IWWU, as well as the female activists engaged with all three movements, feminism, socialism and nationalism. Over 1,000 female workers (out of a total of 20,000 workers in all) were locked out by Dublin employers in an attempt to break the unions. While many IWWU members were strikers themselves, Liberty Hall (headquarters of the ITGWU and IWWU) was where women from all organisations gathered together to provide support for the striking workers. Inghinidhe women, including Molony, Markievicz, Nellie Gifford and Madeleine ffrench-Mullen, as well as Sheehy Skeffington and other IWFL members who had been involved in the LDC, 'provided a similar service during the Lockout'.[26] The Lockout served to politicise many middle class and working class women who would later be involved in the 1916 Rising. As Therese Moriarty has noted, the attendance of middle class women at Liberty Hall during the Lockout reads like a roll call of well-known names from Dublin's feminist and nationalist movements.[27]

After the Lockout, about 500 women workers lost their jobs because of their union activities and many were not re-employed. A number of these women became involved in another organisation which grew out of the Lockout – the Irish Citizen Army. In late 1913 James Connolly announced the formation of a workers militia, a citizen's army which was effectively a defence corps for workers.[28] Women were involved in the Irish Citizen Army (ICA) from the beginning, with many of the more socialist female activists preferring to join the Irish Citizen Army rather than any other militant nationalist organisation. Among the advanced nationalist women who were members of the Irish Citizen Army were Markievicz, Molony, ffrench-Mullen, Perolz, Gifford and Lynn. Beyond these upper and middle class women most of the female activists in Liberty Hall were working class women. As well as joining the IWWU and participating in the Lockout, working women such as Rosie Hackett, Jinny Shanahan, Bridget Brady, Martha Kelly and others joined the women's section of the Irish Citizen Army in 1913 and 1914. The roles played by the Inghinidhe and the IWFL women alongside the IWWU women in feeding the starving families of the striking workers and in attempting to aid hungry children through the 'Save the Kiddies'[29] campaign are striking examples of female cross-class solidarity and activism. The fact that many of the more left-leaning middle class women choose to join the Citizen Army rather than any other female advanced nationalist organisation reflects the combination of their political interests and social activism through trade union politics and in advanced nationalism. Women were now very active in the political and cultural activities in Liberty Hall and throughout 1915 members of the women's section of the Citizen Army were training in first aid and ambulance work under the guidance of the Chief Medical Officer of the Citizen Army, Dr. Kathleen Lynn. The image of the Citizen Army as an egalitarian organisation has been hotly debated. Women joined from the beginning and the organisation did have a distinct women's section for its female members. However, it is telling that some of the female members appreciated the atmosphere of equality that they felt prevailed in the Irish Citizen Army, with ffrench-Mullen telling her friend Rosamund Jacob that 'there was absolutely no difference made between men and women in the Citizen Army'.[30]

The Citizen Army had its appeal for the radical feminist and socialist women, while for the majority of advanced nationalist women, their desire to be involved was more influenced by the formation of the Irish Volunteers in November 1913. The Irish Volunteers was set up in response to the formation of the Ulster Volunteers and to reinforce the claim for Home Rule in Ireland. In November 1913 at their inaugural meeting, many of the male leaders agreed that there would be work for women to do. However, in response to queries about this from advanced nationalist women, Irish Volunteer leader Patrick Pearse rather evasively responded that 'while the women would have ambulance and red cross work to do' he 'would not like the idea of women drilling and marching in the ordinary way, but there is no reason why they should not learn how to shoot'.[31] The contradictions in this statement are symptomatic of the difficulties men had in envisioning the sort of work nationalist women would do and how to incorporate this work within the Irish Volunteers. In *Leabhair na mBan* (1919), Jennie Wyse-Power wrote that advanced nationalist women held informal meetings in the months following formation of the Volunteers 'to discuss the formation of a women's society whose aim would be to work independently, and at the same time to organise Nationalist women to be of service to the Irish Volunteers'.[32] Finally a meeting was called for all interested women, at 4p.m. on Thursday, 2 April, 1914 in Wynn's Hotel meeting room in Dublin city.

This meeting was to announce the formation of a new organisation for women, Cumann na mBan. It was to become the most influential women's organisation in twentieth-century Ireland and had its origins in two powerful ideologies which were driving the socio-political transformation of Ireland in the first decades of the twentieth century, nationalism and feminism. Having no wish to alienate the constitutional nationalist women, initially the Cumann na mBan executive set themselves a moderate course. Their aims were to advance the cause of Irish liberty, to form a fund and raise money to arm and equip a body of men to achieve this and to engage in training in first aid, drill and signalling and rifle practice. However, this aim of 'arming a body of men' to fight for Irish liberty, contained the seeds of the major arguments and divisions between feminists and female nationalists. According to historian Rosemary Cullen Owens it was the formation of Cumann na mBan that 'crystallised the differences between those who sought national freedom first and equal rights second and those who sought suffrage first, before all else'.[33] Among those who derided Cumann na mBan was Hanna Sheehy Skeffington who accused new group members of forming a 'ladies auxiliary committee' of the Irish Volunteers.[34] In the editorials of the *Irish Citizen,* the IWFL maintained the line that suffrage must always come first. The fact that Cumann na mBan (despite the fact that many of its founding members were also feminists) supported the ideal of nationalism first, struck a nerve. In turn, Cumann na mBan members resented the accusations from suffragists that they were auxiliaries or 'handmaidens' to the Volunteers, and put forward a strong counter-argument. Founder member Mary Colum wrote in their defence that:

> from the start we of Cumann na mBan decided to do any national work that came
> within the scope of our aims. We would collect money or arms, we would learn
> ambulance work, learn how to make haversacks and bandoliers... for we are not
> the auxiliaries or the handmaidens or the camp followers of the Volunteers, we
> are their allies.[35]

Despite this staunch defence of their actions, this tension between feminism and nationalism was to continue, among female activists, within and outside of Cumann na mBan. However the need to keep the moderate nationalist members happy was soon unnecessary as Cumann na mBan spilt (as did the Irish Volunteers), over John Redmond's call for the Irish Volunteers to join the British Army and fight on the Western Front.[36] In October 1914 the Cumann na mBan national executive released a manifesto which stated that 'we came into being to advance the cause of Irish liberty... we feel that... to urge... Irish Volunteers to enlist in the British Army cannot be regarded as consistent with the work we have set ourselves to do'.[37] Many of the moderate members who supported Redmond left the organisation at this juncture. As Wyse Power later wrote, the departure of the moderates 'cleared the road' for the work of Cumann na mBan.[38] Pašeta has argued that this split was a seminal moment in the radicalisation of the organisation.[39]

For women who had been involved in Inghinidhe na hÉireann, 1914 and the foundation of Cumann na mBan represented another phase in their development. Many of these more radical women would not have accepted the status of auxiliary to the Volunteers and there had to be a negotiated agreement, facilitated by Countess Markievicz, whereby some (although not all) of the women of Inghinidhe amalgamated with and became a distinct branch of Cumann na mBan, based in the south inner city of Dublin. At the first meeting about thirty members enrolled in this Inghinidhe branch and when the women of Inghinidhe merged with Cumann na mBan 'there was no doubt that it (Cumann na mBan) became more culturally directed and that the intellectual heart of the new organisation also came under the influence of some more advanced 'militant republicans'.[40] Not all the Inghinidhe members joined this branch of Cumann na mBan however. Former Inghinidhe members such as Molony, Perolz and ironically, Markievicz herself remained associated with the Irish Citizen Army and fought in 1916 as members of that organisation. With radical women in the Inghinidhe branch, the split and resignation of many moderate members of Cumann na mBan, as well as the continued associations many of its members had with socialist and feminist networks, especially women within the IWFL, the Citizen Army and IWWU meant that, particularly in Dublin, Cumann na mBan was very much part of a growing and radicalised female cohort engaged in aspects of nationalist, socialist and feminist activism, or indeed in all three.

During 1915 the growing militarism of Cumann na mBan became obvious. One of its first public displays was in August 1915 at the funeral of the old Fenian, Jeremiah O'Donovan Rossa, when the organisation marched in his funeral procession with the Volunteers and the Irish Citizen Army. This event was to prove a major publicity coup for Cumann na mBan; many of the statements in the military pension applications indicate that many young women joined after the funeral. The Cooney sisters mention this funeral as the point where they became interested in Cumann na mBan, as does Bridget Hegarty, Rose Mullally and others. The organisation also engaged in a relentless and effective propaganda campaign, publishing three nationalist pamphlets: 'The Spanish War by Theobold Wolfe Tone', 'Why Ireland is Poor' and 'Dean Swift on the situation'.[41] Between August 1915 and the Rising of 1916, Cumann na mBan consolidated. By the spring of 1916 it was a 'small but reasonably well organised and partially trained, quasi-military organisation'.[42]

As they became more organised, they became more quasi-military in appearance and ideology. At their convention in 1915 they adopted a uniform. The uniform was similar to that of the Irish Volunteers: a coat, skirt, belt and hat made of Volunteer (dark green) tweed. It remained optional for members because of the cost, members who could not afford it could wear a haversack and a hat. They also had designed and adopted a badge: a Lee Enfield rifle crowned by their initials 'CnamB'. The badges were made from silver or cheaper metals and many members could afford and did buy it. In October 1915 Countess Markievicz, writing in the *Irish Citizen*, suggested that women who were involved should 'dress suitably in short skirts and strong boots, leave your jewels in the bank and buy a revolver'.[43] While many of the women of Cumann na mBan did not, like the Countess, have jewellery to leave in the bank, the sentiments expressed are indicative of the militarisation of Cumann na mBan as 1916 approached.

As plans for the Rising were underway some women were entrusted with insight into what was about to happen. In April 1916, Kathleen Clarke was told by her husband Tom and his fellow Irish Republican Brotherhood (IRB) leader, Seán MacDiarmada, to 'select sixteen girls, members of Cumann na mBan, for despatch work, girls whose silence and discretion they could absolutely rely upon'.[44] Around the same time, Markievicz was taken into confidence by James Connolly as she was to be his 'ghost', that is, take his place in the preparations for the rebellion should something happen to him. The wider membership of Cumann na mBan were not taken into the inner confidences of the IRB, nor were they given all details of the plans. However selected women were trusted with secrets and aspects of the plan, especially those women close to IRB men. Despite the lack of exact knowledge, something they shared with the majority of the Irish Volunteers, Cumann na mBan branches continued to train in first aid, drill and signalling and rifle practice. All of these activities were preparing women for participation in a fight they strongly suspected was coming, but just not when. In contrast women of the Citizen Army were more aware, certainly early in 1916, that a Rising was imminent. Weeks before the Rising many of the younger female members were spending more and more time in Liberty Hall preparing field kits, collecting cans for bomb making and helping with preparations where they could. In the week before the Rising, on a final route march, Rosie Hackett remembered that Connolly addressed them and told them to 'buck up', that the day was coming.[45] Then the call to arms came and on Easter Monday, 1916 'Irish men and women declared their belief in their country's right to National Independence and the willingness to die if need be to win that right'.[46]

The 77 Women: route to the Rising

The list of seventy-seven women who were arrested after the surrender in 1916 is not a comprehensive list of all the women who took part in the Rising. It is limited to the women who were involved in Dublin and who were arrested after the surrender and taken to Richmond Barracks (except for Kathleen Browne and Nell Ryan who were arrested in Wexford). Over 280 women played an active role in the Rising, in Dublin, Wexford (Enniscorthy), Meath (Ashbourne) and Galway (Athenry and Tuam), while in other locations like Cork and Kerry, Cumann na mBan women stood ready with the Irish Volunteers to become involved (although both groups eventually stood down). However, the fact that these women were arrested after the Rising, along with their male comrades, marks them as an insurgent group, a defined group of women who were involved in the Easter Rising. Taking a forensic look at these seventy-seven women as a representative sample, a detailed and complex analysis can be made of the route to politicisation of certain women in the early years of the twentieth century. A close analysis of their biographies demonstrates that this was not a homogenous group.[47] While there are discernible patterns and commonalities between the women in terms of the political activities, there are also differences in how these women came to be involved in an armed uprising. Their involvement in one or more of the three movements of nationalism, socialism and feminism is an aspect of this pattern but differences emerge when studied in relation to the class and age of these women.

The women of the Irish Citizen Army fought mainly in two outposts during 1916, at City Hall and at St. Stephen's Green / Royal College of Surgeons. Among them were women who were given leadership roles in the rebellion – Countess Markievicz, who was second-in-command to Michael Mallin at St. Stephen's Green / Royal College of Surgeons and Kathleen Lynn who was second-in-command to Seán Connolly at City Hall. Nellie Gifford, Madeleine ffrench-Mullen, Markievicz and Lynn represent the cohort of older, middle and upper class, educated, politicised women who, by 1916, had been active in feminist, socialist and nationalist politics for a least a decade. Marie Perolz and Helena Molony had joined Inghinidhe na hÉireann in 1900 and 1903 respectively and Markievicz was a member from 1908, while ffrench-Mullen was also a member and a contributor to *Bean na hÉireann*. Nellie Gifford was active in the IWFL while Lynn was on the executive of one of the other suffrage organisations, the Irish Women's Suffrage and Local Government Association (IWSLGA) from 1903 and associated with the militant suffrage organisation, the Women's Social and Political Union (WSPU) in England. All six women had worked in relief work in Liberty Hall during the 1913 Lockout and were members of the Citizen Army from its foundation. As well as coming from similar backgrounds these women knew each other and moved in the same circles. Lynn met Molony through her friendship with Markievicz and, as Lynn herself stated, Molony 'converted [her] to the National movement'.[48] In 1913 Lynn joined Markievicz, Molony and other activists in the soup kitchens in Liberty Hall and it was here that she met her life long partner Madeleine ffrench-Mullen. Along with Markievicz and Molony they both joined the Citizen Army at its formation and Lynn became its chief medical officer, while Molony was 'in actual charge of the girls on the military side'.[49]

The other twelve Citizen Army women arrested became involved in the Easter Rising through different routes to the aforementioned six. These twelve women were younger, working class women, politicised later than the others, many directly through support of and / or membership of the trade union movement. In surviving pension applications and witness statements many mention direct involvement in the 1913 Lockout and in the relief activities in Liberty Hall as their first political awakening. Citizen Army members Rosie Hackett, Bessie Lynch, Jinny Shanahan and Bridget Davis, the Norgrove sisters (Annie and Emily) were involved in trade union activities from 1911, joining the IWWU and were locked out of their jobs in 1913. This group was among the early members of the women's section of the Citizen Army. As well as trade union activism some of these women were involved in cultural nationalism. Katie Barrett was involved in the Gaelic League and was active in the Irish Citizen

Army's cultural group, the Liberty Players, who staged Sunday night revues and concerts in Liberty Hall. While military ranks among the women in the Citizen Army were vague and unclear, Molony mentioned that Shanahan and Barrett were 'sort of ranked as sergeants' under her in the women's section.[50] Hackett, Shanahan, Davis, Lynch, Maggie Joyce, Bridget Goff, the Norgroves and Barrett all volunteered in the soup kitchen at Liberty Hall during the Lockout, where they met many of the older and more experienced, feminist / nationalist activists.[51] Most of them had joined the women's section of the Citizen Army by 1915 and were all involved in the preparations for the Rising in Liberty Hall in the weeks and months prior to Easter Monday, 1916.

The situation with the women of Cumann na mBan demonstrates the similar patterns and differences as are seen with the women of the Citizen Army. The majority of the Cumann na mBan women arrested came from the Inghinidhe branch, most of whom had mobilised and served together, led by Rose McNamara, at the Marrowbone Lane garrison, under the command of the Irish Volunteer leader there, Éamonn Ceannt.[52] McNamara, the daughter of a shopkeeper, was born in Dublin and was an early member of Inghinidhe na hÉireann, joining in 1906, then followed that organisation into Cumann na mBan in 1914. Other members of the Inghinidhe branch included May Gahan, Julia Grenan, Margaret Kennedy, Bridget Hegarty, the Cooney sisters (Lily, Meg and Annie), Rose Mullally, Sheila O'Hanlon, Josie O'Keefe, the Quigley sisters (Maria and Priscilla), Marcella Cosgrove and Josephine Spicer. All of these women were from working class backgrounds, many of them living (according to the 1911 census) in tenements and artisan dwellings in inner city Dublin. Along with McNamara, Grenan, and Cosgrove were long time members of the original Inghinidhe na hÉireann, but most other members who fought in 1916 joined the Inghinidhe branch after 1914 when it had become part of Cumann na mBan. Although some were involved in the Gaelic League prior to 1914, many date their interest in Cumann na mBan and nationalism from the O'Donovan Rossa funeral (August 1915) which heightened interest in advanced nationalism among a young generation of women and men, especially those women who would have witnessed Cumann na mBan marching in the funeral precession. The Cooney sisters and Bridget Hegarty all joined after the O'Donovan Rossa funeral. Using the 1911 census data it is obvious that most of these young women joined the Inghinidhe branch because it was the branch nearest where they lived; all have home addresses on the south side of the city and the Inghinidhe branch was the only branch based in this area. Therefore, in the context of which branch a woman joined, geographical location rather than an ideological specificity seemed more important. However, ideology did become important once these girls joined. The Inghinidhe branch had among its senior members committed feminist and separatists of long standing, and it is unsurprising that this was the first branch to organise itself on military lines similar to the Irish Volunteers. This meant that the branch had a Commandant (Eileen Walsh), Vice-Commandant (Rose McNamara), Quartermaster (Marcella Cosgrove) and Section Commander (May Byrne). The Inghinidhe branch was motivated, well organised, tight knit and closely associated with the 3rd and 4th battalions of the Irish Volunteers, Dublin Brigade, an indication why it provided many of the Cumann na mBan women out in 1916.

Twelve members of the Central branch, five members of the Fairview branch, two members of the Colmcille branch and two members of the Wexford branch of Cumann na mBan were arrested. Unlike the more organised Inghinidhe branch, many members of these branches made their own way to the various outposts in which they served and most obeyed the command to leave and evade capture prior to the surrender. Interestingly, as with the Inghinidhe women, quite a few members of the other three branches had been involved in cultural nationalism through the Gaelic League prior to joining Cumann na mBan. These include Brigid Foley, the Ryan sisters (Mary Kate and Nell), Nora O'Daly and Kathleen Browne. Most of the women in the Central branch had been in Cumann na mBan from the beginning and some, like Pauline Markham, had been present in the funeral procession of O'Donovan Rossa. The Colmcille and Fairview women were also members of their branches from their inception. For example, in 1914, O'Daly was a founder member of the Fairview branch of Cumann na mBan. Like most other Cumann na mBan branches the Fairview women did first aid classes and also learned rifle cleaning and sighting, drill and others things which might prove useful in assisting the men of the 2nd Battalion (Irish Volunteers) to which the Fairview Cumann was attached. O'Daly was involved in hiding arms brought in during the 1914 Howth gun running and also handed out anti-recruitment leaflets during 1915, especially leaflets targeted at young girls 'telling them not to walk out with soldiers'.[53]

The analysis of the biographical data of the arrested Cumann na mBan women demonstrates the politicisation of women through cultural nationalism and feminism prior to 1914. The older women, those in leadership roles, could be considered more radical in their ideologies, and most of these women had prior involvement in radical feminist and separatist politics of Inghinidhe na hÉireann. While the younger women were also involved in cultural nationalism it was usually through the more conservative nationalism of the Gaelic League. It was in the fevered atmosphere of advanced nationalist politics after 1912 (with the passing of the third Home Rule Bill and the formation of the Irish Volunteers) that most of the younger women joined Cumann na mBan. Often they were looking for a place to express their nationalism in the same manner that their brothers found in the Irish Volunteers.

The Easter Rising has often been posited as a revolution of a young generation of idealists who had rejected the older constitutional politics of their parents. This does ring true when the ages of all the c.280 women who participated in the Rising are studied. The majority were born in the years between 1885 and 1900, which means that many were aged between 16 and 30 years in 1916. Of the seventy-seven women arrested, the ages of fifty-nine of the women in 1916 have been established. The oldest woman arrested, at fifty-eight, was Countess Plunkett, mother of one of the signatories to the Proclamation, Joseph Plunkett. Another older woman arrested was forty-one year old Nell Humphreys, sister of Irish Volunteer leader and founder, The O'Rahilly. Also in her forties at the time was Kathleen Browne of Rathronan who, along with thirty-four year old Nell Ryan of Tomcoole, was arrested for sedition at their homes in south Co. Wexford. Interestingly all the women who would be regarded as more radical were among the older group; Markievicz, Lynn, ffrench-Mullen and Molony were over thirty in 1916: Lynn was forty-two, Markievicz was forty-eight, ffrench-Mullen was thirty-six and Molony was thirty-three.

Of the remaining forty-eight women all were aged between fifteen and thirty with the majority (thirty-five women), aged between fifteen and twenty-five. In the Irish Citizen Army all the arrested women except Lynn, Molony, Markievicz and Perloz were under twenty-five which points to the involvement of young unmarried women in trade union politics from 1911. The women of Cumann na mBan were more mixed in terms of age with girls as young as seventeen (Eileen Cooney) in the organisation's branches along with older, more established activists like Julia Grenan (33), Lily O'Brennan (38) and Marcella Cosgrove (41). However, the age range from this sample of female participants in the 1916 Rising shows that it was a youthful rebellion. While the leaders were generally older, most were still only in their thirties or forties. The rest were in their late teens and early twenties, with the majority being young, and unmarried.

Although the middle class is often regarded as the class that produced the Easter Rising, the majority of the seventy-seven women arrested were lower middle class or working class women. These young women, members of both Cumann na mBan and the Irish Citizen Army, came mainly from the north and south inner city areas of Dublin. Of the twenty-four women members of the Irish Citizen Army who took part in the Rising, eighteen were arrested. Of these, only Markievicz, ffrench-Mullen, Nellie Gifford, and Lynn could be regarded as belonging to the middle (and upper) class, educated, revolutionary elite. Molony and Perolz were slightly different in coming from a lower middle class background. The remaining thirteen women of the Citizen Army are more representative of the working class women, younger than the more radical women, politicised later through involvement in trade unionism, then coming to nationalism and feminism through this route. Most were born in Dublin and were daughters of unskilled labourers or tradesmen (among them Katie Barrett, Bridget Brady, Martha Kelly and Rosie Hackett). Brady, Hackett, Jinny Shanahan, Bridget Davis were all workers in Jacob's factory who lost their jobs during the 1913 Lockout and all appear in the 'Freedom's Martyrs' photograph of the IWWU taken with Delia Larkin in 1911.

An analysis of the class affiliations of the seventy-seven women arrested shows there was a distinct divide between those who were the leaders and those who were ordinary members in the Citizen Army. The similarities in the biographical details of Markievicz, Molony, ffrench-Mullen, Gifford, Lynn and Perolz, all from non-Catholic (excluding Molony), middle and upper class (excluding Molony and Perolz) backgrounds, demonstrate the dominance of these radical middle-class women as leaders in the socialist feminist activism. Interestingly, these women either never married (Lynn, ffrench-Mullen, Molony) or had short lived or unconventional marriages (Gifford, Perolz, Markievicz). As well as the eighteen Citizen Army women, forty-nine members of Cumann na mBan were arrested. Of these forty-nine women, twenty-nine were members of the Inghinidhe branch of Cumann na mBan. The Central branch of Cumann na mBan contained the members of the executive committee of Cumann na mBan, and forty-four of its members mobilised for the Rising; of these, twelve were arrested. Those middle class women, members of the Central branch who were among the founders of Cumann na mBan had either ceased involvement in the organisation (Colum had emigrated, O'Farrelly had left Cumann na mBan after the

Remondite split), did not take an active part in the Rising in Dublin (Wyse Power was a dispatch carrier to Wexford, O'Rahilly was pregnant and Bloxham was not in Dublin) or, if they did take part, were not arrested (Louise Gavan Duffy). Senior Cumann na mBan woman Kathleen Clarke had wished to take part but her husband Tom insisted she stay at home and 'carry out her orders, that no matter how things went the work entrusted to me would still be there to be done'.[54] Of the members of Central branch who did participate and were arrested most were from working class or lower middle class urban backgrounds. Among them were Meg Carron and Nellie Ennis, daughters of a general labourers, Annie Higgins, a talented musician, daughter of a cooper, Carrie Mitchell who was working as a clerk at the time, and Nurse Catherine Treston, daughter of a carpenter. As with the Inghinidhe branch, most of the Central branch women were Dublin born, young, working class women. Of the others branches, Fairview and Colmcille, ten and seven women respectively participated in the Rising and six and two respectively were arrested. As with the other branches these women were also working class or in the case of Fairview's Bridget Foley, the daughter of a farmer from Cork. Among those who would be considered middle class was Lily O'Brennan, writer and schoolteacher, and Mary Kate and Nell Ryan, two of the famous Ryan sisters of Tomcoole, Co. Wexford, daughters of a well-to-do farmer. Another middle class Cumann na mBan member arrested was Kathleen Browne of Rathronan, Co. Wexford, taken in by the army in Wexford for raising the tricolour over her family's ancestral castle. Therefore, in terms of female participation, the majority of the female rebels were from working class, urban backgrounds. Analysis also shows that, while leadership roles are most commonly held by middle class women, working class women did function as leaders. In particular, the leaders of the Inghinidhe branch, Eileen Walsh, Rose McNamara, Marcella Cosgrove and May Byrne were all working class women.

This in-depth study of the seventy-seven women arrested serves to elucidate 'the different types of connection between them, and hence how they operated within and upon the social [and political] institutions of their time'.[55] Analysis shows the close connections and networks which existed between the older, middle class and more politicised cohort during the early years of the twentieth century. Most of these women were involved in two or more of the three dominant ideological movements, feminism, nationalism and socialism. Devoted to the causes they espoused and living unconventional and often public lives, all could be considered among the more radical activists of that time. Analysis also shows that the more radical separatist and feminist women were most engaged with social activism, eventually becoming more ideologically socialist in their thinking. These radical women joined the Citizen Army rather than Cumann na mBan. However, in the post-Rising period, as the Citizen Army became less active and Cumann na mBan developed into the largest female nationalist organisation infused with a more defined feminist ideology, most of the Citizen Army women became Cumann na mBan members. Indeed by 1917 one of the most famous members of the Citizen Army, Countess Markievicz, was elected president of Cumann na mBan. The research also vividly demonstrates that this was a youthful rebellion. While the leadership women were generally over 30 and several were in their forties, most of the rank and file members of both Cumann na mBan and the Citizen Army were in their late teens and early twenties. These were young women who had grown up in a world which was rapidly transforming, experiencing a political awakening in nationalist and feminist politics and trade union activism. The biographical data shows what while the leadership of the various organisations was most likely middle class, a growing involvement of working class women in revolutionary politics becomes evident, especially after 1911. Most were politicised through their involvement in the trade union movement and came later to nationalism than their middle class sisters.

The research also highlights the various familial and kinship links among the women and between the women and men. It was not unusual for groups of sisters to become politicised, usually once the eldest got involved the younger siblings followed suit. Among the seventy-seven women are the Ryan sisters, the Quigley sisters, the Foley sisters, the Cooney sisters, the Norgrove sisters, the Listons and the Martins. As well as their female siblings, having brothers or other male relatives involved eased the way for many of these women into revolutionary politics. Kathleen Barrett of the Citizen Army had three brothers out in 1916, including Seán Connolly who was killed at City Hall. Josie McGowan, a member of Inghinidhe branch, had two brothers in the Irish Volunteers, while fellow Inghinidhe member Kathleen Murphy was married to Seamus Murphy, a captain in the 4th battalion of the Irish Volunteers. The Liston sisters served in Marrowbone Lane alongside their brother, Irish Volunteer Michael Liston. James Ryan, a member of the Irish Volunteers, served in the GPO and was brother to Nell, Min and Mary Kate 'Kit' Ryan. Rose McNamara was introduced to Inghinidhe na hÉireann in 1906 by Marie Perolz, whose brother was married to

McNamara's sister. Nora O'Daly's brother-in-law Paddy was one of the Volunteers responsible for the attack on the Magazine Fort in the Phoenix Park at the outbreak of the Rising, while Joseph Murtagh, the younger brother of her friend Brigid Murtagh, served with Na Fianna in the GPO. May O'Moore from Fairview Cumann na mBan had a brother Seán who fought with Ned Daly at the Four Courts. Nell Humphreys' brother, The O'Rahilly, and her son, Richard 'Dick' Humphreys, both served in the GPO. In addition, Douglas ffrench-Mullen, brother of Madeleine ffrench-Mullen, was a captain in the Irish Volunteers, stationed at the South Dublin Union garrison. For the Seerys and the Norgroves the Rising was a family affair. Catherine Seery's brothers Patrick and James, and her father John, all fought, while Annie and Emily Norgrove's father, George and mother, Maria, also participated in the Rising.

Analysis of the seventy-seven women arrested in the aftermath of the Rising show that this group of revolutionary women were a politically and ideologically complex group. They were from different backgrounds, ages, religions and classes and took shifting and varied ideological routes towards involvement in the Easter Rising. These women are not united under one homogenous, uncontested banner but despite their differences there was, certainly after 1913, a sense of comradeship and shared common purpose. By 1913 most of the women involved in feminism, nationalism and socialism had worked together, especially in Liberty Hall during the Lockout. They often shared resources, for example Kathleen Lynn gave first aid instruction to both the women's section of the Irish Citizen Army and to members of Cumann na mBan. In 1911 Markievicz had appeared on the platform when the IWWU was launched. In 1912 the Inghinidhe ha hÉireann women and the IWFL feminists had worked together on the campaign to get female suffrage included in the third Home Rule Bill. This is not to say that ideological differences and debates between the women disappeared. Certainly when Cumann na mBan was established the more militant feminist women were not happy at its 'auxiliary' status. While these political and ideological differences remained and would re-emerge later in the revolutionary period, the pattern that emerges by 1916 is of politicised women of all ages, classes and ideologies becoming more militantly committed to the ideal of a free Ireland and an Ireland in which the political voice of women would be heard and heeded.

Notes

1   BMH WS 185 (Margaret Loo Kennedy)
2   BMH WS 482 (Rose McNamara), p. 8
3   Tom Clonan, 'The Forgotten Role of Women Insurgents in The 1916 Rising' (*The Irish Times*, March 30, 2006). See also Ann Matthews, *Renegades; Irish Republican Women 1900–1922* (Dublin: Mercier Press, 2010), p. 154
4   Mary Cullen, 'Women, emancipation and politics, 1860–1984' in J.R. Hill (ed.) *A New History of Ireland Vol. VII, Ireland 1921–1984* (Oxford, Oxford University Press, 2003), p. 846
5   Roy Foster, *Vivid Faces: The Revolutionary Generation in Ireland 1890–1923* (London: Allen Lane, 2014), pp. xxii–xxiii
6   Senia Pašeta, *Irish Nationalist Women, 1900–1918*, (Oxford, Oxford University Press, 2013), pp.164–165
7   Ibid., p. 17
8   Ibid.
9   Margaret Ward, *In their own Voice: Women and Irish Nationalism* (Cork: Cork University Press, 2001), p.16.
10 D.A.J. MacPherson, *Women and the Irish Nation: Gender, Culture and Irish Identity, 1890–1914* (London: Palgrave Macmillan, 2012), p. 99
11 Hilairí Ó Murchadha, 'The Growth and Decline of the Gaelic League in Co. Wexford, 1900–1950' in *The Past: The Organ of the Uí Cinsealaigh Historical Society* (2005), p. 6
12 BMH WS 384 (J.J. O'Kelly / Sceilg), p. 13
13 Pašeta, *Irish Nationalist Women, 1900–1918*, p. 25
14 Margaret Ward, *Unmanageable Revolutionaries*, p. 86
15 BMH WS 391 (Helena Molony), p. 2
16 Karen Steele, *Women, The Press and Politics During the Irish Revival* (New York: Syracuse University Press, 2007), p. 109. In the suffrage newspaper *The Irish Citizen* in 1913, Countess Markievicz, *Bean na h-Éireann* contributor and later 1916 rebel, identified these three movements of Ireland as the nationalist, women's and labour movements.
17 Steele, *Women, The Press and Politics During the Irish Revival*, p. 109.
18 Sikata Banerjee, *Muscular Nationalism: Gender, Violence and Empire in India and Ireland 1914–2004* (New York: NYU Press, 2012) p. 79
19 Pašeta, *Irish Nationalist Women, 1900–1918*, p. 62
20 Margaret Ward (1995), *In their own Voice*, p. 38
21 Angela Bourke et al (eds) (2001), *The Field Day Anthology of Irish Writing and Traditions, Volume V* (Cork: Cork University Press), p. 92
22 Cullen 'Women, emancipation and politics, 1860–1984' pp. 851–852
23 Pašeta, *Irish Nationalist Women, 1900–1918*, p.116
24 Because the IWFL was determined to remain non-aligned, individual members, rather than the IWFL as a group, cooperated with Inghinidhe, that way the IWFL could preserve it non-aligned status.
25 Mary Jones, *Those Obstreperous Lassies; A history of the Irish Women Workers Union* (Dublin: Gill and Macmillan, 1988), pp.1–6
26 Pašeta, *Irish Nationalist Women, 1900–1918*, p. 125
27 *The Irish Times*, Oct 17, 2012 Special Supplement, *Women and the Vote*. Therese Moriarty 'Suffrage and socialism: links with Labour' http://www.irishtimes.com/culture/heritage/century/century–women–and–the–vote
28 Ann Matthews, *The Irish Citizen Army* (Dublin: Mercier Press, 2014), pp. 18–23
29 The Save the Kiddies campaign was a scheme, to send the children of locked out workers

to England for the duration of the strike. It was organised by Dora Montefiore, an English socialist and feminist, in cooperation with the Irish socialist and feminist women including the IWWU. The plan was opposed by the Catholic Church who feared that Irish children in English homes would lose their religion. The scheme was called off and the funds for it redirected to the soup kitchen in Liberty Hall where around 3,000 children were fed every morning during the Lockout.

30 Pašeta, *Irish Nationalist Women, 1900–1918*, p. 168
31 Rosemary Cullen Owens, *A Social History of Women in Ireland 1870–1970* (Dublin: Gill and Macmillan, 2005), p. 113
32 McCarthy, *Cumann na mBan*, p. 13. *Leabhair na mBan* was published in 1919
33 Cullen Owens, *A Social History of Women in Ireland 1870–1970*, p. 113
34 Pašeta, *Irish Nationalist Women, 1900–1918*, p. 136
35 Ward (ed.), *In their own Voice*, p. 50
36 Redmond made this speech at a public meeting at Woodenbridge, Co. Wicklow on September 20, 1914
37 McCarthy, *Cumann na mBan*, p. 36
38 Cumann na mBan Leabhar na mBan (Dublin, 1919) p. 5
39 Pašeta, *Irish Nationalist Women, 1900–1918*, p. 147
40 McCarthy, *Cumann na mBan*, pp. 26–27
41 Ibid., p. 50
42 Ibid.
43 Countess Markievicz, 'Buy a revolver' in *The Irish Citizen*, October 23, 1915
44 Ward (ed.), *In Their Own Voice*, p. 59
45 BMH WS 546 (Roseanna 'Rosie' Hackett), p. 1
46 Nora Connolly 'from Atlantic Monthly (1916)' in Bourke, et al (eds) *The Field Day Anthology of Irish Writing* Vol. V p. 104
47 See all biographies of the seventy-seven women in Appendix 1
48 BMH WS 357 (Kathleen Lynn), p. 1
49 IE/MA, MSP34REF11739 (Helena Molony)
50 Ibid.
51 See Military Pension applications made by Hackett, Shanahan, Davis, Lynch , Joyce, Goff, the Norgroves and Barrett for information on when they considered they began their association with the Irish Citizen Army.
52 The majority of Cumann na mBan women who were out in Dublin in 1916 came from the Central branch but they served mainly in the GPO and the Four Courts areas, where they either obeyed the order to leave before surrender or they managed to evade capture after surrender.
53 IE/MA, MSP34REF13563 (Nora O'Daly/ née Gillies)
54 Helen Litton (ed.) *Kathleen Clarke: Revolutionary Women* (Dublin: The O'Brien Press, 2008), p. 112 Although Tom Clarke did not know it, Kathleen was also six months pregnant. When she visited him before his execution in Kilmainham Goal, she didn't tell him of her pregnancy as she feared it would add to his anxieties. She later miscarried the pregnancy.
55 K.S.B. Keats-Rohan, 'Biography, Identity and Names: Understanding the Pursuit of the Individual in Prosopography' in Keats-Rohan ed. *Prosopography Approaches and Applications: A Handbook* (University of Oxford, Linacre College, 2007), p. 141

CHAPTER TWO

—

Frightful Insurgents – What the Women Did:
City Hall, the Four Courts and the GPO Garrisons

*When we walked out that Easter Monday morning we felt in, a very
real sense that we were walking with Ireland into the sun.*
(McGarry, *The Abbey Rebels of 1916*, p. 140)

THE EASTER RISING BEGAN ON Monday, 24 April 1916 as a chaotic, shambolic affair. Mobilisation started from 10a.m. that morning with individuals and groups receiving messages from the organisers, many carried by women couriers. In all, almost 280 women, mainly members of Cumann na mBan or the Irish Citizen Army, participated in the Easter Rising. About 200 took part in Dublin, others in Galway, Enniscorthy and Ashbourne, Co. Meath, but many more had been prepared to fight. Cumann na mBan, along with the Irish Volunteers, had planned a large scale mobilisation on Easter Sunday, the planned start of the Rising. However, like the men of the Irish Volunteers, their plans were thrown into confusion by the counter-manding order signed by the Chief-of-Staff of the Irish Volunteers, Eoin MacNeill, which appeared in the newspapers on Easter Sunday. The cancellation of the general mobilisation meant that many women either went home on Sunday or remained at home on Easter Monday.

Some of the women were despondent at the countermanding order. Nora O'Daly didn't quite believe what she read in the Sunday newspapers so she 'went to Father Matthew Park and there learned that the news was only too heartbreakingly true'.[2] Despite this disappointment, as soon as news came through that the Rising was going ahead, the more organised branches of Cumann na mBan such as the Inghinidhe branches or the more determined individuals from the Central, Fairview, Fingal and Colmcille branches in Dublin along with the women's section of the Irish Citizen Army, made their way to various outposts during Easter Monday and Tuesday. On Easter Monday morning the Inghinidhe branch mobilised on the south side of the city in two groups: one of which was attached to the 3rd Battalion of the Irish Volunteers and the other to the 4th Battalion. The women attached to the 3rd Battalion had instructions to mobilise at the corner of Holles Street and Merrion Square, from where they were to join the men under Commandant Éamon de Valera at Boland's Mill.[3] However, de Valera sent a courier informing them that he did not want women in his garrison. Boland's Mill was therefore one of the few outposts in which no woman saw service, although a number acted as couriers to and from units under de Valera's command during the week. Disappointed with the response from Boland's Mill, members of this Inghinidhe group managed to join other outposts and did see service during the week. The second Inghinidhe group mobilised at Cleaver's Gaelic League Hall on Donore Avenue, off the South Circular Road, where they were sent to join 'A' Company, 4th Battalion, Irish Volunteers, to take over Marrowbone Lane Distillery (Jameson's), which was under the command of Éamonn Ceannt, who was stationed in the South Dublin Union.

In some respects women had already provided essential work for the Rising during Easter Sunday and Monday. In the weeks prior to the Rising Cumann na mBan women Kitty O'Doherty, Effie Taafe and Brigid Foley had transported and hidden guns when word had come of an imminent raid on O'Doherty's house, where she had 'a regular arsenal under the floor in [her] sitting-room'.[4] Following MacNeill's counter-manding order several Cumann na mBan women were sent around Dublin city and county by Pearse, Connolly, Clarke and MacDiarmada, carrying news of the plan to rise on Easter Monday. Countess Markievicz had brought Cumann na mBan mem-bers Elizabeth O'Farrell and Julia Grenan to Liberty Hall on Easter Sunday. There they received instructions to carry messages around the country. O'Farrell left to deliver dispatches to Volunteers in Athenry, Spiddal and Galway city, while Grenan went to Dundalk and Carrickmacross. Cumann na mBan Central branch member Brigid Foley was sent in a taxi to Cork carrying a sealed message from the Military Council for Tómas MacCurtain confirming MacNeill's countermand and postponing mobilisation until noon on Monday.

In Dublin, on the north side of the river Liffey, the Central branch of Cumann na mBan were attached to Ned Daly's 1st Battalion, Irish Volunteers and would have expected to join him in the Four Courts area. However, on Monday as the Rising began, the only Cumann na mBan members in position were Winifred Carney in the GPO and the Inghinidhe members who mobilised with Ceannt in Emerald Square, off Cork Street. Over the course of the next few days, individual members from the Central, Fairview and Colmcille branches made determined efforts to get to the various outposts. Some commandants, including Daly at the Four Courts, turned them away at first but a directive came from the GPO that women were to be allowed to join the fight. Fairview branch member Nora O'Daly left her three young children at home and with her friends, May Moore and Bridget Murtagh, made her way by tram into the city centre. On St. Stephen's Green they were spotted by Countess Markievicz, looking to join in the fight. She invited them to serve with the garrison, which they did, and they spent the week in St. Stephen's Green and the Royal College of Surgeons. As the week went on more and more women joined the outposts. May Moore later said they joined Markievicz, as in the confusion, they lost their 'own crowd'. This type of confusion was experienced by many members of Cumann na mBan.[5] Despite this, the women were determined to play their part; the battalion in the GPO started the week with one woman, Winifred Carney, armed with her revolver in one hand and typewriter in the other, but by the end of the week over thirty women had served in the GPO in some capacity or other.

The members of the women's section of the Irish Citizen Army were more organised and disciplined. Twenty-eight female members of the Irish Citizen Army participated in the Rising. Most of them had spent the previous week on duty in Liberty Hall and were aware that something was about to happen. The Citizen Army women spent their time making bandages, bandoliers and bombs, putting together ration packs, learning first aid and generally preparing for the fight. On Easter Sunday, James Connolly, Commandant of the Irish Citizen Army, took his men and women on a route march around Dublin, where their bugler William Oman stopped and blew his bugle at each chosen Rising outpost. That evening many of the women and men were ordered to stay in Liberty Hall until further notice and, as Rosie Hackett later wrote, 'Connolly told us we would have to buck up and get ready, that the day was coming'.[6] On Easter Monday morning just before midday, William Oman stood outside Liberty Hall and again sounded his bugle, this time to call the women and men of the Citizen Army to fall in. At this point most of the signatories of the Proclamation, Tom Clarke, James Connolly, Patrick Pearse, Seán MacDiamada and Joseph Plunkett, had arrived at Liberty Hall. Also present was Irish Volunteer leader, The O'Rahilly, who despite his attempts to call off the Rising decided, if it was happening, he had to take part. It was, he said to Countess Markievicz, 'madness, but it [was] glorious madness'.[7]

City Hall garrison

At midday on Easter Monday, the newly promoted captain of the Irish Citizen Army, Seán Connolly, led his band of thirty men and ten women from Liberty Hall towards Dublin Castle. Having received his orders from James Connolly, he was on his way to take City Hall and Dublin Castle and hold the buildings for the duration of the Rising. Among this group were some of the longest serving female members of the Citizen Army including Abbey actress, feminist and trade unionist Helena Molony. She had spent the previous weeks in Liberty Hall helping with preparations for the Rising and was now marching on City Hall armed with her own revolver and ammunition. She and Jinny Shanahan had actually remained in Liberty Hall during the preparations, sleeping on a pile of men's clothes at the back of the union shop. As the decision was made to begin the Rising on Easter Monday, Elizabeth Lynch recalled that after the Citizen Army Sunday route march, they were ordered to remain in Liberty Hall for the night. Before they set out at noon on Easter Monday, James Connolly 'gave out revolvers to [the] girls saying: 'Don't use them except in the last resort'.[8] Molony remembered that this Citizen Army contingent:

> were instructed to go to Dublin Castle, under Captain Seán Connolly; We were to attack the Castle. It was a very wise move, It was expected that the psychological effect of attacking Dublin Castle, the citadel of foreign rule for seven hundred years, would be considerable when the news spread through the country.[9]

As the group headed off, the Chief Medical Officer with the Citizen Army, Dr. Kathleen Lynn, filled her car with first aid supplies and prepared to join them. Molony marched at the head of her group of Citizen Army women, which included Jinny Shanahan, Katie Barrett (née Connolly, sister of Seán), the Norgrove sisters (Annie and Emily), Brigid Davis, Brigid Goff, Bessie Lynch, Molly O'Reilly and Brigid Brady. She later recalled that as they marched up Dame Street some of the contingent went to occupy City Hall while Connolly and a few men along with Molony and 'her girls' veered off towards the gate of the upper courtyard of Dublin Castle. The policeman on duty at the gate attempted to stop them but Connolly shot him dead and tried to run through the gate. The insurgents managed to seize the guardroom and disarmed the six soldiers inside. Connolly and his contingent did not know that Dublin Castle was very lightly defended at that moment. As well as the six soldiers they had disarmed there was a force of only twenty-five soldiers in nearby Ship Street Barracks. Had they held their position, the insurgents might have succeeded in taking the Castle and capturing the

Under-Secretary for Ireland, Sir Matthew Nathan, who was in the Castle at a meeting with the British Army's chief intelligence officer Major Ivan Price and the Secretary of the Post Office, Arthur Norway. As the three men held their meeting they heard the shots that signalled the attack on the Castle, Price pulled his service revolver and began firing through the window at the insurgents. Nathan, with the constables on duty, managed to quickly lock the upper and lower gates of the Castle thereby preventing the place falling to Connolly and his contingent. With this early setback, Connolly and his men and women made their way to City Hall and joined the rest of the group there. Within a few minutes they had secured the basement and ground floor and were able to get on the roof of City Hall where they had an excellent view over all possible approaches.

In the meantime Lynn, accompanied by Countess Markievicz, arrived at City Hall with her car full of first aid supplies. She had to climb over the iron gates at the front to gain access and, on meeting Connolly, was told to make her way to the roof as they were expecting an attack. Bemused onlookers were startled at the sight of women in long skirts scrambling over the wrought iron fences in front of City Hall. Markievicz, Brigid Davis and others unloaded the medical supplies and Markievicz left in Lynn's car for St. Stephen's Green. According to Emily Norgrove, who noted that women from the Citizen Army had continued on to Christ Church, Markievicz came across them there and ordered them back to City Hall.[10] The women set up a field hospital on the first floor of the building and then Lynn went with Jinny Shanahan to the roof of City Hall where she found several of the group taking up positions. The insurgents were not long in City Hall when gun fire from several buildings around them, including the Castle, began to rain down on them. Nathan had requested reinforcements from Ship Street Barracks which soon arrived in Dublin Castle. Soon after, Citizen Army bugler William Oman noticed, from his elevated position on the roof, 'an ominous-looking force of about 200 khaki uniforms making its way towards Ship St. Barracks'.[11] It became very dangerous to move around the roof of City Hall and within a few minutes Connolly had been wounded in the elbow. Despite the danger Lynn noticed that 'it was a beautiful day' up on the roof with a 'hot sun' beating down on them.[12] However, because they failed to take the Castle, they were in an insecure position and, needing reinforcements, Connolly dispatched Molly O'Reilly and then Helena Molony to the GPO to request that James Connolly send some men to their aid. Having delivered the request, Molony returned to City Hall and climbed back on the roof where she noticed that Connolly, an Abbey actor like her and a close friend, was walking around with his head sticking up above the protection of the parapet. At this stage the sniper fire directed at City Hall was constant and the other insurgents were crawling about keeping their heads below the parapet. Having been slightly wounded some time earlier, Connolly's luck now ran out. Horrified, Lynn, Molony and some of the other women heard a shot and saw him fall back, fatally wounded by a sniper shot to the body. Brigid Davis ran to him and cradled his head in her lap where he lay.[13] Lynn knew immediately that the wound was fatal, she saw that 'first aid was useless. He died almost immediately... Jinny Shanahan whispered an Act of Contrition in his ear'.[14] The death of Connolly, the first rebel casualty of the Rising, had a demoralising effect on the City Hall garrison. His sister, Katie, and his younger brother Mattie, who was only fifteen at the time, witnessed his death. While Mattie cried bitter tears, the Citizen Army snipers returned fire on the soldiers in the Bedford Tower inside Dublin Castle. Joe Reilly, Lynn and other senior officers immediately took command and tried to instil some morale and fighting spirit back among their contingent.

The attack on City Hall had taken the Dublin Castle authorities by surprise but as the day wore on they began to formulate plans to retake the building. At dusk on Monday, a battalion of soldiers from the Curragh arrived at the Castle and assumed positions for an attack. As soon as the troops arrived, Nathan and the officers in Dublin Castle began to put their plan into action. A.H. Norway was still in the Castle and recalled hearing the bullets and bombs going off and seeing the Castle Yard crowded with soldiers and among them 'from time to time was carried in a woman, caught in the act of carrying ammunition to the insurgents and fighting like trapped cats'.[15] Inside City Hall the insurgents were coming under sustained fire while the 'bullet[s] fell like rain'.[16] Elizabeth 'Bessie' Lynch had been dispatched to Liberty Hall to bring back some reinforcements and a few men returned with her. However, as Lynn noted, the death of Connolly had taken some of the heart out of the Citizen Army men and women. They continued to fire on the British troops but she:

> often thought afterwards that it was surprising that those soldiers were allowed to enter the Castle yard unmolested by our men. I think that Seán Connolly's death had a demoralising effect on the City Hall men. It was a pity some attack was not made on them because immediately after their arrival the fusillade started.[17]

Despite the bombardment all round them Molony, who was in charge of food supplies, managed to find some oats and make porridge for the tired, hungry and demoralised garrison. As night fell the British troops secured their positions on nearby buildings and targeted the insurgents on the roof of City Hall. The shelling from the Castle was intense, with the concentration of fire on a large window at the rear of the City Hall building. Mattie Connolly heard from a woman on sentry duty on the ground floor that a breech in the wall was about to happen. Annie Norgrove noted that the bullets hopped 'like hail off the chimney pots' and just as she heard a warning shout to keep her head down 'a chimney pot smashed in smithereens around me'.[18] A hole opened up in the rear of the building and members of the Citizen Army rushed down from the roof to try and stem the tide of incoming British soldiers. Bullets were flying everywhere and chunks of plaster fell from the ornate ceiling and wall decorations. Women and men took shelter where they could, often crouching behind the huge stone columns. British troops began to flood in through the hole they had blasted in the rear wall. The insurgents fired back but were overwhelmed by the sheer number of troops coming towards them. They began to fall back towards the first floor of the building. Molony had gone onto the roof to check on her comrades and on coming back down found the building beginning to collapse around them. The big cornices were falling all round creating a very dangerous situation and, as she said, she 'would not mind being shot, but... would not like to be crushed'.[19] The situation in the building was now becoming untenable. After her lucky escape from injury earlier, Annie Norgrove took shelter between pillars in the great hall on the ground floor. The British soldiers called out to the insurgents to surrender. Norgrove grabbed Molony by the arm and said 'Miss Molony... we are not going to give in? Mr. Connolly said we were not to surrender... She was terrified, but there was no surrender about her'.[20]

However, they could no longer hold out against the overwhelming numbers of British troops now inside the building, so the men and women on the ground floor surrendered. Lynn described the moment where she was:

> suddenly told by a voice in the dark to put up my hands which I did. I was asked by an officer who was there. I said some women and a wounded man. I found out afterwards that men were there too, but I did not know it at the time.[21]

She told the officer in charge that she was a doctor and he presumed that she had come in to offer medical aid. He was surprised to find out she belonged to the Citizen Army and was an insurgent. To Molony's considerable annoyance 'the British officers thought the girls had been taken prisoner by the rebels... They asked them 'Did they do anything to you'.[22] As she wrote later 'the women in the Citizen Army were not first-aiders, but did military work, except where it suited them to be first-aiders'.[23] Once the women and men on the ground floor were taken into custody and removed into Dublin Castle, the British troops secured that floor but the insurgents still held the upper floors and roof of the building. As the troops moved upstairs they met Jinny Shanahan and the few remaining women on the first floor. Again not believing that women could be rebels, they presumed she and the others had been taken hostage by the Citizen Army men when the Rising began. They asked Shanahan if she knew how many more men were on the upper floors and she told them 'There are hundreds upstairs - big guns and everything'.[24] As a result of her misinformation the remaining Citizen Army contingent on the roof held out longer than expected as the British troops thought they faced many more insurgents than were actually there. This caused them to proceed slowly with care and caution. Shanahan told Molony that when the British officer later found out she was a member of the Citizen Army he was very angry at her ruse. Shanahan, Brigid Brady and Brigid Davis were the last women arrested in City Hall and taken into Dublin Castle.

It was dawn on Tuesday morning before the final assault on the roof of City Hall began when there were only about a dozen exhausted Citizen Army men left on the roof. British troops clambered up the stairs and onto the roof through the skylight. The men on the roof fired back, but worn out and outnumbered, with comrades falling wounded alongside them, they surrendered. City Hall had fallen. The insurgents still standing and able to walk were arrested and taken to Dublin Castle where they were all, men and women, removed to Ship Street Barracks at the back of the Castle. As the Rising was still in full fury all over the city, the British authorities had to secure the City Hall insurgents and kept them in Ship Street Barracks until the surrender on Saturday, 29 April. At Ship Street the women were all put into a 'large room which seemed to be underground, because we could see the people passing above through a grating'.[25] Lynn said that they got a good dinner on the first day but as the days wore on the food got worse and worse. The conditions in the room were horrible. Molony wrote that they had to sleep on 'old bits of mattresses... used by the soldiers. They were covered with vermin; and before a day had passed we were all covered with vermin too'.[26] Lynn called these mattresses 'biscuits' and they were given grey blankets, also covered in lice, and while the 'scratching was not so bad in the daytime… in the night-time it was perfectly awful'.[27] The sanitary conditions were primitive and they had to be escorted by a soldier to use the lavatories; the women found this lack of privacy difficult to accept.[28]

Later in the week other arrested women joined them in the filthy room. Conditions deteriorated and by Friday, 28 April, the women were getting nothing to eat or drink other than hard biscuits, dry bread and water. Brigid Foley and Marie Perolz of Cumann na mBan and Kathleen Clarke, also of Cumann na mBan, wife of Tom Clarke, were all arrested after the surrender and brought to Ship Street Barracks. Foley described their big room as a terrible place 'there were no sanitary arrangements. A sergeant came with a bucket which he placed behind the door. We became infested with fleas and lice'.[29] This is where Kathleen Clarke spent the hours waiting for the call to visit her husband, before his execution. Her ordeal cannot have been made easier with the din created by some prisoners. Foley described one woman who was making a row:

> When I asked her why she was there she said she had run after one of the Volunteers with a loaf of bread and a soldier had hashed it out of her hand. She lifted a stone and threw it at the soldiers who arrested her. I told her that one of our friends – Mrs. Clarke – was very ill and asked her to shut up and give her chance to rest. She replied that if she made enough row and we objected, they would let her go. She told the policeman that she had left a young baby at home and wanted to feed it. She was let out after that.[30]

On Saturday, 29 April after the general surrender, the City Hall women were marched with the men to Richmond Barracks. There they encountered the many dozens of other women who had fought in other outposts and they were able to find out what had been happening while they were imprisoned in Ship Street Barracks.

Nine women had been arrested at City Hall and all were members of the Irish Citizen Army. They were Katie Barrett, Brigid Brady, Brigid Davis, Elizabeth 'Bessie' Lynch, Dr. Kathleen Lynn, Helena Molony, Annie Norgrove, her sister Emily Norgrove and Jinny Shanahan. They had served as couriers and dispatch carriers, first aid assistants with their chief medical office, Dr. Lynn, they ran the food commissariat and served as sentries and look-outs on the roof. After Seán Connolly was killed, Lynn became the senior officer in City Hall and was the person who offered the surrender on Tuesday, 25 April 1916. These women experienced dreadful conditions in Ship Street Barracks for almost a week, then a march through hostile crowds to Richmond

Barracks and further imprisonment in Kilmainham Gaol. Most of the City Hall women were released on 8/9 May along with the bulk of the other seventy-seven imprisoned women. However, Helena Molony and Kathleen Lynn, continued to be incarcerated as they were regarded as dangerous subversives and were moved to Mountjoy Gaol. Molony was then transferred, firstly to Lewes Prison in England and later to Aylesbury Prison. She was eventually released in December 1916. Lynn was deported to England under the conditions of the Defence of the Realm Act (DORA) and remained there for some months. By 1917 she was back in Ireland and working for the national cause, as were most of her female comrades.

The Four Courts garrison and North King Street outpost

On Easter Monday 1916 Commandant Edward Daly, O/C 1st Battalion Dublin Brigade, Irish Volunteers set up his headquarters in St. John's Convent, situated just off North King Street. Daly's orders were to hold open a secure line from the Four Courts on the river Liffey through to Cabra, which would provide an escape route out of the city for the Volunteers if needed. His orders were also to prevent or delay any British military advancing into the city from west Dublin. Because of Eoin MacNeill's countermanding order, Daly only had 130 men and women at his disposal on Easter Monday. In order to hold such a vast area with such limited numbers, he deployed his Volunteers to positions he believed would be strategically important. Divided into five companies, Daly's men took over several buildings in the Church Street, North King Street and Four Courts areas. They set about securing the area, constructing barricades and moving to the south-side of the river to occupy the Mendicity Institute. The Mendicity was an extremely important outpost. Seán Heuston's orders were to delay the advance of British troops coming from the Royal (now Collins) Barracks and reinforcements expected from the Curragh who would arrive at Kingsbridge (now Heuston) Station.

Cumann na mBan women expected to be called up to serve in the Four Courts. Phyllis Morkan recalled that Ned Daly told her that 'if there was going to be fighting, they would need all the women they could get.[31] However, once his men were in the Four Courts area, Daly never sent a direct order for women to join him. Despite this, many women succeeded in getting to the Four Courts and serving the week there. Unlike the Volunteers who mobilised at certain points around the city that morning, word generally filtered through to Cumann na mBan women that operations were underway. For example, Anne Fahy, a member of the Central branch, heard from Pauline Morkan that she was to mobilise at their allotted location – the Black Church, near Parnell Street. On reaching the church she found some of her comrades there. Phyllis Morkan, sister-in-law of Pauline Morkan, also mobilised at the Church. She recalled:

> When we got there we saw members of the C. na mB. [*sic*] about 14 or 15, walking around in twos and threes. The orders were, not to stand around in groups. We were all in mufti – uniform would have attracted too much attention. We could not wear even a badge. All day, or rather all afternoon, we walked about and hearing in the distance a good, deal of shooting. During that time all sorts of rumours were going around, people coming and telling us that O'Connell St. was strewn with dead Lancers. We waited on and presently an order came from Daly to dismiss and report again the following morning.[32]

On their way home Phyllis and Pauline came along North King Street and seeing the Volunteers there managed to get through the barricade at the junction at North King Street and Church Street and went to St. John's Convent. They were sent to a comrade living in Phibsboro and stayed the night, and Phyllis returned to Church Street the next morning.

On reaching Church Street on Tuesday morning, Morkan was asked to fetch May Kavanagh who was living in Ranelagh. Making her way through the city, she succeeded in locating Kavanagh and the two women returned to Church Street. There they met Commandant Daly who asked the women to set up an emergency hospital in the Fr. Mathew Hall. Morkan remembered:

> We went around to all the nearby houses with some of the volunteers and asked for material and bed clothes – we had no difficulty getting those things we required as everyone was most willing to help – in a short time we had a big 'ward' ready with the dressings, etc. cut, and waited for our first patient.[33]

The women quickly realised that they had no stimulants to give to the patients and with Daly's permission, they set off to Morkans' home on Arran Quay (the family owned two pubs) to collect these necessities. However, due to the increasing British presence they were unable to get back to Church Street. On Tuesday, Brigadier-General Lowe arrived at Kingsbridge station. He commanded the Reserve Cavalry Brigade and brought with him 1,000 troops from the Curragh and took over command of operations. That day Daly moved his head-quarters from the convent to the Fr. Mathew Hall on Church Street.

Also on that day, Anne Fahy managed to make her way to the GPO where she found a number of her comrades. Like Anne they had mobilised on Easter Monday and, on being dismissed, many returned home only to make their way into the city the next day to see where they could serve. Eilís Ní Riain, like Pauline and Phyllis Morkan, did not return home that night. With Emily Elliott, she instead decided to go to the GPO on Monday evening and from there she was sent to Reis' Chambers/ Hibernian Bank on the east side of O'Connell Street. Captain Thomas Weafer was in charge of the garrison there. Throughout Tuesday Ní Riain was sent to the GPO on numerous occasions with dispatches and to get supplies:

> There was no food or facilities for cooking in the building. We eagerly awaited daylight on Tuesday morning to go across to the GPO for rations for the men. With great difficulty we crossed O'Connell Street, as it was a mass of barbed wire and barricades. However, we were admitted after detailed interrogation. We explained our mission and were escorted to the food controller. Here the late Desmond Fitzgerald was in charge. I explained our position. We required food for so many Volunteers occupying an outpost in Reis' Chambers. He said he could not supply food without a written order from the officer in charge of the outpost. We again stressed the great difficulty we had encountered in reaching the GPO and I said we could not possibly return without some food. At first he was reluctant to comply with the request but we were so persistent that he ultimately yielded to our appeal. When we returned it was necessary to apologise for our long absence and 'Blimey' [O'Connor] greeted us with, 'Up the Republic!'[34]

Fahy, Ní Riain and a number of other women including Emily and Eilís Elliott, Louisa and Mary O'Sullivan were then asked to go to the Four Courts. Fahy was more than happy to go there as it meant that she would be with her husband Frank who was a member of Daly's 1st Battalion and was stationed in the courts. Throughout Tuesday and Wednesday members of Cumann na mBan continued to arrive at the courts. Brigid Lyons arrived on Wednesday. She had come from Co. Longford and went to the Four Courts where she found her uncle Joe McGuinness, also a member of the 1st Battalion, Irish Volunteers. Describing the scene in the Courts, Lyons recalled:

> I saw Mrs. Fahy and the two Sullivan girls, sisters of Seamus. I went to the big kitchen. There were piles of silver and plate. The only lights were candles on the floor. There was a great deal of noise of fighting, rumours and reports.[35]

On Wednesday, some of the women, including Anne Fahy, Eilís Ní Riain and the Elliott sisters were sent to give assistance at the medical post in Fr. Mathew Hall. There were quite a number of Cumann na mBan there, mainly from the Central branch, however later on they were joined by members of the Colmcille branch, including Kathleen Martin, Bríd Martin, Lily Murnane and Margaret Martin. The women were each given a white armlet to identify that they were attached to the hospital staff and as Eilís Ní Riain remembered

> we were allotted our duties by the senior members of our branch. The Volunteers supplied the hospital with plenty of food including ham, tomatoes, tea and sugar and, I think, milk. I there sampled tomatoes and sugarless tea for the first time in my life'[36]

During the first days of the Rising the women helped in the kitchens and tended to the wounded. At that time there were not many serious injuries to deal with, as full scale attacks had yet to begin on Daly's command. With the surrender of Seán Heuston's outpost in the Mendicity Institute, that would all change. On Wednesday the 59th Division arriving at Kingstown (now Dún Laoghaire) proceeded to Ballsbridge. Some of the troops were held at the RDS while the rest advanced towards the city centre via Mount Street. That day Seán Heuston's garrison surrendered and as a result the British began to take up positions along the Liffey opposite the Four Courts. The encircling of Daly's command had begun. That day Daly ordered the capture of Linenhall Barracks, situated between North King Street and Bolton Street, to prevent the military gaining a foothold there.

As the battle intensified, the number of wounded grew and as the fight wore on, the type of wounds the women were treating became more serious. Eilís Ní Riain stated, 'as time went on the number of more seriously wounded patients increased and we carried them on stretchers into the hall and dressed their wounds'.[37] But while the atmosphere was quite serious in the outposts surrounding the Courts, there was still a relaxed atmosphere amongst the garrison in the Four Courts complex. Brigid Lyons wrote:

> We spent a lot of time making tea and sandwiches. I remember Frank Fahy drinking tea and wondering politely how he was going to get it down. When we investigated the reason we discovered that the tea had been made with the turnip water that was left from the dinner. I saw Sean Flood appearing with sides of bacon and mutton. He was a great provider. These things were got from the hotels and shops around.[38]

Although there were no wounded to treat in the Four Courts building, there were prisoners to be looked after. A number of Dublin Metropolitan Police (DMP) had been arrested by the Volunteers early in the battle, as was Lord Dunsany. Pauline Keating remembered his treatment:

> The first day we laid an ordinary tray for him, but the next day the girl who did it decked it out in great style to show what we could do. We thought it good fun. I think she was able to produce some silver implements to make a splash. There may have been other prisoners, but I did not know of them.[39]

The women were kept very busy with food provisioning. The Volunteers, in the Four Courts complex, had to be fed, as had the men manning the barricades along Church Street and North King Street. This hazardous work was undertaken by the women in the Fr. Mathew Hall. Under fire they climbed across the barricades, some of them very intricate, to get to the men. Fearing for their safety, the women were accompanied on these excursions by Fr. Augustine from the Capuchin Order on Church Street. On Thursday morning Eilís Ní Riain and her comrades visited the Four Courts where they found a number of women including Nellie Ennis, Máire Carron, Brigid Lyons, Rose McGuinness and Maggie Derham, amongst others. They were also visited every day in the Fr. Mathew Hall by Daly. That day Catherine Byrne (*née* Rooney) arrived at North King Street. She had been bringing dispatches to and from the GPO to Daly from Patrick Pearse. Unable to get back to the GPO she returned to North King Street and remained with the garrison in Brunswick Street, where she was nearly killed in the battle. Recalling her lucky escape she wrote:

> Seán Moore occupied a tall house at the corner of Church St. [*sic*] and Brunswick St. [*sic*] He was in a top room watching through field glasses the military garrison at Broadstone station. I asked him to let me have a look. I was half way back in the room looking through the glasses when we heard the whistling sound of a bullet. I turned around to a Volunteer who had been staring near the door but had jumped aside to avoid the bullet which he pointed out to me embedded in the door. He asked me was I hurt as the bullet went very near my head. I took off my beret and found two holes in it, so it was a narrow shave all right.[40]

Later Brigid Lyons and Annie Derham were sent to Peadar Clancy who had set up an outpost in No. 5 Church Street. This was a dangerous journey for the women to undertake as they had to make their way 'over broken glass and with bullets flying, taking shelter from time to time'.[41] They reached their destination safely, but soon discovered a completely different atmosphere to the one they had experienced in the Courts. They were coming under heavy fire from the British and quite quickly were treating their first casualty, a Mr. Lennon, a member of the Volunteers who happened to live in No. 5. They were constantly on the go as Lyons recalled:

> We cooked joints of meat, tea, fried potatoes for constant relays of men, Sean Flood again being the provider. We cut up the meat with bayonets. I think that Mr. Lemon had stored water in various vessels in case the water might be turned off. Miss Derham and myself lay down on a bed for a couple of hours, and the men also went to bed from time to time in relays.[42]

In order to remove the Volunteers from their positions in Sackville Street and its surrounding areas, the British decided to shell the outposts rather than risk frontal assaults. The gunboat, the *Helga*, stationed on the Liffey began, on Wednesday, to shell strategic buildings including Liberty Hall, the GPO and the Four Courts.

On Thursday afternoon the 2 / 6th Sherwood Foresters were ordered to Dublin Castle. By now, there were 16,000 troops in Dublin. Major-General Friend had also arrived and took command of the British forces and continued to press the encircling action. In order to link his forces from Gardiner Street to Kingsbridge, Friend needed to break the Volunteer stronghold at North King Street. Under the cover of two improvised armoured cars, the Sherwoods moved out from Dublin Castle and came under attack at Capel Street from the Four Courts garrison. They pressed on, reaching Bolton Street thus cutting the Volunteer line of communication from the GPO to the Four Courts. The 2 / 6th, under the command of Lieutenant-Colonel Henry Taylor, was ordered to approach North King Street from Capel Street, while the 2 / 5th was to attack from Queen Street. Taylor established a command post in Bolton Street Technical College and ordered his men to advance towards North King Street. Immediately they came under attack from the Volunteers in Langan's Pub and 'Reilly's Fort' and many troops were wounded. Scattering in all directions many ran into Beresford Street and came under attack from the Volunteers in Jameson's. In order to attack the Reilly's Fort successfully the troops began tunneling through houses in order to reach it. Mrs. Martin Conlon, a member of the Central branch and who was serving with her husband in the Fr. Mathew Hall, recalled the atmosphere in the hall that night:

> That Friday night was terrible. The Church St. priests were with us and gave us general absolution and I think we received Holy Communion. The only lights we had in the Hall were little night lights. The bombing and the firing continued all that night and the next day till about 4p.m. when the surrender message came from Pearse.[43]

On Saturday morning the Volunteers evacuated both Reilly's and Langan's. Despite taking these buildings the military still came under attack from the Volunteers in Jameson's, Beresford Street and North Brunswick Street. Eilís Ní Riain, stationed in the Fr. Mathew Hall remembering the last day of fighting wrote:

> Rosary after rosary was recited during the last twenty-four hours as the British military were closing in on the area. The firing was intense on Saturday. The noise of rifle firing was deafening. Soon we learned that the military were closing in on the outskirts of our area and that our dear comrades were vacating their outposts and retreating to their headquarters in the Four Courts. The noise was still deafening. Father Augustine was still on his knees; he consoled the wounded and staff alike and prayed for the success of the men in action.[44]

That afternoon Daly, who by now had established his headquarters in the Four Courts, received orders from Patrick Pearse to surrender and although the garrison in the Courts did comply, those Volunteers in and around North King Street continued to fight on until Sunday, 30 April 1916. As with all the garrisons there was a mixed reaction from the rank and file. There were many heartbreaking scenes, not believing the orders many broke down and cried, some smashed their weapons, most wished to fight on but, as stated by their officers, they were an army and should act as such and follow the orders of their superior officers. The women were to witness so many of these scenes. Brigid Lyons who was stationed in No.5 Church Street recalled:

> A Volunteer rushed in and asked me for a hatchet – we had been using it for chopping wood – and he started to hack the butt of his rifle rather than surrender it. Some others of the Volunteers tried to cut a hole through the wall of the backyard, though I don't know where that would have brought them to. Tom Walsh was among them and he and others cried bitterly. Three fellows came to me and gave me their revolvers to keep for them, thinking that I would get away. Eventually, quite suddenly, I found myself alone.[45]

By Sunday, 30 April, the fighting was over. The men of the Four Courts garrison had left the building on Saturday and were marched to the Rotunda and held there overnight before being marched to Richmond Barracks. Many believed that the women would not be arrested and they were told as much in the Four Courts by a British soldier, a Lieutenant Lindsay. The women had stayed overnight in the Courts thinking that they would be allowed to go home on Sunday morning but this proved not to be the case. Brigid Lyons, who had returned to the Courts on Saturday night, remembered, 'one of the Church St. priests, Fr. Columbus, stayed in the room with us till morning by way of protection. We were only allowed to the bathroom in twos and threes under escort. Two were allowed to the kitchen to make tea, also under escort'.[46] The women were then removed in a lorry and taken to Richmond Barracks.

Some women like the Elliot sisters, Eilís Ní Riain and Catherine Byrne managed to escape. Ní Riain and her comrades, having removed the wounded to the nearby Richmond Hospital returned to Fr. Mathew Hall. Finding the hall empty they were allowed stay in the church overnight and were able to leave unnoticed amongst those going to mass the next morning. In all, twelve women who had served in the Four Courts/Church Street/North King Street area were arrested and detained in Richmond Barracks and later Kilmainham Gaol. They were Máire Carron, Brigid Lyons, Nellie Ennis, Kathleen and Bríd Martin, Florence Meade, Carrie Mitchell,

Pauline Morkan, Kitty Fleming, Maggie McLoughlin and Louisa and Mary O'Sullivan. All were released on 8 / 9 May. Most of these women remained involved in revolutionary activities up to and including the Civil War.

The GPO garrison and Sackville Street area outposts

Early on Easter Monday afternoon Patrick Pearse stepped out of the GPO and read the Proclamation of the Republic to the crowd around him, insurgents and civilians. That Proclamation, addressed to Irishmen and Irishwomen, called on the allegiance of every man and women in Ireland and guaranteed equal rights for all in the new Republic:

> The Irish Republic is entitled to, and hereby claims, the allegiance of every Irishman and Irishwoman. The Republic guarantees religious and civil liberty, equal rights and equal opportunities to all its citizens.[47]

Earlier that morning Pearse along with James Connolly, Joseph Plunkett, Thomas Clarke and Seán MacDiarmada had gathered at Liberty Hall with members of the Irish Volunteers, the Hibernian Rifles, Cumann na mBan and the Irish Citizen Army. Belfast branch Cumann na mBan member Winifred Carney, personal secretary and trusted comrade of James Connolly, had been in Dublin since April 15, helping with the plans for the Rising. Now as Connolly prepared to lead the Citizen Army towards Sackville Street and the GPO, only one woman was to accompany them. This was Winifred Carney who, it is said, marched into the GPO with a Webley revolver in one hand and a typewriter in the other.

The GPO was taken very quickly and within the hour the building had been secured by the Volunteers. As the insurgents broke their way into the building one Volunteer exclaimed that this 'ain't no half-arsed revolution, this is the business'.[48]

While Connolly (Commandant-General of the Dublin Division of the insurgents) and Pearse (Commander-in-Chief) and the other leaders set up in the great hall on the ground floor, The O'Rahilly assumed command of the top floor and roof of the GPO. Within the first thirty minutes a tricolour was raised over the Henry Street end of the building and a green banner inscribed with the words 'Irish Republic' over the Prince's Street side. After the hoisting of the flag of the new Republic, Pearse stepped out to the front of the GPO, proclaimed the Provisional Government of the Irish Republic and read the Proclamation. Margaret Skinnider, arriving with dispatches from St. Stephen's Green, had to ride 'through great crowds of people who had gathered to hear Patrick Pearse read the Proclamation of the republic at the foot of Nelson's Pillar'.[49] The Rising had now officially begun and within thirty minutes the women and men in the GPO were in action, firing on a party of Lancers who had been sent from Marlborough Barracks to investigate the disturbances in Sackville Street.

Aoife de Burca, a nurse and member of Cumann na mBan, was in Malahide, Co. Dublin on Easter Monday morning when she was told that 'The Sinn Feiners [sic] have taken the GPO, City Hall and Dublin Castle – there are two horses lying dead in Sackville Street belonging to the Lancers and terrible work is going on in town'.[50] With great difficulty and great determination she managed to get into the city centre on Tuesday and took up duty 'at Reis', on the Sackville Street side of Lower Abbey street where there was a wireless station'.[51] Throughout Tuesday Cumann na mBan members arrived at the GPO individually or in small groups. Soon Winifred Carney was joined by over thirty women who served all or part of the week in the GPO. On Monday and Tuesday groups of Cumann na mBan women were bringing supplies from arms dumps all over the city to the Volunteer outposts.

Some women found it difficult to access the outposts. Bríd Dixon and Leslie Price, who had been told to go home by Ned Daly at the Four Courts, walked over to Sackville Street and they saw 'Seán MacDermott, Tom Clarke, Seán McGarry, Gearóid O'Sullivan, Michael Staines and all those we knew in the Gaelic League, and we flew over to them'.[52] Other members of the Volunteers were glad to see the women. As Ruaidhrí Henderson recalled:

> The women of the Central branch, Cumann na mBan, mobilised in Wellington Street at noon. Disbanded temporarily, they were called in later, some reported to Commandant Daly at Church Street, the others to Commandant Connolly at G.H.Q. The latter were assigned mainly to the nursing and kitchen staffs in the GPO and outposts in O'Connell Street, a number, were selected for despatch work. They were a necessary and welcome addition…[53]

When Dixon and Price arrived in the GPO they were told that Louise Gavan Duffy was in the food commissariat and were sent to help her. Other women had to smash their way in. Catherine Byrne, who claimed she was the first member of Cumann na mBan in the GPO, was told by the sentry at the door to go home when she tried to get in. She refused to accept this and instead walked round the building, eventually kicking in the glass of a side window and jumping in.[54] There she helped with nursing and soon had cases of wounded Volunteers to deal with, starting with Liam Clarke who was severely wounded when a homemade bomb he was carrying exploded. While

Clarke was lying on the ground she washed his head and 'discovered he had a very nasty wound at the side of his head, which I dressed. Afterwards his eye had to be removed'.[55] Later on Monday, Byrne noticed that more members of Cumann na mBan were arriving at the GPO:

> between 5 and 4 o'clock, I should think. I saw Statia Toomey and Molly Reynolds coming in with several others. I should have mentioned that after I arrived I noticed Winifred Carney, a member of the Citizen Army, sitting working at a desk in the main hall towards the Henry Street side.[56]

Senior leaders of Cumann na mBan such as Molly Reynolds and Stacia Toomey had come to the GPO to insist that the women be formally mobilised. Late on Monday evening that formal mobilisation order was drafted and issued, calling on Cumann na mBan women to join the fight. Over the following days women continued to make their way into the city and joined where they could and where they were allowed. As they arrived at the GPO they were allocated to the kitchens, to nursing duties or as dispatch carriers by Connolly and Clarke. The women often found that the roles they could play were demarcated mainly along gender lines, despite the promise of equality in the recently read Proclamation. Unlike the other outposts, in the GPO a man, Desmond Fitzgerald, was in charge of the food commissariat and he strictly controlled the women and their access to and preparation of the food.

Despite these obstacles the women were determined to play their part. More and more Cumann na mBan and a few Irish Citizen Army women arrived, some of the Cumann na mBan women bringing arms in from arms dumps they had been in charge of. Women were now also with the insurgents in the other buildings around Sackville Street – in the Hibernian Bank, Reis' Chambers, the Imperial Hotel and other occupied buildings. At Reis' a radio broadcasting set was erected and broadcast news on the progress of the fighting from Tuesday afternoon to midday on Wednesday. Late on Monday, Catherine Byrne went with Leslie Price to the Hibernian Bank and spent the night with the Volunteers there. On Tuesday morning Martha Kelly also left the GPO to help the men in the Imperial Hotel where she remained for the rest of the week. Brigid Foley, who had been in Cork delivering dispatches, arrived in Dublin and got into the GPO. Molly Adrien arrived on a bicycle from the Fingal Battalion in Ashbourne, Co. Meath with dispatches from Thomas Ashe. Adrien returned to Ashbourne, scouting the coastline as she went and was back in the GPO with more dispatches on Wednesday. During Tuesday Brigid Foley went from the

GPO with messages to Reis' and the Hibernian Bank, although 'it was harder to get across this time on account of the increased firing'.[57] Once she delivered her dispatches Brigid, her sister Nora, and Máire Lawless went to set up a first aid station at Skelton's, 14 Lower Sackville Street, where they had to treat a badly wounded civilian the following day. Foley's reaction details the trauma these women faced when dealing with the bloody results of war. She wrote:

> He was an awful sight as he was frightfully badly wounded in the stomach. I stuck it out as long as the doctor was doing his part, but when I took away the bowl of water I got good and truly sick. I think he died soon after.[58]

As the violence and gunfire increased, the women carrying out their dispatch duties found it more and more dangerous. Foley remembered going to the GPO on Wednesday evening 'with a white flag on a stick, with bullets flying around me'.[59] Marie English helped evacuate Reis', while carrying supplies under fire across the road to the GPO. Others like Leslie Price used stories of sick relatives to get around the barricades manned by British troops:

> My two sisters... and myself and Mrs. Conlon made our way to Church St. to try and see my brother Michael and Martin Conlon, and also to see whether we could give any help there. I think we stayed in Church St. that night. We had no difficulty in getting through as we made up all sorts of pitiful stories about sick relatives, &c.[60]

Despite the growing danger and the increasing bombardment of the city, especially of the GPO, women were still trying to join in the fight. On Wednesday Cumann na mBan member Brigid O'Driscoll heard that Cumann na mBan were in the GPO and looking for helpers in the Hibernian Bank:

> After breakfast we went down to the Hibernian Bank, where we remained until that afternoon, when the firing became so severe that we had to abandon it by making a hole in the next house north of it. We went across to the GPO.[61]

Earlier that day James Connolly sent Cumann na mBan member Mary Cullen to the men holding 25 Northumberland Road, to warn them of the approaching British reinforcements, while Tom Clarke sent Veronica Ní Riain to north Co. Dublin to contact Volunteers there who had not yet mobilised. Clarke sent orders that they were to mobilise and join the Ashbourne garrison. Heavy firing continued throughout Wednesday and later that night the British fired shrapnel into Sackville Street. Rifle and machine gun fire was ceaseless from the direction of Trinity College and Great Brunswick Street (now Tara Street) Fire Station. The gunboat *Helga* added to the artillery fire and a heavy gun was in position on the corner of D'Olier Street and College

Street, forcing the insurgents in the Metropole Hotel to withdraw to the GPO.

By Thursday it was clear that the rest of the country had not risen in support of the insurgents. As Molly Reynolds later related 'that Thursday night [was] beyond description. It was the night the *Helga* shelled us from the Liffey'.[62] Despite this, Pearse continued to send dispatches around the country. Nora Daly, sister of Ned Daly and Kathleen Clarke, was sent with dispatches to Terence MacSwiney in Cork while her sister Laura delivered dispatches to Limerick. Both managed to deliver their messages and get back to the GPO by Friday. Annie Higgins was sent north towards Carrickmacross, Bailieboro and Cavan with dispatches. She cycled to Carrickmacross and used public transport from there. However, she was arrested in Kingscourt, Co. Cavan, imprisoned and transported to Richmond Barracks after the final surrender.

In Dublin the women in the GPO were dealing with an increasing number of serious casualties. Captain Thomas Weafer was fatally shot on Wednesday in the Hibernian Bank where he was attended by Aoife de Burca, Leslie Price and Marie Mapother. On Thursday Connolly was wounded in the leg by a sniper as he checked outposts in Liffey Street. Leslie Price saw him being brought to the GPO on a stretcher and said to herself 'Here's goodbye to you', although as she looked at his 'courageous old face' she thought 'alright'.[63] The shot had shattered almost two inches of his shinbone and the pain was intolerable, he had to have frequent injections of morphine and could no longer stand up. By Thursday evening huge fires were blazing around Sackville Street, an inferno that was 'like the song of a great dynamo' according to a Volunteer.[64] The women and men in the GPO and other smaller outposts prepared for the final assault. Louise Gavan Duffy, like so many others in this situation was becoming desperate and 'thought we were going to retire into the cellars, but I did not ask and nobody told me'.[65]

On Friday, the situation inside the GPO was becoming very dangerous. Connolly dictated a message to Winifred Carney which was read out to the garrison, 'Courage boys – we are winning'.[66] By midday howitzer shells had set fire to the roof of the GPO and the plans for evacuation were put in action. Pearse called the women together in the hall (between twenty and thirty of them) and asked them to leave the GPO. The women were angry and protested. 'No, no', they said 'we'll stay with the men… you told us we were all equal… what about women's rights'.[67] Pearse, it was reported, was shaken by this but insisted that they leave and in addressing them said that:

> When the history of the week would be written, the highest honour and credit should

be given to the women whose bravery, heroism and devotion in the face of danger surpassed that of the women of Limerick in the days of Sarsfield. He then order-ed them, except those of the nursing section to proceed under a red-cross flag to their homes.[68]

About twenty women left in the first group, leaving about fifteen more women still in and around the GPO. Gavan Duffy mentioned that Pearse did not force those women who chose to remain behind to leave as 'he said he did not think he had any right to prevent anybody taking part in the Rebellion who wanted to stay'.[69] The first group who left around midday on Friday were soon stopped by British soldiers, arrested and held for a brief time at Broadstone Station. However as Price reported they were soon released as 'although the British held us up at the barriers, they let us through when we said we were going home to Cabra Road'.[70] The fires in the GPO were worse by Friday evening and the remaining fifteen or so women in the GPO prepared to leave, with 'two trained nurses [Julia Grenan and Elizabeth O'Farrell] and General Connolly's secretary [Winifred Carney] only being retained at G.H.Q'.[71]

A member of the group, Molly Reynolds, described their hard, slow journey out 'through holes in the walls... [carrying] wounded men in blankets, [carrying] the stuff we had with us'.[72] When they got out near the top of Moore Street, one of the women forgetting herself, stepped out and was met by a shower of bullets fired by the British at the Parnell Street end of Moore Street'.[73] Gingerly they made their way to the Coliseum on Prince's Street (at the side of the GPO) and there they were able to hoist a Red Cross flag, 'they were [then] conveyed via the Coliseum, Princes Street and Abbey Street to Jervis Street hospital'.[74] The women remained under guard in Jervis Street hospital until after the surrender. After that, on their way home, they were recognised as members of Cumann na mBan. A DMP detective made to search Reynolds, who was terrified as her bag contained 'a copy of the Proclamation and several Cumann na mBan badges'.[75] Luckily the military were too busy and the women were told to go on their way. Rather than return home some of the women found ways to continue in the fight. Molly Adrien and Leslie Price were among two who made their way to Ashbourne and north Dublin respectively, where they remained with the Fingal battalion until they surrendered.

By Friday evening the GPO was engulfed in flames and the garrison, including the three remaining women, Winifred Carney, Elizabeth O'Farrell and Julia Grenan, began to evacuate the building. They left the GPO by the side entrance on Henry

Street and made their way, under constant fire, to Moore Street. An advance party led by The O'Rahilly was to make their way to Williams and Woods jam factory on Parnell Street and set up a new headquarters there, with the rest of the garrison following to join them. O'Rahilly and his men ran down Moore Street into a hail of fire and several of the men, including The O'Rahilly, were badly wounded. He crawled into a laneway near Parnell Street and, bleeding profusely, wrote a farewell note to his wife, Nanny, a founder member of Cumann na mBan, who was six months pregnant and waiting at home for news of the Rising and her husband. By 8p.m. the main body of the GPO garrison began to leave the building after Pearse made his final speech and they had sung The Soldier's Song. Crossing from the GPO to Moore Street was very dangerous as the British had the street covered by machine guns on the roof of the Rotunda hospital on nearby Parnell Square. Winifred Carney 'plain, strong, determined, brusque',[76] remained doggedly by James Connolly's side, bending over his stretcher, shielding his body as he was carried across Henry Street.

As they ran down Moore Street they forced their way into houses, accidentally killing young Brigid McKane and wounding her father as they shot open a front door. As they took cover in the house, the three women were looking after Connolly and any of the other wounded. They would spend the night caring for the wounded men 'amid the roar of burning buildings, machine guns playing on the houses, and, at intervals, what seemed like hand grenades'.[77] On Saturday, the leadership of the Provisional Government (minus Ceannt and MacDonagh), pinned down in small houses on Moore Street, discussed their options. It was decided to seek terms from the British 'in order to prevent further slaughter of the civilian population and save the lives of as many as possible of our followers'.[78] At about 12.45p.m. on Saturday 29 April, Seán MacDiarmada hung a white flag outside No. 15 Moore Street and out stepped Elizabeth O'Farrell, 'a very pretty girl and very pale' holding a while flag.[79] Inside Julia Grenan, her lifelong companion, was desperately agitated but assured by Connolly that the British would not fire on a woman holding a white flag. Slowly O'Farrell made her way to the barricade at the top of Moore Street. There she asked to be taken to the British officer in charge. She was searched and found in possession of:

> two pairs of scissors one of which he afterwards returned to me, some sweets, bread, and cakes, etc. Being satisfied that I wasn't dangerous he then took me of all places in the world to Tom Clarke's shop as a prisoner – all this procedure occupied about three quarters of an hour. I was kept in the shop for about another three quarters of an

hour, when another military man came to me – whom I learned was Brigadier General Lowe.[80]

Lowe insisted that O'Farrell return and bring Pearse out to offer unconditional surrender.

On the way back to Moore Street, she passed by the body of The O'Rahilly lying in Sackville Lane and 'gave both the verbal and written message to Commandant Pearse, and told him I was to be back in half-an-hour'.[81] At about 3.30p.m. O'Farrell then went with Pearse to General Lowe at the top of Moore Street and standing by his side watched as he handed over his sword and surrendered. O'Farrell later mentioned that General Lowe was most anxious to find out if Countess Markievicz was in the GPO with Pearse. He then suggested that the British detain O'Farrell overnight to take the notice of surrender to the other outposts the next day. Pearse and O'Farrell agreed. Pearse was then taken away down Sackville Street and as O'Farrell recalled, after he shook her hand and stepped into the awaiting car, 'I saw him no more'.[82] Back in Moore Street, Julia Grenan and Winifred Carney prepared James Connolly for surrender; they combed his hair, washed him, redressed his wounds and made his stained dusty uniform as presentable as possible.[83] Putting him on a stretcher, the women, with the men from the Citizen Army and the Volunteers moved out into Moore Street under a white flag. Connolly was then taken under escort to Dublin Castle hospital.

The rest of the garrison, along with the two women, surrendered their arms and, placed under guard, they were marched to the green area in front of the Rotunda Hospital where they spent a long and bitterly cold night out in the open. Sometime after 9a.m. the following morning they were marched to Richmond Barracks, where the women were separated from the men and imprisoned with the women who had fought in the other outposts. As her comrades from the GPO were being marched to Richmond Barracks, O'Farrell delivered the surrender order from Pearse and Connolly to all the outposts throughout Sunday. When she got to St. Stephen's Green she was met by Markievicz and asked to see Mallin but was told he was sleeping and that Countess Markievicz was next in command:

I saw her and gave her the order – she was very much surprised and she went to discuss it with Commandant Mallin, whom I afterwards saw. I gave her a slip with the directions as to how to surrender – the Southern sides being ordered to surrender at St. Patrick's Park.[84]

After she delivered the surrender to Jacob's Factory and was going towards the Castle with her British escort, she saw Éamonn Ceannt come down 'the Ross Road at about 6 o'clock p.m. and surrendered with his men and also with the members of the Cumann na mBan who were attached to his command'.[85] She was then taken to Ship Street Barracks, even though General Lowe had given his word she would not be taken prisoner. The soldiers accused her of shooting six policemen and she was stripped and searched. On hearing of her protestations of her treatment General Lowe had her brought into the Castle and apologised to her. O'Farrell was then released onto nearby Dame Street and left to make her way home. Much to her distress, many of her comrades in arms, as well as her partner Julia Grenan, were all now in Richmond Barracks.

Because most of the women had obeyed Pearse's order to evacuate the GPO on Friday, only four women were arrested in Moore Street and the surrounding area. They were Cumann na mBan members Winifred Carney, Julia Grenan, Martha Kelly and Catherine Treston. Their comrade Annie Higgins had earlier been arrested on a dispatch journey to Co. Cavan and Brigid Foley, who had made it home to Phibsboro, was arrested there. Carney and Grenan were held with the men through Saturday night, out in the open on the green area in front of the Rotunda Hospital. Early the next morning they were marched to Richmond Barracks. They were separated from the men and taken to Kilmainham Gaol the next day. There they were joined by Treston, Kelly, Foley and Higgins. While they were in Kilmainham they heard the shots that killed some of the comrades they had fought with in the GPO, including the Pearse brothers, Patrick and William. Higgins, Kelly, Treston and Grenan were released in the mass release on 8 / 9 May while Brigid Foley and Winifred Carney were transferred to Mountjoy Gaol where they spent a few weeks. They were then deported, with others like Helena Molony, Marie Perloz, and Nell Ryan, to Lewes Prison in England. Foley was released in August 1916 and, as with all her other GPO comrades, resumed her republican activism immediately. Unlike Foley, Winfred Carney was kept longer in prison, being transferred to Aylesbury Gaol along with Helena Molony and Nell Ryan. She was released on Christmas Eve, 1916.

Notes

1. Nell Regan, 'Helena Molony' in Mary Cullen and Maria Luddy (eds) *Female Activist: Irish Women and Change 1900 – 1960,* (Dublin: The Woodfield Press, 2001), p. 152
2. O'Daly 'The Women of Easter Week', p. 3
3. MA/MSPC/MSP34REF21047 Ann Devlin
4. BMH WS 355 (Kitty O'Doherty), pp. 8 – 14
5. MA/MSPC/MSP34REF47647 May Wisely
6. BMH WS 546 (Rosie Hackett), p. 3
7. Michael Foy and Brian Barton, *The Easter Rising* (London: The History Press, 2011), p. 73
8. BMH WS 391 (Helena Molony), p. 33
9. Ibid.
10. Matthews, *The Irish Citizen Army* (Cork: Mercier Press, 2014), p. 90
11. Molyneux and Kelly (eds), *When the Clock Struck in 1916* p. 29
12. BMH WS 357 (Kathleen Lynn), p. 5
13. The nurses apron that Brigid Davis was wearing that day and which she kept for many years is now in the Kilmainham Gaol archives.
14. BMH WS 357 (Kathleen Lynn), p. 5
15. Foy and Barton, *The Easter Rising*, p. 75
16. BMH WS 357 (Kathleen Lynn), p. 6
17. BMH WS 357 (Kathleen Lynn), p. 6
18. Matthews, *The Irish Citizen Army,* p. 109
19. BMH WS 391 (Helena Molony), p. 38
20. Ibid.
21. BMH WS 357 (Kathleen Lynn), p. 6
22. BMH WS 391 (Helena Molony), p. 39
23. Ibid.
24. Ibid.
25. BMH WS 357 (Kathleen Lynn), p. 6
26. BMH WS 391 (Helena Molony), p. 40
27. BMH WS 357 (Kathleen Lynn), p. 7
28. BMH WS 398 (Brigid Martin, née Foley), p. 14
29. BMH WS 398 (Brigid Martin, née Foley), p. 13
30. Ibid.
31. BMH WS 210 (Phyllis Morkan), p. 1
32. BMH WS 210 (Phyllis Morkan), p. 2
33. Ibid.
34. BMH WS 568 (Eilís Ní Riain), p. 8
35. BMH WS 259 (Brigid Lyons/Thornton), p. 3
36. BMH WS 568 (Eilís Ní Riain), p. 9
37. Ibid.
38. BMH WS 259 (Brigid Lyons-Thornton), p. 3
39. BMH WS 432 (Pauline Keating), p. 4
40. BMH WS 648 (Catherine Byrne), p.
41. BMH WS 259 (Brigid Lyons/Thornton), p. 3
42. Ibid.
43. BMH WS 419 (Mrs. Martin Conlon), p. 9
44. BMH WS 568 (Eilís Ní Riain), p. 12
45. BMH WS 259 (Brigid Lyons/Thornton), p. 5
46. Ibid.
47. The Proclamation of the Irish Republic, 1916

48   McGarry, *The Easter Rising, Ireland: Easter 1916* (Oxford: Oxford University Press, 2010), p. 132

49   Margaret Skinnider, *Doing My Bit For Ireland (New York: Century, 1917), p. 106*

50   BMH WS.359 (Aoife de Burca), p. 2

51   Ibid.

52   BMH WS 1,754 (Leslie Price), p. 7

53   BMH WS 1,618 (Ruaidhrí Henderson), p. 5

54   BMH WS. 646 (Catherine Rooney), p. 2

55   Ibid.

56   Ibid.

57   BMH WS 398 (Brigid Martin, née Foley), p. 9

58   Ibid., p. 10

59   Ibid., pp. 10-11

60   BMH WS 1,754 (Leslie Price), p. 11

61   BMH WS 484 (Brighid, Bean Ui Fheaidh, (Ni Dhiscin)), p. 4

62   Ferghal McGarry, *Rebels: Voices from the Easter Rising* (London: Penguin Books, 2011), p. 227

63   McGarry, *The Rising,* p. 137

64   Foy and Barton, *The Easter Rising,* p. 189

65   BMH WS 216 (Louise Gavan Duffy), p. 8

66   Ibid., p. 192

67   Joe Good, *Inside the GPO 1916; A first-hand account* (Dublin: The O'Brien Press, 2015), p. 91

68   BMH WS 618 (Ruaidhrí Henderson), p.15

69   BMH WS 216 (Louise Gavan Duffy), p. 8

70   BMH WS 1,754 (Leslie Price), p. 11

71   BMH WS 1,618 (Ruaidhrí Henderson), p.15

72   Miss M. Reynolds, 'Cumann na mBan in the GPO: Heroic work of girls during the fighting of Easter Week' in *An tÓglach,* March 27th, 1926, p.3

73   Ibid.

74   BMH WS 1,618 (Ruaidhri Henderson), p.15

75   Reynolds, 'Cumann na mBan in the GPO', p. 5

76   Good, *Inside the GPO 1916,* p. 107

77   Foy and Barton, *The Easter Rising,* p. 201

78   Ibid., p. 205

79   Good, *Inside the GPO 1916,* p. 111

80   Elizabeth O'Farrell, 'The personal Account of the surrender at the GPO and others posts', Allen Library, Dublin, IE/AL1916/95/2

81   Ibid.

82   Ibid.

83   Good, *Inside the GPO 1916,* p. 114

84   Ibid.

85   Ibid.

CHAPTER THREE

—

Marrowbone Lane Distillery, St. Stephen's Green, Royal College of Surgeons Garrisons and other Areas

I told the girls to get into whatever outpost they could. Some of them succeeded.[1]

Marrowbone Lane (Jameson's) Distillery garrison

The Marrowbone Lane (Jameson's) Distillery was an outpost attached to Éamonn Ceannt's 4th Battalion, with headquarters in the South Dublin Union (SDU), now St. James's Hospital. Like several of the garrisons throughout the city, the Union was taken to prevent British forces entering the city centre from the south-west from Richmond Barracks, Wellington Barracks, the Royal Hospital Kilmainham and the Curragh. At about 11am on the morning of Easter Monday, members of the 4th Battalion, Irish Volunteers mobilised at Emerald Square, off Cork Street. Twenty-five members of the Inghinidhe branch, Cumann na mBan had mobilised at the Cleaver Gaelic League Hall, Donore Avenue and made their way to Emerald Square. As was the case with the entire Dublin Brigade of the Irish Volunteers, Ceannt's battalion was greatly depleted due to Eoin MacNeill's countermanding order. In all, approximately one hundred Volunteers mobilised that morning, although by the end of the week his numbers increased to a little over two hundred men. If MacNeill had not issued his countermanding order, Ceannt would have had approximately 700 men under his command.

Eileen Murphy, O/C of the Inghinidhe branch, had mobilised the whole branch at No. 6 Harcourt Street on Easter Sunday. They waited and waited but they received no word of where they should go or what they should do, so Murphy dismissed the women and they went home. Early next morning she did receive word that her women were to mobilise for action. She stated:

> I stayed at home on Sunday night and on Monday morning early Josie Kelly, now Mrs. Green, came to me on her bicycle with a message from Commandant Ceannt to mobilise all our branch of Cumann na mBan at the Cleaver Hall in Dolphin's Barn at eleven o'clock. This upset me because the arrangement already made was that only half our members were to cooperate with the 4th Battalion. I decided to go to see the Commandant, Josie and I went to his house in South Circular Road and asked him did he mean me to mobilise all our branch for the Cleaver Hall. He said no, only those who were already appointed to operate with the 4th Battalion. We proceeded, Josie and I, on our bicycles to mobilise those, and they all turned up at Cleaver Hall.[2]

Margaret 'Loo' Kennedy had only heard about the mobilisation by accident when she was at mass on Easter Sunday. She went to No. 6 Harcourt Street but was later dismissed. On Monday morning she received a mobilisation order and:

> we were mobilised for Cleaver Hall Donore Avenue, at 10 o'clock a.m. Six or eight of us were sent to O'Hanlon's, 7 Camac Place, Dolphin's Barn, to collect stretchers, lanterns and other goods stored there. Two girls of this family were with us. When we returned to Cleaver Hall we were ordered to proceed to Emerald Square to link up with the 4th Battalion. We moved off at the rear of 'A' Company in the Battalion; all the girls on parade went together to Marrowbone Lane Distillery with 'A' Company…[3]

While half of the branch, twenty-five women in all, mobilised at Cleaver Hall, the remainder of the Inghinidhe branch went to Harcourt Street. They were meant to be attached to the 3rd Battalion, under the command of Éamon de Valera, but as Eileen Murphy later said 'we did not get in', so she told them to go and find where they could get in. 'Four or five of them, Elizabeth O'Farrell, Julia Grennan [sic] and Josephine 'Joe' Walsh and at least one of her sisters were in the GPO'.[4]

Éamonn Ceannt led his contingent of men and women from Emerald Square to take over their target, the South Dublin Union. These included a group of women led by Rose McNamara, vice O/C of the Inghinidhe branch, who was dressed in full uniform. With McNamara at their head they marched with the Volunteers to their designated outpost, Marrowbone Lane Distillery. Seamus Murphy, captain of 'A' Company, 4th Battalion led his section into the distillery. Rather than split into smaller groups and go with each section of Ceannt's battalion, the women chose to stay together en masse with Murphy's unit:

> We marched behind until we reached the Distillery in Marrowbone Lane (used as forage stores for the British Government) at 12 o'clock. I next saw Captain Murphy who was in charge of Volunteers, 4th Battalion knock at small gate and demand same to be opened in the name of the Irish Republic. As soon as we got in prisoners were made of the Lodgekeepers, also a soldier in khaki. We remained in an old cellar all day, waiting for work to do.[5]

As Murphy's men were allocated their positions so too were the members of Cumann na mBan. A number of the women were detailed to each sniper in the upper levels of the building.

Ceannt and his group marched on towards what was to be his headquarters, the South Dublin Union. Other sections were detailed to take over other buildings. A small party under Con Colbert, captain of 'F' Company, 4th Battalion took over Watkin's Brewery in Ardee Street, while another section, under the command of Patrick Egan, took over Roe's Distillery at Mount Brown. Of these three outposts Marrowbone Lane was the most important strategically. It protected Ceannt's position as it had commanding views of the vast area surrounding the South Dublin Union. Those inside could see all possible advances by the British on Ceannt's headquarters. It was a veritable fortress, four stories high, with numerous windows and surrounded by a twelve-foot-high wall with the added advantage of a crow's nest which was impossible to take by surprise.

Murphy had roughly sixty-five men and women under his command (forty Volunteers and twenty-five Cumann na mBan) in the distillery and they quickly prepared the building for battle. Robert Holland later described the scene:

> They were all in good spirits there and they had posted the small garrison that they had to the best advantage, one man to each room. The rooms were like dormitories about 80 feet long by about 40 feet wide. These rooms were used as stores for kiln-drying wheat. The building lay between Marrowbone Lane at one end, Forbes Lane on one side and the Canal in front. At the right-hand side was the 'Back of the Pipes'. There were eight windows on each side of each room with ceilings about 9 feet high. There was a lot of air ventilators in each wall about 12 inches from the floor level and these had small wooden shutters which could be pulled to one side. The walls of the buildings were about 2 feet thick, and we used the ventilators as port holes to fire out through.[6]

Ceannt's men in the Union did not have long to wait before they had their first experience of battle. Around 12.30p.m. a party of troops of the 3rd Royal Irish Regiment, stationed in Richmond Barracks, were ordered to make their way to Dublin Castle which had just come under attack from Seán Connolly's garrison. Predicting that soldiers from the Barracks would be passing their position, Ceannt sent a party of his men to McCaffrey's Estate, a vast tract of open ground stretching from the Union down along Mount Brown. Approximately one hundred troops under the command of Major Holmes proceeded towards Mount Brown. Despite seeing the Volunteers, Holmes' men came under attack from the men in McCaffrey's. The British responded with machine-gun fire. Patrick Egan, stationed in Roe's, saw what happened:

> [I] saw three Volunteers lying in a group under the hedge across the road… Two were lying face down, while Owens was on his back. He was wounded and was making great efforts with his right hand to move his waterbottle to his mouth; he got it to his neck, when it tumbled over and fell down beside his head; his hand slipped down to his side; his face had the pallor of death; he was slowly dying. By this time, the enemy machine guns had come into action and were whipping the hedge and field. A fourth man (McDowell?) lay on his back, with his knee up and arms outstretched, near the Union wall; he was dead. The sight was depressing; their position was hopeless - no back or cover to protect them.[7]

The Volunteers came under attack from British troops in the Royal Hospital, Kilmainham. While this was happening some troops tried to gain entry to the Union via Rialto. However these soldiers came under attack from the Volunteers in Marrowbone Lane. Volunteers Robert Holland and Mick Liston were waiting in the upper levels in the distillery. Liston, whose sisters Catherine and Mary were also in the distillery, had a commanding view from his position in the crow's nest of the distillery. On seeing the troops, they immediately opened fire. Each sniper had at least one woman with him keeping watch. Robert Holland was assisted by Josie O'Keeffe and, as he remembered, she did a lot more than keep watch:

> I would teach her to load them and leave them on the floor at my hand, as I might have to fire from either side of the building. She brushed away all the wheat into the middle of the floor. I opened up all the ventilators and she went away and brought back with her a Lee Enfield and a Mauser and haversack full of ammunition… I showed Josie how to load the two rifles and she remarked how heavy the Mauser or 'Howth' rifle was. She learned the job of loading them very quickly.[8]

The British soldiers did manage to enter the grounds of the Union but immediately realised it would be no easy task to take the complex which was made up of a series of small buildings. Coming under fire from both Murphy's men in the distillery and Ceannt's men in the Nurses' Home and McCaffrey's Estate and other buildings, they suffered heavy casualties. Sadly it was at this time that Nurse Margaretta Keogh, who worked in the Union, was fatally wounded while trying to tend to the injured soldiers. That night the garrison in Marrowbone Lane were reinforced by another sixty Volunteers, including some from Roe's Distillery. Some women brought much needed supplies for the garrison. It fell to Rose McNamara and her Quartermaster, Marcella Cosgrove, to prepare breakfast for the garrison early the next morning. Marrowbone Lane proved to be one of the more well-fed garrisons during the Rising. On Tuesday morning the Volunteers commandeered some bread and milk but as the week went on, their menu improved. Later that day two priests from Mount Argus Church arrived and most of the women and men went to confession. By now there were twenty-two women in the Distillery, three having left on courier work.

Despite the effort it had taken for the British troops to gain a foothold in the South Dublin Union, that day they were ordered to withdraw. As they made their way to the western wall of the complex,(the wall near what is now the dry canal), they came into view of the Marrowbone Lane garrison who again opened fire. The British quickly realised that in order to take the Union, Marrowbone Lane Distillery had to be immobilised. However, it would be no easy task and reinforcements were called in including cavalry units. More troops were in position in Fairbrother's Field near Rialto and the canal and units of infantry were mobilised in James Street and Thomas Street. The distillery was virtually surrounded. The Cavalry unit was fired on by volunteer Thomas Young who had twenty men in position on a footbridge overlooking Cork Street. They succeeded in halting the advance of the troops trying to attack from nearby Cork Street. He stated:

> On Tuesday, while I was changing the guard on the bridge, I looked out on to the Lane and noticed a party of soldiers coming towards us from Cork Street direction. I took up a firing position, aimed at a soldier in the front rank and opened fire on him. The soldier fell, mortally wounded, and his comrades retreated around a bend in Marrowbone Lane before I could fire a second shot.[9]

Because the distillery was such a large complex, communication between the sections was difficult especially with so few men. To combat this, Young developed a signal system with Sergeant Ned Neill who was guarding the main gate of the building:

> These signals would indicate to him the type of person wishing to enter, the movements of animals, vehicles and suchlike, the reason being that it was considered unsafe to open the gates without prior knowledge of the person seeking admission, and it was a means of diverting foodstuffs which might be en route to other British garrisons, the Vice-Regal Lodge and suchlike places.[10]

It was through this system that the garrison were able to eat so well. In the time they were there, they commandeered three cows and at least twenty-eight chickens. The next morning, Wednesday, Con Colbert arrived with his section from Watkin's Brewery. Also to arrive that day was Seamus Murphy's wife Kathleen, and that night the garrison ate well, they cooked the chickens for dinner, the women having to improvise... having to take them [chickens] out of the pots with bayonets, not having any forks or utensils for cooking'.[11]

Kathleen Murphy took charge of the kitchen. Volunteer Seamus Kenny remembered, 'Captain Seamus Murphy's wife was there cooking and some of the Cumann na mBan girls were giving her a hand. She was a great woman and a great cook'.[12] On the whole, Wednesday was a quiet day but throughout the evening the British soldiers had begun to dig trenches all along the canal in preparation to storm the distillery. They concentrated fire on the Volunteers positioned in the windows and forced the Volunteers to pull back. Michael Liston was slightly wounded in the head, but had his injury treated by the women and went back to his post in the crow's nest. Although it was not a serious head wound, seeing him shot affected the women. Bob Holland remembered the atmosphere when he was brought to the women, 'Our hearts sank and I saw the tears run down Josie McGowan's face and Josie O'Keeffe's as they brought him down'.[13] Taking advantage of the volunteer's pull-back from the windows, the British soldiers advanced on the distillery and managed to reach the outer wall. Con Colbert, who was on one of the upper floors, saw the troops trying to dash towards the building. Armed with canister bombs he took some of his men and raced downstairs, throwing the bombs at the soldiers with deadly effect. His quick thinking held the British soldiers off, for a while at least. Realising they would suffer heavy losses if they continued their assault, the troops retreated.

Thursday began like the previous two days. Soldiers were still trying to encircle the distillery but with the Volunteers in such strategic positions, the chances of making any headway were slim. The 2 / 7th Sherwood Foresters, under the command of Lieutenant Colonel Oates, were now deployed to take the South Dublin Union. While crossing Rialto bridge they were fired on by the Volunteers in both the Union and Marrowbone Lane. They made their way into the Union complex and once again the advance towards Ceannt's position in the Nurses' Home began. On reaching the Nurses' Home a fierce battle between the British forces and the Volunteers ensued:

> The gunfire was so intense that the rooms in the Nurses' Home soon filled with dense clouds of plaster dust. Bullets flew through the back windows, entered the rooms and exited through the front of the building… Khaki figures darted across the front of the building and the Volunteers opened a rapid fire.[14]

It was during this assault that Cathal Brugha, vice O/C of the 4th Battalion was seriously wounded when a grenade was thrown into the building and exploded. Having ordered his men to leave, he waited for the soldiers to storm the building. Ceannt and his men were in the boardroom nearby. Believing their comrade dead, they knelt and said a decade of the Rosary. But the firing from the Nurses' Home continued and above the racket they could hear someone singing '*God Save Ireland*'. Seeing that the soldiers had not actually entered the building, Ceannt went back to see for himself what was happening. On reaching the Nurses' Home he found that Brugha was still alive, barely, and the barricade was still intact. Immediately Ceannt ordered the retaking of the Nurses' Home and his men, boosted by the fact that their vice O/C was still alive, continued the fight with renewed intensity.

By Friday, the fighting in the area had quietened, although those in Marrowbone Lane could hear the battle raging in the city centre. The garrison enjoyed this lull in the fighting. Robert Holland, who was an apprentice butcher, was called from his post to slaughter one of the cows. Even though it was due to him that the garrison ate so well, he did not get to sample the fruits of his labour, 'I have, however, no recollection of getting any meat for my dinner and I asked for some. I was told it was Friday and handed a can of soup and some bread'.[15] The atmosphere amongst the garrison was upbeat. They were there for the long haul and as Holland remembered, 'The whole garrison on this day more or less relaxed and the chaps were finding their bearings and making themselves acquainted with the different parts of the buildings'.[16] That night the entire garrison congregated in the main hall of the building and said a decade of the Rosary, after which the women suggested that they should hold a ceili on Sunday night. Returning to his post, Holland looked out onto the city and was disturbed by what he saw, '...the City looked like an inferno; every place seemed to be burning and there was the usual firing and heavy explosions. We now knew that the British were using artillery and we expected that we would be the next to come under artillery fire'.[17]

On Saturday morning the British forces were nowhere to be seen. The only event worth mentioning was the capture of what the garrison thought was a British spy. Throughout the week the Volunteers had noticed a woman standing at the canal observing the distillery. Eventually Captain Murphy ordered her arrest and she was taken prisoner into the distillery. As she was a woman, Murphy ordered the women to search her. Rose McNamara stated:

> We were afraid this person might be a man, in women's clothes, so we had to be careful as she was a very masculine-looking woman. We each of us had our knives in case of a fight, but she was harmless. We did not find anything on her, so she was let go with a warning.[18]

That night, McNamara slept for the first time that week. On Sunday morning Éamonn

Ceannt in the South Dublin Union received word of the surrender from Thomas MacDonagh who, on the arrest of both Pearse and Connolly, was now in overall command of the Dublin Brigade. MacDonagh himself brought the order to the garrison. When they heard the news there was a mixed reaction from Ceannt's men. After some discussion they agreed to obey their orders.

Meanwhile in the distillery, as it was Sunday, the garrison was getting ready to say morning prayers. They were called together by Murphy who asked them, 'if they were prepared to fight to the last, even tho' [sic] the old enemy whom we were fighting, played her old game and starved us out. They all shouted "Yes"'.[19] Later that afternoon, MacDonagh and Fr. Augustine arrived with the news of the surrender. As Annie Cooney recalled:

> The news was received very badly and there was great disappointment. There was dreadful grousing; they were saying "Was this what we were preparing for and living for all this time? Is this the end of all our hopes?" They were flinging their rifles around in temper and disgust.[20]

The women were tasked with getting the men from the upper levels down to the hall. While up in the barley loft, Cooney saw Éamonn Ceannt come into the yard:

> He was like a wild man; his tunic was open, his hair was standing on end and he looked awful. He evidently hated the task of asking the garrison to surrender. He put his two hands on the barricade, with his head bent, and presented a miserable appearance.[21]

Robert Holland heard the news from Con Colbert. He then told some of his comrades who, he stated, 'were all dumbfounded and a dejected appearance replaced the previous good spirit'.[22] At about 6.30p.m. the garrison from the South Dublin Union arrived at the distillery. Those inside now realised that the fight was definitely over. Holland wrote:

> When I heard this I felt kind of sick in my stomach, putting it mildly, and everybody else felt the same, I'm sure. It came as a great shock. Colbert could hardly speak as he stood in the yard for a moment or two. He was completely stunned. The tears rolled down his cheeks. I glanced at Captain Murphy and he had turned a sickly yellow. Harry Murray bowed his head.[23]

The garrison was ordered to line up in formation in the yard. Ceannt, Fr. Augustine and a British Officer, Major Rotherham, were present. Rose McNamara recalled, '... We (Cumann na mBan) all collected in front of the fort and shook the hands of all the men and gave them all "God Speed", and told them to cheer up. Some were sad and some trying to be cheerful'.[24]

The order was given to march and with that, the members of the 4th Battalion and the Inghinidhe branch, Cumann na mBan began their journey to St. Patrick's Park, beside St. Patrick's Cathedral. When they reached Bride Street they were met with a wall of soldiers with fixed bayonets and machine guns trained on them. The men laid down their arms but the women managed to hold on to some. Thinking that the women would not be imprisoned, many of the Volunteers had given them their handguns to hold. The men pleaded with the women to go home, but they were resolute, '...we were not going to leave the men we were with all the week to their fate... we decided, to go along with them and be with them to the end whatever our fate might be'.[25] Soon, however, the whole garrison, men and women were marched to Richmond Barracks. On the journey the women did their utmost to keep spirits up by singing all the way. On reaching the Barracks the women were separated from the men and were split into two groups. They were not ill-treated and early next morning, 1 May, they were moved to Kilmainham Gaol.

In all twenty-five Inghinidhe branch members, and Central branch member Lily Brennan, were arrested. The arrested women were Rose McNamara, Marcella Cosgrove, Margaret Kennedy, the Liston sisters Catherine and Mary, the Cooney sisters Annie, Lily and Eileen, as well as May Byrne and Bridget Hegarty. Also arrested were Josephine Kelly, Josie McGowan, Kathleen Murphy, Rose Mullally and Margaret 'Cissie' O'Flaherty. Lily O'Brennan, sister in law of Éamonn Ceannt, who had kept a diary of her week in Marrowbone Lane Distillery, was among their number. As she was now under arrest, she 'decided it would be better to destroy it [the diary], so on the way to Richmond Barracks she tore it up into small pieces'.[26] Other women arrested were Sheila O'Hanlon, sisters Josie and Emily O'Keeffe, the Quigley sisters Maria and Priscilla, Agnes MacNamee, Katie Byrne, Bridy Kenny, Kathleen 'Katie' Maher and Josephine Spicer. At Richmond Barracks they were separated from the men and held in the married quarters until they were transferred to Kilmainham Gaol. While in Kilmainham Gaol they heard the executions every morning. Despite their imprisonment, they tried to keep up morale by Irish dancing in the exercise yard, and when that was forbidden, they danced in their cells. On the night of 7 May, while attending mass in the chapel in the Gaol, the women saw their comrades and leaders. Annie Cooney recalled:

> We were on the gallery from which we had only a view of the altar and the front seat. We were able to see Eamon [sic] Ceannt, Michael Mallin, Con Colbert and Sean

> Heuston, who were kneeling in the front seat. They were the only ones to receive Holy Communion, which we thought significant. That affected us all and I began to cry. We craned our necks to try to see more, but the wardresses pulled us back.[27]

Rose McNamara, remembering what it was like to be in the Gaol at the time of the executions, wrote:

> Loud reports of shots at daybreak. We say prayers for whoever it was; heard terrible moans; then a small shot; then silence. We heard from one of our members that poor Con Colbert, E. Ceannt, Mallin and Heuston had been shot.[28]

The Inghinidhe branch was an especially close and unified group. They proved this throughout the Rising when on Easter Monday they chose to stay together rather than be split up amongst Ceannt's other outposts. After the surrender, when they had the chance to leave and go home, they refused en masse and when given the opportunity to leave Kilmainham Gaol on the night of 8 May, the majority of them remained until the next morning. The Inghinidhe branch had proven their determination and loyalty to the cause of Irish freedom during Easter Week. Over the coming years, during the War of Independence and the Civil War, they would show just exactly how determined and loyal they were to that cause.

St. Stephen's Green/Royal College of Surgeons garrison

On Easter Monday, Mrs. Margaret Joyce marched with Commandant Michael Mallin as he led his section of the Irish Citizen Army towards St. Stephen's Green. Her husband James was already in position in Davy's pub, Portobello with a small contingent of the Citizen Army. Margaret Skinnider, a member of Glasgow Cumann na mBan but attached to the Citizen Army that morning, cycled ahead of the insurgents scouting for British soldiers or police along their route to St. Stephen's Green. By 12 noon, without encountering any opposition, Mrs. Joyce noticed that 'they were already in Grafton St.' and about to take the Green.[29]

St. Stephen's Green was chosen as an outpost as four major routes into the city converged there, 'those being Baggot Street/Merrion Row, Lower Leeson St., Harcourt Street, and Cuffe Street, which made its capture a priority' for the insurgents.[30] In taking Davy's pub, James Joyce was among the garrison who were to protect the route from Portobello through Harcourt Street into the Green from any advance by British troops coming from Portobello (later Cathal Brugha) Barracks. As the insurgents approached the Green, their Commandant Michael Mallin instructed them to secure the area. On that quiet bank holiday Monday, the response of the population and administration of Dublin to a group of uniformed, armed men and women moving about the city was not yet serious. People were accustomed to seeing the Volunteers, Cumann na mBan and the Citizen Army on route marches and the sight of armed groups of men and women in the city was not unusual. In fact most people seemed to be intrigued by the spectacle. Certainly the sight of women in uniform and in particular Countess Markievicz, second-in-command to Mallin, in her self-designed uniform which consisted of 'an Irish Citizen Army tunic, a pair of riding breeches and puttees and a lady's hat with an ostrich feather' initially caused more amused comment than fear.[31] As the insurgents entered the Green, they set about clearing the few members of the public out of the area, closing and locking the gates and securing positions for themselves.

The first controversial event at the Green happened within the first few minutes of occupation, as the insurgents were securing the park. An unarmed member of the Dublin Metropolitan Police (DMP), constable Michael Lahiff of College Street Station, tried to enter the park at the north-west gate. He was ordered to leave and told he would be shot if he did not do so. Constable Lahiff kept advancing, trying to force the gate and a couple of shots rang out. He fell backwards, fatally wounded. Who shot Constable Lahiff has always been a cause of debate and controversy. Many accept that he was shot by Countess Markievicz who supposedly gloried in the killing, shrieking in delight 'I killed him, I killed him'.[32] However, the first, uncredited, mention of her involvement in this shooting was in Max Caulfield's 1965 book *The Easter Rebellion*. Indeed, if the shooting occurred that early in the occupation of the park, then the balance of evidence suggests that Markievicz was not yet there, as she had first gone with Dr. Kathleen Lynn to deliver supplies to the garrison at City Hall. At 12 noon, around the time Lahiff was shot, both Lynn's and Markievicz' later accounts confirm that she was at City Hall, after which she made her way to St. Stephen's Green. In her recollection of the events of that day Markievicz recalled reaching City Hall in Lynn's car as Seán Connolly attacked Dublin Castle and killed the sentry.[33] When she reached the Green, she reported to Mallin who showed her how the barricading of the Green was progressing. She made no mention of Constable Lahiff. Once she had arrived at St. Stephen's Green, the work of securing the area continued.

In those early hours of the occupation the youthfulness of the insurgents was evident. A civilian witness, Diarmaid Coffey, noted how young they were, stating that 'many of those in the green were mere boys and a few girls, one of whom was distributing oranges to the boys'.[34] Douglas Hyde, former President of the Gaelic League and future President of Ireland, had a home nearby and was on St. Stephen's Green when the attack began. He also noted the youth of the insurgents, commenting that a young girl with a bandolier looked as if 'she would have liked to kill him'.[35] Markievicz mentioned that some of the 'young girls' had guns and 'with these they sallied forth and held up bread vans'.[36] By this time Mallin and Markievicz were endeavouring to secure the Green with far fewer men and women than previously expected or planned. The plan had been to take control of the Green and the larger buildings around it with a large contingent of men and women. However, in the wake of the countermanding order, Mallin and Markievicz had fewer than sixty men and women under their command. Markievicz mentioned that Mallin left her in charge of the trench-digging in the Green while he oversaw the erecting of barricades, created from hijacked motorcars and drays, to block off the streets into the area. At the same time, under the command of Madeleine ffrench-Mullen, the Citizen Army women began to set up the first aid station in the summer house in the Green, to organise the food supply and distribute ammunition and arms to the defenders around the park.

By Monday afternoon four Cumann na mBan women had arrived at the Green – Nora O'Daly, Brigid Murtagh and May Moore from the Fairview branch and, a little later, Katie Kelly from Galway. The women decided to join the action there, although Nora O'Daly mentioned that the Green 'even to a mind untrained in military matters, looked like a death trap'.[37] At this stage civilians in the area were still bemused by what was happening, O'Daly was surprised that some were actually sightseeing and commenting on the women insurgents 'running, with no hats on them'.[38] As the day wore on the insurgents settled into their assigned positions in the park. Mallin sent Margaret Skinnider to the GPO with a dispatch for Connolly and began to organise the taking of positions in a few houses surrounding the Green, including the Royal College of Surgeons, taken by a raiding party led by Frank Robbins. As night fell the women bedded down as best they could in the summer house, along with the few prisoners taken by the insurgents. The night was cold and damp but Brigid Goff entertained the women with 'comical remarks about the snipers who were disturbing her sleep'.[39] It was relatively quiet until about 4a.m. when machine gun fire suddenly opened on their positions from the Shelbourne Hotel. Skinnider later wrote that this gun fire wakened the 'girls in the summer-house' who 'ran for safety behind one of the embankments'.[40] The British Army troops visiting the Shelbourne had been reinforced and had also managed to get a Maxim machine gun and ammunition onto the hotel roof and opened fire on the insurgents in the park.

It soon became obvious that the situation in the Green was untenable and a decision was made to retreat to the more defensible Royal College of Surgeons on the west side of the park. On Tuesday morning the evacuation began, with the women sent to the College first, although their long skirts and uniforms hampered their progress and 'the bullets were flying everywhere and sending the gravel up in showers off the path'.[41] Skinnider said that the machine gun fire seemed deliberately aimed at the women attempting to cross as they 'made excellent targets in their white dresses, with large red crosses on them'.[42] As the women were crossing to the College, a hostile crowd of civilians tried to bar their way and Christina (Chris) Caffrey had to scare them off with her gun. Rosie Hackett was in the group Caffrey helped across and mentioned that as they left the Green 'the crowd was making attempts to attack us, but Chris held them up. When anyone showed a gun, that was enough for the crowd. She got us to a point opposite the College', they then made a run for it and got to the College.[43] Skinnider was sent by Mallin to bring the sixteen men guarding Leeson Street Bridge into the College. On this trip she experienced the increase in violence as she cycled her bicycle towards Leeson Street:

> Soldiers on top of the Hotel Shelbourne aimed their machine-gun directly at me. Bullets struck the wooden rim of my bicycle wheels, puncturing it; others rattled on the metal rim or among the spokes. I knew one might strike me at any moment, so I rode as fast as I could. My speed saved my life, and I was soon out of range around a corner.[44]

She returned with the men to the College and once all but a few men who remained in the trenches in the Green got inside the College the doors and windows were locked and barricaded. Chris Caffrey was sent with dispatches to Connolly in the GPO to let him know that while the Green was lost, the battalion were now secure in the College of Surgeons. The college was a good stronghold with solidly built walls which proved impregnable to the gun fire from the Shelbourne. As Skinnider said, the British may as well have been firing 'dried peas' at the walls for all the damage they did.[45] A tricolour, which Skinnider brought from the GPO on one of her dispatch missions, was hoisted over the College.

The immediate concern for the women was to re-establish their first aid station, which they did in the large College Hall on the first floor. There was a secluded area behind the large blind on which lantern slides were shown for the medical students and this was cordoned off as an improvised first aid station. No one but the first aid assistants and casualties were allowed in there. Madeleine ffrench-Mullen was in charge of first aid, assisted by Nora O'Daly, Brigid Murtagh and Rosie Hackett. Ffrench-Mullen kept a calm demeanour throughout the week which was most welcome as the numbers of casualties increased, many with severe wounds. She was, according to O'Daly, a woman to inspire confidence and trust, an honest, brave, quiet person.[46] They soon had their first serious casualty when Michael O'Doherty, who had been on the College roof, was raked by machine gun fire from the Shelbourne and seriously wounded. The women managed to get him bandaged and he was subsequently taken by the Dublin Fire Brigade to Mercer's Hospital where he recovered from his wounds. Caffrey and Skinnider continued to carry dispatches between the College of Surgeons and the GPO for the next few days. While the insurgents in the College were now relatively safe, and had ammunition and arms, their major problem was a lack of food. Caffrey returned with some food from the GPO and then went on a food run to Camden Street. Noted feminist and pacifist Hanna Sheehy Skeffington, although not participating in the Rising, turned up with young Clann na nGael girl scout May McLoughlin, Cumann na mBan member Nancy Wyse Power and Volunteer Thomas McEvoy, bringing with them a very welcome supply of food from the GPO.

Although the insurgents were relatively safe in the College of Surgeons, Mallin now had to deal with the British soldiers who had taken over strategic buildings around the Green. His plan was to burrow through the houses between the College and the Shelbourne and try to burn out the British troops. Already his men had burrowed through to the Turkish Baths next door, from which they had removed mattresses, stretchers and other items to make themselves more comfortable in the college. The plan was to tunnel from the Turkish Baths towards South King Street and Grafton Street and set some houses on fire to cut the British line of sight from the Shelbourne Hotel to the College. However, with few men and fewer resources this was not going to happen quickly, so on Wednesday, Skinnider proposed a frontal bomb attack on the Shelbourne. She wanted to 'go out with one man and try to throw a bomb attached to an eight-second fuse through the hotel window'.[47] Mallin was reluctant to let a woman participate in such a front line attack but Skinnider argued that women 'had the same right to risk our lives as the men; that in the constitution of the Irish Republic, women were on equality with men'.[48] While Mallin did not permit this attack, Skinnider did lead another attack. By Thursday British army snipers had taken up positions on the roof of University Church, which hampered any movement by the insurgents in and out of RCSI and around their strategically held positions on the Green. Mallin decided these new positions had to be taken out. Led by Margaret Skinnider and trade union organiser and Citizen Army member William Partridge,[49] a small group of insurgents, including young Fred Ryan, moved stealthily towards the Russell Hotel at the intersection of the Green and Harcourt Street. As they reached Harcourt Street they were fired on by soldiers stationed in the Sinn Féin Bank, opposite their position. Ryan was killed and Skinnider was shot several times in the back. She was brought back to the college where the women at the first aid station jumped into action. They had to probe the wounds without anaesthetic to remove the bullets but 'all the while Madam [Markievicz] held [her] hand'.[50] Despite her injuries, Skinnider refused to leave the College. Later that day Skinnider recalled that Markievicz and William Partridge left the college to retrieve the body of Fred Ryan. They were fired on and returned fire, Markievicz, reputedly, killing two soldiers. On returning to the College, Markievicz said to her 'You are avenged, my dear'.[51]

By Thursday the food situation for the insurgents in the College of Surgeons and the men manning nearby posts was so bad that several of the women were sent out on food runs. They only had a few cream crackers supplied by the garrison in Jacob's Biscuit factory.[52] On Tuesday Nellie Gifford and Chris Caffrey were sent to the Jacob's and GPO outposts for food and ammunition. Nellie Gifford had trained as a domestic economy instructor and her skills were put to use as the director of the garrison's food stores and kitchen in the college. Gifford organised the food runs, the commandeering of food from shops in the vicinity and the cooking of what they had in the kitchens. She was assisted by several of the other women present including Brigid Goff and Katie Kelly from Galway, another Cumann na mBan woman who requested to join the garrison once the Rising broke out. Markievicz described the almost miraculous way Gifford produced 'a quantity of oatmeal from somewhere and made pot after pot of the most delicious porridge which kept us going'.[53] On Thursday Gifford received some flour from a food run to Jacob's and some more food, including four or five pounds of bacon, was delivered from local shops. Newspaper reports from the aftermath of the Rising mention that sweet stuffs were found in the space where Markievicz and the women slept and that 'she and the others seemed to have a partiality for chocolates'.[54]

By Thursday, British forces were taking more control of the city, the college garrison could see flames and smoke to the north of their position, indicating that large parts of the city were on fire. Caffrey was arrested briefly on Thursday as she tried to deliver dispatches to the GPO, but had the presence of mind to eat the piece of paper and was soon released without charge. She then made her way back to the college. From then on none of the female dispatch carriers could get through the city and the college was more or less cut off from headquarters. Mallin and his garrison failed to dislodge the British troops from the Shelbourne Hotel and by Friday the British had control of most of St. Stephen's Green and surrounding areas. The college was under constant fire and the numbers of dead and wounded rose. Rosie Hackett wrote of a close escape she had when a man lay on the mattress she had just been resting on. Murray, she wrote, threw himself down to rest but 'whatever way it happened, this bullet hit him in the face. We attended him there for the whole week. He was then brought to Vincent's Hospital where he died after a week'.[55] Despite the worsening situation, discipline and morale inside the college were still high. Mallin was a respected but firm commander, broking no displays of indiscipline or disrespect, even to the portrait of Queen Victoria which hung in the College. Some young Citizen Army men who had slashed at the portrait were severely reprimanded.

Against overwhelming odds the garrison kept up the fight. They continued to return fire on the British troops, especially after they uncovered the college's Officer Training Corps stock of arms and ammunition which greatly boasted their meagre supply of arms. The women were also determined to participate to the end and did their best to keep morale high. O'Daly wrote that on Wednesday Madeleine ffrench-Mullen asked if anyone wanted to leave, but none of the women left. She also mentioned that seeing the 'always cheerful' Rosie Hackett about 'was a tonic' for all the women.[56] Markievicz composed an uplifting poem, 'Our Faith', which was published in the *Workers Republic* that week, exhorting her comrades to fight and die for Ireland. Skinnider also described the way the garrison kept themselves entertained in the evenings, gathering in the large lecture theatre to sing rousing songs including a poem composed by Markievicz, set to a Polish air:

Armed for the battle,
Kneel we before Thee,
Bless Thou our banners,
God of the brave!
Ireland is living
Shout we triumphant,
Ireland is waking —
Hands grasp the sword![57]

However, as Friday dawned the college garrison could see the fires increasing all over the city and the movement of more British troops in and around the Green. Mallin and Markievicz began to prepare for a final assault. The wounded, excluding Skinnider, were transferred to local hospitals. By mid-afternoon firing increased from the Shelbourne and the men and women in the college prepared for an attack. This attack did not come, but the continuous sniping and the depleted food supplies wore on the nerves and the energy of the insurgents.

Because they were cut off from the GPO and the rest of the city, Mallin and his garrison did not know of the surrender of the leaders at Moore Street on Saturday, 29 April. Throughout that day the women and the men of the college garrison continued with business as usual, exchanging fire with the British troops around them, tending to the wounded and feeding the garrison. The men had tunnelled into a pastry shop nearby and also received more supplies from Jacob's, so Gifford and her helpers kept everyone fed. They decided to keep the bacon they had received during the week for a big Sunday dinner which, in the end, they never got to eat. Then, on Sunday morning they received word of the surrender from Elizabeth O'Farrell, who arrived at the College with Major de Courcey Wheeler. Rosie Hackett described the atmosphere as the news was delivered. She found

> Madam… sitting on the stairs, with her head in her hands. She was very worried, but did not say anything. I just passed on as usual, and she only looked at me, but I knew there was something wrong. Mr. Mallon [sic] went round, shaking hands with all of us.[58]

Not everyone was happy to surrender. As O'Daly wrote, 'there were many who would have preferred the alternative of the enemy's bullet, but obedience is one of the first essentials of a good soldier and they obeyed, bitter and hard though it was'.[59]

Skinnider heard Markievicz urging Mallin to fight on, but he had received the order to surrender from his commanding officer James Connolly and therefore would surrender. The tricolour which Skinnider brought from the GPO and which flew over the college for a week was lowered and a white flag hoisted in its place. Skinnider was taken by ambulance to the nearby St. Vincent's Hospital. As she was being taken out, Markievicz slipped her final will and testament into her coat lining for safe keeping in case she, Markievicz, was executed. As the moment of surrender approached Mallin and Markievicz called all the officers, men and women of the garrison into the large lecture theatre. Many did not want to surrender, they were:

> Strong, brave, upstanding men and women, all of whom had taken risks of one kind or
> another during that week, not knowing and not caring if they would forfeit their lives,
> [and] were broken-hearted.[60]

But soon, the moment of surrender was upon the garrison. The insurgents gathered at the York Street entrance of the college where Mallin offered their surrender to Major de Courcey Wheeler. Markievicz kissed her revolver before handing it over to Wheeler (who was related to her by marriage). Later newspaper reports of the surrender sensationalised this moment of a militant, unrepentant Countess 'fantastically dressed in male attire' surrendering.[61] The rebel garrison was lined up and marched towards Ship Street, through a hostile crowd of onlookers. May Gahan remembered that the prisoners were pelted with bottles and horse dung as they walked to Richmond Barracks.[62] James O'Shea remembered how the soldiers made a 'jeer and a joke of Madame Markievicz' and how 'there was a great display of soldiers' women shouting "bayonet them" etc'.[63] They were then taken to Richmond Barracks where the women were separated from the men. The women were held in Richmond Barracks while being sorted and then transferred to Kilmainham Gaol where most remained for about ten days.

Twelve women were arrested at the Royal College of Surgeons. They were Citizen Army members Madeleine ffrench-Mullen, May Gahan, Nellie Gifford, Brigid Goff, Rosie Hackett, Margaret Joyce, Kathleen Seery, Countess Markievicz and Cumann na mBan members Nora O'Daly, May Moore, Brigid Murtagh and Katie Kelly. Markievicz was the only woman put on trial for taking part in armed rebellion. Her court martial was held on 4 May in Richmond Barracks. Her defence was short and to the point: 'we dreamed of an Irish Republic' she said 'and thought we had a fighting chance'.[64] She was found guilty and sentenced to death, but her sentence was commuted to life imprisonment on account of her gender. Others from the Royal College of Surgeons tried included Mallin, who was sentenced to death and executed, as well as William Partridge and James Joyce, husband of Margaret Joyce who was in Kilmainham Gaol with the rest of the women. Both men received terms of imprisonment. Most of the women arrested remained in Kilmainham until the 8/9 May. Nora O'Daly described the boredom, which they relieved by singing; the bad food, the overcrowding and, as the days wore on, the trauma of hearing the early morning shots which signalled the execution of their comrades in arms, including, on the morning of 8 May, the execution of their commandant, Michael Mallin. Madeleine ffrench-Mullen, Nora O'Daly and Nellie Gifford were held on in prison after the bulk of the women were released. All three women were known to the authorities for their activism prior to 1916 and were regarded as dangerous subversives. They were transferred to Mountjoy Gaol and held there until their release in June 1916 while Markievicz was held in Aylesbury Gaol until she was released under the general amnesty in June 1917.

Further arrests in Dublin and Wexford

As soon as word arrived in Wexford that the Rising had begun, members of the Irish Volunteers and Cumann na mBan there came out in support. Reports sent to the Intelligence Division of the RIC had previously stated that 'around Enniscorthy and Ferns the Irish Volunteers and the Sinn Féin Party with the GAA and the Gaelic League are the most influential'.[65] Patrick Pearse had delivered a speech at Enniscorthy on 1 March 1916 which made it clear that rebellion was imminent. He told Seamus Doyle of the Enniscorthy Volunteers that 'the Insurrection is near at hand' and he arranged a 'code' with Doyle which would 'signify that the orders for the Rising were to be put in force'.[66] Eily O'Hanrahan was only a teenager at the time and a member of Cumann na mBan who 'dressed in furs and [posing] as an adult'[67] was sent to Enniscorthy. She arrived in Enniscorthy on Holy Thursday, 20 April, with an order, written and signed by Pearse, containing instructions and a call to arms. She delivered her dispatch and returned to Dublin. However, like all the Volunteer Brigades around the country, there was confusion amongst the Wexford Volunteers because of MacNeill's countermanding order. Jenny Wyse Power, a member of Cumann na mBan executive and Central branch, brought another dispatch from Pearse to Seamus Doyle on Easter Monday stating that 'we start at noon today, carry out your orders'.[68] Later that evening, confirmation came that the Rising was in progress in Dublin.

On Wednesday over one hundred and fifty members of the Irish Volunteers and Cumann na mBan were gathering in Enniscorthy. Only about twenty men had rifles but many were armed with pikes as their ancestors had been in 1798. Cumann na mBan member Máire Fitzpatrick recalled her emotions on the day, seeing Enniscorthy under the control of the Irish Volunteers:

> As long as I live, that morning sight will never leave my mind. A glorious day, Mike Moran (no relation) was standing at White's corner with a rifle covering the police barracks... Dad with a can of tea and he feeding the sentries. He was an old man then with snow white hair. Nobody else about but an old man with a bucket of tea, two

young men with rifles, and I knew then all our work was not in vain. We were on the road to freedom.[69]

Vice Commandant of the Wexford Battalion, Irish Volunteers, Paul Galligan recalled that 'large numbers of men were presenting themselves to join us and our biggest problem was feeding these men'. The local Cumann na mBan, for whom Galligan felt 'nothing but admiration and appreciation is due, helped to house and feed the new arrivals'.[70] The Volunteers had set up headquarters in the Athenaeum theatre in the town centre, where a 'tricolour was hoisted... by Mrs. Robert Brennan, Miss Marion Stokes and Miss Gretta Comerford, and was saluted by a firing party'.[71] Cumann na mBan then set up food stores, first aid stations and canteens in the building, although some like Máire Fitzpatrick felt that 'it's the rifle I would have preferred'.[72] By Thursday, 27 April a message arrived from James Connolly instructing the Volunteers to hold the railway line from Rosslare to prevent British Army reinforcements reaching Dublin. By midday, the Volunteers had succeeded in destroying the railway line.

During the week the Enniscorthy Cumann na mBan ran the first aid stations, cooked and carried dispatches and arms. When news came of the surrender, the Enniscorthy garrisons would only do so if they got a direct order from Patrick Pearse. Volunteer leaders Seamus Doyle and Seán Etchingham got permission to travel to Dublin and see Pearse at Kilmainham Gaol, where he told them to surrender but hide their weapons as they would be needed later. In Enniscorthy the news that the fight was over came as a shock. Máire Fitzpatrick recalled seeing 'men and boys that day who worked and drilled and dreamt of the fight for freedom break down. But Dad said "Surrender, but not defeat"'.[73] The garrison surrendered, several of the men were arrested but all the Cumann na mBan women went home to await further orders.

Wexford Cumann na mBan members Nell Ryan and Kathleen Browne had not managed to make it as far as either Enniscorthy or Dublin during the week of the Rising. Family stories indicate that both intended and tried to join the fight either in Enniscorthy or Dublin. The *Wexford People* of 13 May 1916 gives the first hint of Ryan and Browne's fate during this period. In a description of 'Incidents of Rebellion in Co. Wexford' the reporter writes that

> The work of lining up the rebels in the Co. Wexford is still proceeding. In addition to the commanders – Brennan (journalist), Etchingham (journalist), de Lacey (Labour Exchange Agent), Doyle (Labour Exchange Agent), King (clerk) and Raiter (publican) nearly 300 insurgents and their sympathisers have been captured including six women; prominent amongst whom are Miss Browne, Rathronan Castle

(whose brother is a lieutenant in the army), and Miss Nellie Ryan, secretary of the Co. Wexford Insurance Committee.[74]

This confirms that both Kathleen Browne and Nell Ryan were arrested in Wexford before they could join any outpost. The *Wexford People* article states that Waterford Gaol was 'fitted up' to receive these prisoners. It further states that 'Miss Browne, Rathronan Castle and Miss Ryan... who were arrested last week, were removed from Waterford to Dublin on last Monday'.[75] Both Ryan and Browne were obviously arrested during Easter Week, possibly as they made their way to join the fight.

In Dublin, Kit Ryan, sister of Nell, was arrested at home. She had not taken an active part in the Rising, unlike her sisters Min and Phyllis and her brother Jim, but she was part of the group of people who had come to the attention of the authorities prior to the Rising. No. 19 Ranelagh Road, where Kit and Min Ryan shared a flat, was a meeting place for many of the participants and planners of the Rising. Their open house in Ranelagh extended to many involved in cultural and advanced nationalism:

> Miss Kit Ryan (afterwards Mrs. Seán T. O'Kelly), who kept open house every Sunday evening for young and old who were Sinn Féiners, Gaelic Leaguers, Volunteers, etc. Here, we met people like Seán McDermott, Seán T. O'Kelly, Liam Ó Briain (now Professor Romance languages, Galway University), Fr. Paddy Browne (now President, Galway University), Pádraig Ó Conaire.[76]

Seán MacDiarmada was a very good friend of the sisters and in his final letter admitted that had he lived, he would have married Min. Kit Ryan's arrest had more to do with the people she was associated with than with any activities during the Rising.

Kathleen Browne and Nell Ryan spent over a week in Waterford Gaol before being transported to Dublin. By the time they were being transported from Waterford to Dublin, the executions of the leaders of the Rising were already underway in Kilmainhan Gaol. They were first taken to Richmond Barracks and then to Kilmainham where they spent a few days (probably until 10 May), when they were moved, along with Kit, to Mountjoy Gaol. Conditions in Mountjoy were an improvement on those in Kilmainham. The women were allowed 'to exercise twice a day, to have visitors, and accept clothes and food parcels. They were given the concession of a room in common so they could spend evenings together'.[77] Letters from Kathleen Browne to her family during her imprisonment mention the conditions. On 11 May, as prisoner 1014, she wrote to her mother from Mountjoy:

> We are really comfortable here, have good food, good beds, baths etc. and plenty of good books. It is very much like being in a convent on retreat. We get out exercising

together, but having nothing whatsoever to do with ordinary prisoners. The place is splendidly kept and the attendants very kind. I should be quite content if I knew that you and all at home were taking the matter quietly and logically. I am not the least bit nervous myself as I hope to get out very soon.[78]

Markievicz, who was in Mountjoy as well at this time, also wrote of improved conditions. On 16 May she wrote to her sister, Eva Gore-Booth:

It is very economical living here... everybody is quite kind, and though it is not a bed of roses, still many rebels have much worse to bear. The life is colourless, the beds are hard, the food peculiar but you might say that of many a free person's life.[79]

However, some of the women were not dealing well with imprisonment and on 27 May in a letter home, Browne mentioned that Kit Ryan was struggling, 'Kit is very delicate and is feeling prison life very much. It is very unjust and cruel to keep her here as whatever charges may be against the rest of us there is nothing against her'.[80] Min Ryan obviously kept in touch with the Browne family as Browne thanked her mother for sending 'Min the money as they have been supplying me with everything and are very good to me'.[81] On 4 June, Kathleen Browne was released from Mountjoy. Also released that day were Madeleine ffrench-Mullen, Annie Higgins, Nellie Gifford and Kit Ryan, much to the delight of her sister Nell who wrote that:

Katie [Kit] and Kathleen Browne were released on Sunday 4... I was happy once Katie was set free for she looked so badly, I was afraid she would not be able to stand it much longer... there are only five of us women prisoners here now.[82]

Nell Ryan was deported to England on 20 June 1916 to Lewes Prison with a number of other women. She was then sent, with Winifred Carney, Helena Molony and Brigid Foley, to Aylesbury Gaol where Countess Markievicz was already interned and was not released until 13 October 1916. On their release Kathleen Browne, Kit Ryan and Nell Ryan resumed their revolutionary activism.

A number of women who were regarded by the authorities as subversive were also arrested after the Rising, despite the fact that none of them had taken part in the Rising. In Dublin, the Humphreys household had been thrown into chaos from Easter Monday. Nell Humphreys and her sister Áine O'Rahilly (sisters of The O'Rahilly) had, like him, accepted the countermand issued by Eoin MacNeill. However Nell Humphreys soon found out that both her brother and her teenage son, Richard 'Dick' Humphreys had joined the GPO garrison. Like their brother, Nell and Áine were members of the Gaelic League and outspoken nationalists. Áine had been at the first meeting for the formation of Cumann na mBan and she had been an active member and organiser ever since. Nell, widowed at a young age, had brought her family to Dublin to be near her brother. Dick had joined the Volunteers in 1914 and assisted his uncle in transporting guns from the *Asgard* during the Howth gun running. Some of the guns were hidden in the Humphreys house at 54 Northumberland Road.

Mrs. Humphreys was not inclined to accept her brother's decision and on the afternoon of Easter Monday she went to the GPO to try and persuade her family members to come home. She also wanted to try to persuade Pearse to call off the Rising. She brought with her a number of medals of Our Lady of Perpetual Succour and distributed them among the Volunteers in the GPO. She persuaded Dick to come home but as soon as he got the chance, he returned to the GPO. Mrs. Humphreys returned to the GPO on Tuesday looking for her son. She was, her sister recalled, very brave because the bullets were flying all round but 'she always had great courage'.[83] Mrs. Humphreys returned home but the violence of the Rising soon came to her doorstep. From their home at No. 54 Northumberland Road the Humphreys family were witness to some of the bloodiest fighting of the Rising: the Battle of Mount Street Bridge. 'C' Company of the 3rd Dublin Battalion, Irish Volunteers had orders to stop British reinforcements coming along this route and in order to do so, they took over a number of positions near Mount Street Bridge, including 25 Northumberland Road. Her daughter Sighle witnessed the ambush of the British troops by the men in No. 25:

> On Wednesday, we heard the tramp of marching men and looking out the window saw lines and lines of soldiers with full military kit marching towards the city. Suddenly a volley rang out from No.25 and all threw themselves on the ground. Many never rose again… The soldiers had no idea from whence the firing was coming.[84]

They saw many soldiers killed at this ambush, most of whom were young boys no older than her brother, 'just rank and file cannon folder for their imperial masters' as Sighle Humphreys later described them.[85] In searches of the houses in the area, Bristish soldiers arrested Nell Humphreys, as a known supporter of the Volunteers. She was held in a horse box in the RDS for the rest of the week. After the surrender she was taken to Richmond Barracks and then to Kilmainham Gaol where she remained until 8 May when she was released. On her release, one of her first tasks was to go to the mortuary to identify the body of her brother, The O'Rahilly, and alongside him, another Kerryman, Patrick Shortis from Ballybunion, who had also been killed in the charge up Moore Street. After the Rising, her sister and Cumann na mBan member, Áine

O'Rahilly, also had an arduous task. With Lily O'Brennan and some other Cumann na mBan women, she worked to identify the temporary burial places of Volunteers killed during the Rising. These men were subsequently re-interred in family graves or in Glasnevin cemetery. Áine O'Rahilly, Nell Humphreys and Sighle Humphreys were all active during the War of Independence and their home, at Ailesbury Road, Dublin, was used as a safe house by the IRA.

Two other women arrested at home were Countess Plunkett and Mary Partridge. Neither had taken part in the Rising but both were closely related to known insurgents. Plunkett was the mother of Joseph Plunkett, signatory to the Proclamation and one of the planners of the Rising. Her other sons, Jack and George, were also in the Irish Volunteers and fought in the Rising as well. She was arrested along with her husband, Count Plunkett. Mary Partridge was the wife of William Partridge, a senior trade union organiser and member of the Irish Citizen Army. Both women were taken to Richmond Barracks and then to Kilmainham Gaol. The last time the Plunketts saw their son Joseph was in Richmond Barracks; he was executed on 4 May in Kilmainham. Kathleen Lynn described meeting the distraught Countess, whom she knew, in Kilmainham:

> Countess Plunkett was in the next cell to mine. Of course, she was in a terrible state about her son having been executed, and she used get awfully lonely and upset at night. We would lie down on the floor and talk; and that would make her better.[86]

Mary Partridge and two other women, Lizzie Mulhall and Barbara Reitz, who had been arrested for supporting the insurgents as they walked to Richmond Barracks, were released on 8 May. Countess Plunkett was deported to Oxford with her husband. They returned to Ireland in 1917 when Count Plunkett contested and won the North Roscommon by-election. The Countess also remained very active in republican politics.

Notes

1   BMH WS 480 (Eileen Murphy), p. 6

2   BMH WS 480 (Eileen Murphy), p. 6.

3   BMH WS 185 (Margaret Kennedy), p. 3

4   BMH WS 480 (Eileen Murphy), p. 6

5   BMH WS 482 (Rose McNamara), p. 4

6   BMH WS 280 (Robert Holland), pp. 18 – 19

7   BMH WS 327 (Patrick Egan), p. 22

8   BMH WS 280 (Robert Holland), p. 22

9   BMH WS 531 (Thomas Young), p. 6

10   Ibid., pp. 4-5

11   BMH WS 482 (Rose McNamara), p. 5

12   BMH WS (Seamus Kenny), p. 8

13   BMH WS (Robert Holland), p. 32

14   Paul O'Brien, *Uncommon Valour: 1916 and the Battle for the South Dublin Union* (Cork: Mercier Press, 2010), pp. 78 – 79

15   BMH WS 280 (Robert Holland), p. 37

16   Ibid., p. 39

17   Ibid., p. 40

18   BMH WS 482 (Rose McNamara) p. 6

19   Ibid., p. 7

20   BMH WS 805 (Annie Cooney), p. 8

21   Ibid., p. 9

22   BMH WS 280 (Robert Holland), p. 42

23   Ibid.

24   BMH WS 492 (Rose McNamara), pp. 7 – 8

25   Ibid.

26   BMH WS 264 (Aine Bean E. Ceannt), p. 41

27   BMH WS 805 (Annie Cooney), pp. 12 – 13

28   BMH WS 492 (Rose McNamara), p. 10

29   IE/MA MSP34REF1861 (Margaret Joyce)

30   Molyneux and Kelly (eds) *When the Clock Struck in 1916*, p. 62

31   Ferghal McGarry, *The Easter Rising, Ireland: Easter 1916* (Oxford: Oxford University Press, 2010), p. 131

32   Ibid., p. 137

33   Constance Markievicz, 'Some women of 1916 (1926)' in Dennis L. Dworkin (ed.), *Ireland and Britain, 1798 – 1922* (London: Hackett Publishing, 2012), p.211

34   Brian Hughes, *16 Lives: Michael Mallin* (Dublin: O'Brien, 2012), p. 113

35   Foy and Barton, *The Easter Rising* (London: The History Press, 2011), p. 82

36   Markievicz, 'Some women of 1916', p. 212

37   O'Daly 'The Women of Easter Week' p. 3

38   Ibid., p. 4

39   Ibid.

40   Skinnider, *Doing My Bit For Ireland p.119*

41   O'Daly, 'The Women of Easter Week', p.4

42   Skinnider, *Doing My Bit For Ireland*, p. 124

43   BMH W.S. 546 (Rosie Hackett), p. 7

44   Skinnider, *Doing My Bit For Ireland*, p. 121

45   Ibid., p. 116

46   O'Daly, 'The Women of Easter Week', p. 4

47   Skinnider, *Doing My Bit For Ireland,* p. 142

48   Ibid., p. 143

49   William Partridge (1874 – 1917), trade unionist and revolutionary nationalist, was a founding member and treasurer of the Inchicore branch of the Gaelic League and was active locally in the temperance movement. In August 1912 he became a full-time paid official of ITGWU. A prolific contributor to the ITGWU publication, the *Irish Worker,* he was acclaimed as the best public speaker in Dublin apart from Larkin and noted for his strong, clear, resonant voice. He enlisted in the Irish Citizen Army at its formation and in the post-lockout reorganisation he was elected to the first Citizen Army council as one of five vice-chairmen (March 1914). By the time of the 1916 Easter rising he held the rank of captain. He was appointed ITGWU travelling organiser (April 1915) in an effort to rebuild strength in provincial branches, over the winter of 1915. During Easter Week he served in the Irish Citizen Army's St. Stephen's Green command. Praised for his efforts to maintain morale, he led the garrison in nightly recitations of the rosary in the Royal College of Surgeons. After the surrender he was court-martialled and sentenced to ten years' penal servitude. He was imprisoned in Dartmoor and Lewes prisons. Severely ill with kidney disease, he was released from Lewes prison (April 1917) and entered a Brighton nursing home. Returning to Ireland in May, he died 26 July 1917 in his brother's home at Tower House, Ballaghaderreen. His funeral to Kilcolman cemetery, where Markievicz delivered the oration beside the Partridge family grave, was one of the first post-Easter-Week demonstrations of renewed strength by radical nationalism (*Cambridge Dictionary of Irish Biography*).

50   Skinnider, *Doing My Bit For Ireland*, pp. 147

51   Ibid., p. 148

52   J. Shannon, 'Remembering RCSI and the Rising of 1916', *The Irish Journal of Medical Science*, Vol. 175, No. 2, 2006, p. 7

53   Ruth Taillon, *When History was Made; The Women of 1916* (Dublin: Beyond the Pale Productions, 1999), p. 69 and Markievicz, 'Some women of 1916', p. 212

54   'Inside the Royal College of Surgeons; After the Rebels left', 20 May, 1916, *The Weekly Times*

55   BMH W.S. 546 (Roseanna 'Rosie' Hackett), p. 8

56   O'Daly 'The Women of Easter Week', p. 5

57   Skinnider, *Doing My Bit For Ireland,* p.140

58   BMH W.S. 546 (Rosie Hackett), p. 8

59   O'Daly, 'The Women of Easter Week', p. 5

60   BMH W.S. 585 (Frank Robbins), p. 81

61   *The Irish Times* 'The Cease Fire and the Surrender', April 28th, 1916

62   IE/MA MSP34REF10326 (May Gahan /O'Carroll)

63   McGarry, *Rebels: Voices from the Easter Rising* (London: Penguin Books, 2011), p. 296

64   Seán Enright, *Easter Rising 1916; The Trials* (Dublin: Irish Academic Press, 2014), p.188

65   RIC Intelligence 'Notes for the Co. Wexford, 1915' CSO, Judicial Division (Dublin Castle)

66   Henry Goff, *Wexford has Risen: A short account of the 1916 Easter week rebellion in Wexford* (Wexford: 1916 Trust Ltd., 2007), p. 10

67   Sinéad McCoole, *No Ordinary Women: Irish Female Activists in the Revolutionary Years 1900 – 1923* (Dublin: O'Brien Press, 2003), p. 35

68   Goff, *Wexford has Risen,* p. 15

69   BMH WS 1, 344 (Maire, Bean Mhic Giolla Phadraig,), p. 5

70   BMH WS 170 (Peter Paul Galligan), p. 9

71   Goff, *Wexford has Risen,* p. 17

72   BMH WS 1, 344 (Máire, Bean Mhic Giolla Phadraig), p. 6

73   Ibid., p. 7

74   *Wexford People*, 13 May1916

75   Ibid.
76   BMH WS 416 (Mrs. James Ryan/Mairín Cregan), p. 2
77   McCoole, *No Ordinary Women*, p. 55
78   Mary McAuliffe, *Senator Kathleen A. Browne (1876–1943): Patriot, Politician and Practical Farmer* (Roscrea: Roscrea Publications, 2008), pp. 13–14
79   Anne Marreco, *The Rebel Countess: The Life and Times of Constance Markievicz* (London: Phoenix Press, 1967), p. 219
80   McAuliffe, *Senator Kathleen A. Browne*, p. 15
81   Ibid.
82   Ann Kinsella, *Women of Wexford, 1798–1998* (Wexford: Courtown Publications, 1998), p. 96
83   BMH WS 333 (Áine O'Rahilly), p. 5
84   Sigle Humphreys papers, P106/384 (UCDA)
85   Ibid.
86   BMH WS 357 (Kathleen Lynn), p. 4

CHAPTER FOUR

—

Beginning Again: 1916 – 1919

It was immediately after Easter Week that the women came into their own. Proving, if proof were needed, that this was no romantic affair of a couple of headstrong and flamboyant personalities, but a full-fledged and broadly based movement.[1]

BY MAY 1916 AFTER THE EASTER RISING, much of Dublin city centre had been reduced to a pile of rubble. The majority of the city's population remained hostile to the insurgents at least until after the executions of the leaders began. But the behaviour of the authorities to those now in custody helped change public opinion in Ireland from one of anger to one of sympathy. As well as executing fifteen men over what seemed like a never-ending series of days (from 3 – 12 May 1916), in what one historian has called the disastrous 'staccato rhythms of the executions'[2], the authorities began a process of mass arrests of republican activists and sympathisers throughout the country. In all, sixteen men were executed: fourteen men in Kilmainham Gaol, Thomas Kent in Cork on 9 May 1916 and Roger Casement in Pentonville Prison on 3 August 1916; 134 men were sentenced to penal servitude and 2,654 men were deported to camps in England and Wales. Most of the seventy-seven women arrested and taken to Richmond Barracks were released on 8 / 9 May 1916. The women in Kilmainham Gaol were told of their release late one evening, when they 'were lined up and our names were called from a list that one of the officers had'[3]. Annie Cooney recalled that the officer in charge:

> announced that the persons whose names he had called were to be released. I can't say whether all the women prisoners' names were on that list, but certainly all our garrison [Marrowbone Lane] were on it. He also announced that curfew was on and that if we chose to go that night we would have to take the risk of passing the barricades and being arrested again, or we could wait till morning. Some of the girls who had long distances to go chose to wait till morning, but we [she and her sisters] decided to go.[4]

Women who had further to go remained an extra night and were released the next morning. Twelve women were taken to Mountjoy Gaol, including Countess Markievicz, Kathleen Lynn, Nell and Kit Ryan and Brigid Foley. Six more women would be released from Mountjoy by June, while the rest were taken to jails in England or deported there. Those who were released found themselves in a very different Dublin. Many of their male comrades were either dead or in prison. The first thing the Cooney sisters had to do when they arrived home was to tell their mother that 'Con [Colbert] is gone'.[5] Colbert was a family friend as well as a revolutionary comrade. While her sisters were in jail, Min Ryan had gone to Kilmainham to say a final farewell to Seán MacDiarmada, the man she most likely would have married had he lived. Lily O'Brennan's sister Áine Ceannt had been widowed on 8 May, when Éamonn Ceannt was executed. Ceannt had sent his wife his last message in which he asked God to grant her comfort, as he faced his 'noble death, for Ireland's freedom'.[6] Nellie Gifford's sister, Grace, had married her fiancé Joseph Plunkett in the chapel in Kilmainham Gaol on the night of 3 May 1916, a few hours before he was executed. Cumann na mBan leader, Kathleen Clarke, then six months pregnant, had to bid farewell to both her husband, Tom Clarke (executed on 3 May), and her brother, Ned Daly (executed on 4 May). As Elizabeth Bloxham, a member of the Cumann na mBan executive remarked:

> Then came the time when each day's paper brought news of the executions…
> There was great agony of Spirit in Ireland at that time.[7]

Others such as Lily O'Brennan, aided by Áine O'Rahilly and a few Cumann na mBan women, had the onerous task of identifying the temporary burial sites of Volunteers killed during the Rising. This work allowed the families to have the men reburied in family graves or in Glasnevin cemetery. As soon as Nell Humphreys was released she had to identify the body of her brother, The O'Rahilly, in the morgue.

The process of politicisation, motivated by nationalism, feminism and socialism, in which women had been involved in the years prior to the Rising, now intensified. As most of the remaining leaders were in prison or camps, it was up to the women to keep the republican cause alive. As well as dealing with the grief and sorrow at the loss of so many of their friends and comrades, the women had to deal with the vast number of grieving and destitute families of those who had been swept up in the mass arrests and who were now interned in England. The organisations they had belonged to were also in disarray. Now was the time for reorganisation, locally and nationally.

Reconstruction and reorganisation post-Rising

After the Rising it was difficult to begin the process of rebuilding the nationalist groups, but the women began almost immediately, with fundraising for destitute families of imprisoned Volunteers. One of the first groups they organised was the Irish Volunteers' Dependents' Fund (IVDF) which was founded by the widowed Kathleen Clarke and Áine Ceannt, along with Sorcha McMahon. While this group was nominally independent of Cumann na mBan, most of the work it undertook fell to Cumann na mBan members and indeed, in many ways it was a cover for the reorganisation of Cumann na mBan.[8] The IVDF was not the only organisation set up to assist Volunteer families in which Cumann na mBan women such as Louise Gavan Duffy were key figures. The Irish National Aid Association (INAA) was a bigger, more widespread organisation composed of influential men, women and clerics from all walks of Irish nationalist life. Both organisations were doing similar work and after much negotiation and persuasion, especially with Clarke, the two groups amalgamated to form the Irish National Aid and Volunteer Dependents' Fund (INAAVDF) around July 1916.

From an early stage the Royal Irish Constabulary (RIC) warned of the political repercussions because of the activities of the aid associations. A report from the RIC in Monaghan in June 1916 stated that:

> Sympathy for the rebels has been strikingly shown by the readiness with which Nationalists are subscribing to collections in aid of the families of those who were imprisoned or shot for taking a leading part in the rebellion, or who were deported… These collections show general sympathy with the rebels in places where it was not expected and will strengthen the Sinn Féiners.[9]

A photograph taken in the summer of 1916, some weeks after the majority of the seventy-seven women had been released from Kilmainham Gaol, shows many of them at an Irish National Aid and Volunteer Dependents' Fund fundraiser held in the home of Mr. and Mrs. Ely O'Carroll in Peter's Place, Dublin. Included in this photograph, taken in the garden, are Cumann na mBan members Marcella Cosgrove, Rose McNamara, Kathleen Murphy, Martha Kelly, Lily O'Brennan, Elizabeth O'Farrell, Julia Grennan, Nora O'Daly, Brigid Foley, the Quigley sisters, the O'Sullivan and Cooney sisters among others. Also included are Irish Citizen Army women Brigid Brady, Jinny Shanahan, Brigid Davis, Chris Caffrey, Rosie Hackett, Kathleen Lynn and Madeleine ffrench-Mullen. This is an important visual record of the continued participation of the 1916 women in post-Rising activism and evidence that the unity of purpose between the middle class more radicalised feminist, advanced nationalist and the working class trade union women was continuing.

As well as dedicated fundraising for destitute and bereaved families of Volunteers, and for Volunteers and Cumann na mBan members who lost their jobs because of their activities during Easter Week, many of the seventy-seven women were also vital in ongoing propaganda work. In Ireland and elsewhere, the contribution of these women to the development of republican propaganda was immense. Several republican women toured America to raise awareness of what had happened during the Rising and to fundraise among the large Irish American communities. Min Ryan, Nellie Gifford, Nora Connolly and Margaret Skinnider all toured the US soon after the Rising and all engaged in propaganda work. Perhaps the biggest impact came from the American tour undertaken in October 1916 by Hanna Sheehy Skeffington, widow of the murdered Francis Sheehy Skeffington. Although not a member of Cumann na mBan, she agreed to 'deliver a message from the organisation to the American president when she became the first Sinn Féiner to meet him in January 1918'.[10] Her talks, focused on the injustices done to herself, her husband and Ireland generally, had a huge impact on the Irish-American audiences, despite some negative publicity.

Back home, the women of Cumann na mBan and the Irish Citizen Army were regrouping as a political force. In 1917, the trauma of the Rising was receding slightly and reorganisation and expansion were of concern to both Cumann na mBan and the Citizen Army. By the autumn of 1916 the Citizen Army was re-organising in Dublin. Numbers swelled as more and more radicalised working class young people were drawn to republicanism. Through 1917 women who had been members of the Citizen Army before and during the Rising stayed on as members. Helena Molony and Rosie Hackett worked on the reorganisation of both the Citizen Army and the Irish Women Worker's Union. Liberty Hall, which had been badly damaged during the Rising, became a centre of radical activity again. The Citizen Army continued to drill weekly and held training camps.[11] On the first anniversary of the Rising, Helena Molony and the Citizen Army women in Liberty Hall participated in a reprinting of the Proclamation, copies of which they posted around the city. On 12 May 1917, the first anniversary of the death of James Connolly, four members of the Citizen Army decided on a major display of commemoration. Helena Molony, Jinny Shanahan, Rosie Hackett and Brigid Davis printed a huge banner which read: 'James Connolly Murdered 12th May 1916', and hung it from the top parapet of Liberty Hall. As this display was illegal, they barricaded themselves on the roof of the building:

> Getting up on the roof, she [Molony] put it high up, across the top parapet. We were
> on top of the roof for the rest of the time it was there. We barricaded the windows. I
> remember there was a ton of coal in one place, and it was shoved up against the door
> in case they would get in. Nails were put in.[12]

Hackett remembered that thousands of people gathered across the river Liffey to see their banner. It took '400 police' hours to break down the barricade and get the banner down. [13] Some of the other Citizen Army women went to the Royal College of Surgeons to commemorate the Rising. As Kathleen Lynn remembered:

> We marched from Liberty Hall to O'Connell Street. I remember quite well seeing
> the boy getting up on the roof of the GPO and hanging the Tricolour from the
> corner. I don't know who he was. Miss French Mullen (sic) and Helena Molony
> were determined to hang out a flag at the College of Surgeons. They failed to get
> in there, so they induced the caretaker of a house on the corner of York Street, just
> opposite the College of Surgeons, to open the door of the 'Wild Geese' Club for
> them and they hung out their flag.[14]

However, as time went on most of the Citizen Army women drifted away from membership of the organisation and many of them joined Cumann na mBan between 1917 and 1919. By 1920 Frank Robbins found that 'practically all the women who had taken part in the 1916 Insurrection were not now members of the Citizen Army'.[15] Motivated as they were by both trade unionism and nationalism, the long standing female members of the Citizen Army were not pleased that new members lacked 'the same spirit, the understanding and the discipline' as the older members and 'had very obnoxious pasts as far as Trade Union matters were concerned; at least two of them had actually scabbed in the 1913 strike'.[16] This was too much for women 'who had lost their jobs fighting to uphold trade unionism... [and]... the trials and tribulations endured in the performance of their national duty' during the Easter Rising.[17]

Cumann na mBan also organised effective propaganda campaigns in the months following the Rising. They produced Easter week memorabilia, postcards, posters and flags which commemorated the executed and imprisoned leaders of 1916. They submitted articles to newspapers describing the heroics and sacrifice of the men and women of 1916. The widows and mothers of 1916, especially the widows of the executed signatories, became very effective emblems of the sacrifice of the men. The younger widows (especially those left to raise children on their own) such as Áine Ceannt and Kathleen Clarke, the romanticised widows like Grace Gifford and Muriel MacDonagh, and the bereaved mothers such as Margaret Pearse and Maria Heuston, became public figures in their own right, as well as potent figures on republican platforms. Such was the effectiveness of the Cumann na mBan propaganda campaign that, 'by the time the first batch of prisoners were allowed home in December 1916 they had, to their great amazement, become heroes, their release being marked by burning of bonfires on the hillsides and general celebration'.[18] On the first anniversary of the Rising, Cumann na mBan women helped reprint and redistribute copies of the Proclamation and also tried to fly tricolours at the various 1916 outposts.

Cumann na mBan and Sinn Féin

The Rising had been popularly known as the 'Sinn Féin Rising' even though Sinn Féin as a group had little to do with it. However the appellation remained and post-Rising republicanism coalesced around Arthur Griffith's small Sinn Féin party. Women had been members of Sinn Féin since its early years and many of the leaders of Cumann na mBan had been associated with Griffith (Jennie Wyse Power was an executive member of three groups: Inghinidhe na hÉireann, Sinn Féin and Cumann na mBan). From early 1917, as Sinn Féin became the party of republicanism, women were involved at the highest level. Countess Markievicz, Countess Plunkett, Kathleen Clarke, Wyse Power and Áine Ceannt were all on the executive. Women from Cumann na mBan and the Citizen Army now began to join Sinn Féin in greater numbers. These included Lily O'Brennan, Kathleen Lynn, Winifred Carney, Annie Higgins, Madeleine ffrench-Mullen, Katie Kelly, Lizzie Mulhall, Nell Humphreys, as well as Kathleen Browne and Nell Ryan in Wexford.

Women were determined that their voices would be heeded in Sinn Féin. The Proclamation of 1916 guaranteed equal rights and equal opportunities to all citizens and women were concerned that this would be forgotten. The signatories of the Proclamation may have included 'Irishmen and Irishwomen' on an equal basis but the women knew they would have to battle to keep the spirit of equality alive into the future. The danger of being marginalised was ever present. When it was being decided whether Sinn Féin or any other group would be the vehicle for future republican activist politics, only one woman, Countess Plunkett, was included on the council set up to consider this. The more radical politicised women were not pleased with this situation. In order to address this, a group of women from the executive of Cumann na mBan, Inghinidhe branch of Cumann na mBan, the Citizen Army and the Irish Women Workers' Union met in Countess Plunkett's house. This group became the

League of Women Delegates (Cumann na dTeachtaire) and included Helena Molony, Kathleen Lynn, Áine Ceannt, Madeleine ffrench-Mullen and Jennie Wyse-Power. They wrote to Sinn Féin:

> Taking into consideration the number of members of your executive, we, representing the various interests of the great bulk of the women of Ireland, propose a representation of six, to be chosen by our body.[19]

A battle ensued between the League and Sinn Féin with the women consistently insisting on their inclusion and being consistently refused. After much argument, the women wrested a concession whereby four of their chosen delegates would be co-opted onto the Sinn Féin executive – Áine Ceannt, Jennie Wyse Power, Helena Molony and Fiona Plunkett. This gave the women a significant presence at the Sinn Féin convention in 1917, the first major convention of a political party after the Rising. The League of Women Delegates proposed a motion to the convention, that 'the equality of men and women in this organisation be emphasised in all speeches and leaflets'. [20] The motion was accepted.

Cumann na mBan emerged from the Rising stronger, more radical, more explicitly feminist and more militant. The Proclamation of the Republic guaranteed equal citizenship to all and by 1918 the Cumann na mBan manifesto was changed to reflect this. At the 1918 Cumann na mBan convention, women reaffirmed their role in 'arming a body of men and women to fight for an Irish Republic', but they also insisted that they would 'follow the policy of the Republican Proclamation by seeing that women take up their proper position in the life of the nation'.[21] The women also continued to protest at the ill-treatment of Irish prisoners held in English Gaols and prisons camps. In particular, they protested at the treatment of Countess Markievicz, held in Aylesbury Prison. At a public meeting, Madame O'Rahilly, widow of The O'Rahilly, demanded 'that she [Markievicz] be accorded the same treatment given German prisoners in England'.[22] A letter circulated and signed by Madame O'Rahilly, Áine Ceannt, Mrs. Margaret Pearse and others

> Appealed to the men of Ireland to raise their united voice in condemnation of the cruelty being perpetrated against a noble Irish lady, whose love for her people moved her to leave the highest social rank and take her place with the poor and the oppressed. They demanded equality of treatment with the men who received the same sentence as herself.[23]

The return to Dublin of Countess Markievicz was turned into a triumphant parade of resurgent republicanism. Interned prisoners from Frongoch and Lewes and other camps also received riotous welcomes as they arrived home, but no one, the papers said, could forget the demonstrations which welcomed Markievicz home in June 1917. An immense throng had gathered and escorted her to Liberty Hall and among the welcome committee were many of the women she had fought with during Easter Week, especially her comrades from the women's section of the Citizen Army. She was accompanied by her sister Eva Gore-Booth, her Citizen Army comrade Kathleen Lynn and many women from political organisations along the route from Kingstown (Dún Laoghaire) to Liberty Hall. Markievicz had been elected President of Cumann na mBan in late 1916 and was also appointed to the executive of Sinn Féin. As another effort to crack down on growing support for Sinn Fein began in 1917, Cumann na mBan offered its support for imprisoned men by organising demonstrations outside Mountjoy Gaol.

While imprisoned, a group of Volunteers, led by Thomas Ashe head of the revitalised IRB, went on hunger strike, demanding prisoner of war status. The men were force-fed and Ashe was badly injured during the procedure and died. He had commanded the Ashbourne garrison during the Rising and his funeral became deeply symbolic in propaganda terms. His funeral cortège, from City Hall through the city to Glasnevin cemetery, included all the organisations which had participated in the Rising, including Cumann na mBan. As Eilis Ní Riain recalled:

> the Cumann na mBan took part in the public funeral. I helped to mobilise our branch. We met on the Sunday morning I think it was at 12 o'clock in Exchequer Street and we were there a considerable time before we moved off to join the procession in Dame Street en route for Glasnevin.[24]

Many of the seventy-seven women took part in the funeral procession including Citizen Army women Brigid Brady and Jinny Shanahan, as well as Cumann na mBan women Meg Carron, the Cooneys, Brigid Foley, Bridget Hegarty, the O'Keeffes and Rose McNamara. The Ashe funeral, attended by thousands of Irish Volunteers, including over 700 from Ashe's native Kerry, and many hundreds of members of Cumann na mBan and the Citizen Army, galvanised all three organisations and provided a boost for recruitment. The then Chief Secretary for Ireland, Ian MacPherson, said that Ashe's death did 'more to stimulate Sinn Féinism and disorder in Ireland than anything I know'.[25]

Cumann na mBan, 1918 – 1919: a year of strength

Separating the women who were involved in political activity with Sinn Féin and involved with Cumann na mBan is a difficult task. There was a lot of overlap between both groups and in many areas Cumann na mBan members were also members of Sinn Féin or supporters and campaigners for Sinn Féin candidates. One of the major areas of activism where membership of both organisations intersected was the anti-conscription campaign of 1918. Conscription was 'the greatest and final unifying issue in pre-independence nationalist Ireland and women played a vital role in opposing it'.[26] When Prime Minister Lloyd George announced that the government was going to extend the Military Service Bill to Ireland, a united campaign of all shades of nationalism and republicanism came together to oppose it. These groups included the Labour Party, Sinn Féin, the Irish Parliamentary Party, Cumann na mBan, the Irish Citizen Army, the Irish Women Workers' Union, the Irish Volunteers and the Catholic Church. Cumann na mBan organised flag days and anti-conscription meetings. In May 1918 the IWWU, whose members included Helena Molony, Jinny Shanahan, Rosie Hackett and Marie Perloz, supported a one day work stoppage in protest against conscription. Cumann na mBan organised nationwide anti-conscription meetings, distributed pamphlets and collected signatures for the anti-conscription pledge.

'Lá na mBan' (Women's Day) was a major, all-Ireland anti-conscription event which took place on 9 June 1918 and involved thousands of female activists from several organisations. Women collected signatures of people opposed to conscription and the *Freemans's Journal* reported that 40,000 had signed the anti-conscription pledge in Dublin's City Hall alone.[27] Over 700 uniformed Cumann na mBan members who, 'from the spectacular point of view, provided the leading features of the days' proceedings' were present at City Hall.[28] Over 2,400 IWWU women also marched to City Hall, including many women involved in the Citizen Army. The campaign included a 'solemn pledge for the women of Ireland' signed by an estimated two-thirds of Ireland's women as they believed that, 'the enforcement of conscription on any people without their consent is tyranny'.[29] Many women, both from Cumann na mBan and the Citizen Army, were involved in collecting signatures for this anti-conscription campaign. These included dozens of the seventy-seven women: Katie Barrett, Jinny Shanahan, Rosie Hackett and others from the Citizen Army as well as Meg Carron, the Cooney sisters, Nellie Ennis, Brigid Foley, May Byrne, Josie Kelly, Rose McNamara, Margaret Kennedy and many others from Cumann na mBan. The women participated in the collecting of signatures, they signed the anti-conscription pledge, they arranged and acted as stewards at meetings, most spectacularly on 'Lá na mBan' in City Hall.

In May 1918 several prominent women activists were arrested as part of the so-called 'German Plot'. Lord French, the Lord Lieutenant of Ireland, claimed Sinn Féin was plotting with Germany to restart armed insurrection in Ireland and ordered the arrests of many leaders and members of that organisation. Among those arrested were Countess Markievicz, Maud Gonne McBride and Kathleen Clarke. Campaigns against the arrests and the treatment of those arrested now became the focus of activities among political women. One such meeting was organised by Cumann na mBan at Foster Place, off Dame Street in Dublin on 22 September 1918. *The Irish Times* reported that a crowd of 300 people gathered to 'protest against the treatment of female Sinn Fein [*sic*] prisoners who have been interned in England'.[30] The speakers included Hanna Sheehy Skeffington, Helena Molony and a Miss Mullan [*sic*]. The DMP surrounded the crowd and baton-charged it. Several women were badly beaten, including several Inghinidhe branch members such as Emily O'Keeffe, Priscilla Kavanagh, Maria Quigley, May Byrne, the Cooney sisters and Josie McGowan. While several of the women were roughed up, Josie McGowan received a blow to the head and had to be taken to the Inghinidhe first aid station which the branch had established at Ticknock in Dublin. She died a week later on 29 September; she was twenty years old. As the DMP broke up the meeting they arrested Molony and Mullan. Sheehy Skeffington went to Great Brunswick Street police station to inquire about them and was also arrested.

Much had changed between 1916 and 1918. Markievicz articulated the transforming role of women in society in a lecture in 1918 entitled 'A call to the women of Ireland' in which she said that 'the old idea that a woman can only serve her nation through her home is gone… you must make the world look upon you as citizens first, as women after'.[31] At its convention in 1918 Cumann na mBan changed its constitution to one which reflected its growing independence and assurance of its place in the fight for Irish freedom and the equality of women. Its new manifesto pledged:

1. to follow the policy of the Republican Proclamation by seeing that women take up their proper position in the life of the Nation
2. to develop the suggested military activities in conjunction with the Irish Volunteers
3. to continue collecting… funds… to be devoted to the arming and equipping of the men *and women* [author's emphasis] of Ireland[32]

The opportunity to pursue this policy came at the end of 1918. In August 1918 the Prime Minister, Lloyd George, called a general election for December of that year. Also in August the Representation of the People Act (1918) was passed, which gave the vote to all males over twenty-one and all women over thirty (with certain property qualifications). The female electorate was going to be an essential factor in the outcome of the election. Sinn Féin and the Irish Parliamentary Party made a determined bid for the female vote, but Sinn Féin had the advantage because of its close co-operation with the largest women's organisation in the country, Cumann na mBan.

Cumann na mBan were determined to play their part in a successful election for Sinn Féin. Despite the disappointment of having only two female candidates, Winifred Carney and Countess Markievicz, run in the election, most members were active in the campaign for male candidates in their constituencies. The organisation issued a pamphlet entitled the *Present Duty of Irishwomen* which called on potential women voters to use the 'weapon' (the vote) which 'generations of Irishwomen' fought to gain, 'in order to show the world… our determination to be free':

> Irishwomen, your country calls to you to do your share in restoring her to her rightful place among the nations. No great sacrifice is asked of you. You have merely to secure the votes, to which you are entitled, and use them on behalf of SF [Sinn Féin] candidates at the next general election.[33]

This weapon (the vote) that women had fought so long to obtain could now be used by republican women in the pursuit of national freedom. In Dublin, many of the seventy-seven women put their energies into the election campaign. From its head-quarters in 6 Harcourt Street the Inghinidhe branch mobilised again. Sheila O'Hanlon, the O'Keeffe, Cooney and Quigley sisters, among others, participated in printing and distributing leaflets, organising public meetings which were addressed by Sinn Féin speakers and, most importantly, canvassed door to door to get the electorate out. In Fairview, Nora O'Daly and her friends May O'Moore and Bridget Murtagh camp-aigned for Sinn Féin candidates. In Wexford, Kathleen Browne and the Ryan sisters supported local candidates there. Margaret 'Loo' Kennedy was given the responsibility of setting up first aid stations around the city on election day and these were staffed by members of Cumann na mBan. Other activists involved who helped get the female vote out included Lily O'Brennan, Nell Humphreys and Marie Perloz. Citizen Army women also supported Sinn Féin in the election campaign, including Kathleen Barrett, Kathleen Lynn, Rosie Hackett, Madeleine ffrench-Mullen and Helena Molony.[34]

Given the atmosphere at the time, Citizen Army and Cumann na mBan women were prepared for any violence that might break out.

The size of the electoral gain by Sinn Féin, taking 73 out of 105 seats, indicates that women voters supported the party to the detriment of the Irish Parliamentary Party – perhaps, as was written in the *Irish Citizen*, there was 'an element of ironic justice in the fact that women, whose claims it [the IPP] so long opposed with such unbending hostility, should have played so large a part in its final annihilation'.[35] Countess Markievicz was elected for Sinn Féin, becoming the first women elected to the British House of Commons though she did not take her seat: she followed the Sinn Féin policy of abstention. For Cumann na mBan the victory signalled that the Irish people:

> voted for the complete severance of the English connection... the republican candidates fought the election on one issue only, that of complete separation...[and] there is no justification for the continuance of the British government in Ireland.[36]

Countess Markievicz as a Sinn Féin candidate (albeit one still in prison) and President of Cumann na mBan followed the policy of abstention and supported the creation of the First Dáil which met on 21 January 1919 in the Mansion House in Dublin. At this meeting Countess Markievicz was appointed Minister for Labour, a position that bridged her prior and ongoing activism in the republican and labour movements.

The women of Cumann na mBan had reorganised and expanded after the Rising; they now had new branches in the city and branches in towns and villages in every county through the country. They had fully embraced the sentiments expressed in the Proclamation of 1916 and by 1918 saw themselves as fighting side by side with their male republican counterparts for the cause of Irish freedom. No longer auxiliaries, many saw themselves as allies battling for a Republic in which men and women would take their rightful and equal place. As the first Dáil met on 21 January 1919 the first shots of what would become the War of Independence were fired by Irish Volunteers at an ambush in Soloheadbeg in Co. Tipperary. This signalled the start of a new phase for Cumann na mBan, a phase in which many of the seventy-seven women again participated in violent conflict. Most of them, having experienced the violence of the Easter Rising and now fully committed to the fight for Irish freedom, would play as full and pivotal a part in this period of Irish history as they had during Easter Week, 1916.

Notes

1   Brian Farrell, 'Markievicz and the Women of the Revolution', in F. X. Martin (ed.) *Leaders and the Men of the Easter Rising; Dublin 1916* (New York: Cornell University Press, 1967), p. 229

2   Alvin Jackson, *Home Rule: an Irish history, 1800–2000* (Oxford: Oxford University Press, 2004), pp. 153–4

3   BMH WS 805 (Annie Cooney / O'Brien), p. 14

4   BMH WS 805 (Annie Cooney / O'Brien), p. 14

5   BMH WS 805 (Annie Cooney / O'Brien), p. 14

6   National Library of Ireland, NLI Ms. 13,069 / 9

7   Elizabeth Bloxham Papers, UCD Archives, p. 31

8   McCarthy, *Cumann na mBan,* p. 76

9   Caoimhe Nic Dháibhéid, 'The Irish National Aid Association and the radicalisation of Public Opinion in Ireland, 1916–1918', *The Historical Journal*, Vol. 55, Issue 03, September 2012, p. 711

10   McCarthy, *Cumann na mBan*, p. 83

11   Brian Hanley, 'After the Rising' in *The Irish Citizen Army* (Dublin: Stoneybatter and Smithfield People's History Project, 2015), p. 24

12   BMH WS 546 (Roseanna 'Rosie' Hackett), p. 10

13   Ibid.

14   BMH WS 357 (Kathleen Lynn), p. 8

15   BMH WS 585 (Frank Robbins), p. 157

16   Ibid.

17   Mary Muldowney, 'In their own right and as Equals' in Rising' in *The Irish Citizen Army in Stoneybatter, Smithfield and the Markets* (Dublin, Smithfield and Stoneybatter People's History Project, 2015) p. 14

18   Margaret Ward, *Unmanageable Revolutionaries: Women and Irish Nationalism* (London: Pluto Press, 1983), p. 121

19   Ann Matthews, *Renegades: Women in Irish Republican Politics 1900–1922* (Cork: Mercier Press, 2010), p. 187

20   Margaret Ward, 'The League of Women Delegates & Sinn Féin' in *History Ireland*, Issue 3, Autumn 1996, http://www.historyireland.com/20th-century-contemporary-history/the-league-of-women-delegates-sinn-fein/

21   Ward, 'Cumann na mBan Convention, 1918' in *In their Own Voice* pp. 94–17

22   *Leinster Express*, 21 April, 1917

23   *Nenagh Guardian*, 5 May, 1917

24   BMH WS 568 (Eilís, Bean Uí Chonaill, (Ní Riain), p. 23

25   Michael Laffan, *The Resurrection of Ireland*: *The Sinn Féin Party, 1916–1923* (Cambridge: Cambridge University Press, 1999), p. 269

26   Pašeta, *Irish Nationalist Women*, p. 237

27   McCoole, *No Ordinary Women*, p. 67

28   McCarthy, *Cumann na mBan,* p. 96

29   Jones, *Those Obstreperous Lassies*, p. 26

30   *Irish Times,* 28 September 1918

31   Countess Markievicz, 'Women, Ideals and the Nation', delivered to the National Literary Society, Dublin (Dublin: Fergus O'Connor, 1918), p.12, NLI Rosamund Jacob Papers, MS 33, 127 (2)

32   Ward, *In Their Own Voice*, pp. 96–97

33   Cumann na mBan*, The Present Duty of Irishwomen*, Dublin 1918, copies held in the National Library of Ireland (NLI)

34   All of these women talk about their General Election activism in the military pension

application documents.

35   *Irish Citizen*, April 1919

36   McCarthy, *Cumann na mBan*, p. 103.

BIOGRAPHIES
—
77 Women of The Easter Rising

Seventy-seven women arrested in the aftermath of the Easter Rising were taken to Richmond Barracks and then to Kilmainham Gaol. Where the records allow, the following are biographies of these women, arranged by the garrison in which they served.[1]

CITY HALL

Kathleen 'Katie' Barrett (*née Connolly*)
BORN: Dublin, 1887
ORGANISATION: Irish Citizen Army
POSITION DURING EASTER RISING: City Hall

Kathleen 'Katie' Barrett was a member of the Irish Citizen Army and a sister of Captain Seán Connolly, also Irish Citizen Army, who was in command of the unit which took over Dublin's City Hall at Easter 1916. Her brothers George, Eddie and Matt were also part of that unit, while another brother Joseph fought with Michael Mallin and Countess Markievicz at the Royal College of Surgeons and St. Stephen's Green. Barrett was in City Hall during the Rising, attending to the wounded with Helena Molony and Dr. Kathleen Lynn. She was one of eight daughters and eight sons of Michael Connolly, a seaman and dock worker, and Mary Connolly (*née* Ellis). In the 1901 census the family was living at 2 Bella Street, Dublin 1. Michael Connolly was then working as a dock porter while his wife practiced midwifery and ran a shop from a front room. With her brother Seán, she was involved in the Gaelic League and was active in the Irish Citizen Army's Liberty Players. The Liberty Players were popular for their Sunday night revues and concerts, in which satires and patriotic dramas by James Connolly and Arthur Griffith were performed for the workers and Irish Citizen Army members in Liberty Hall. These cultural evenings helped created a network of activist friends and indeed fostered several relationships and marriages between Irish Citizen Army members.

In the week preceding the Easter Rising Barrett was on continuous duty in Liberty Hall with the men and women of the Irish Citizen Army. When the Rising broke out she was with the Irish Citizen Army contingent her brother Seán lead towards Dame Street. The first objective of this Irish Citizen Army battalion was to take Dublin Castle and Captain Connolly fired on and killed the policeman guarding the gates of Dublin Castle – this policeman was the first casualty of the Rising. However Connolly and his men were unable to take the Castle before the gates were shut so the entire garrison of sixteen men and nine women retreated to City Hall next door. One section of this company entered City Hall, where the women helped barricade the doors and snipers took up position on the rooftop. When Kathleen Lynn and Countess Markievicz arrived with first aid supplies for the garrison, Barrett was on hand to help secure the provisions in the outpost. During the period the insurgents were in City Hall she carried arms for the Irish Citizen Army and was a trusted messenger.

Within an hour, while occupying a position on the roof, her brother Seán was killed by a sniper's bullet, fired from the Castle tower; Barrett was on the roof when her brother was shot. Within hours the British had counter-attacked and forced their way into City Hall. With casualties mounting the men and women of the garrison discussed what they should do, and on Tuesday night they surrendered. Lynn, Barrett and the rest of the garrison were then taken into custody and marched off, under guard, to Ship Street Barracks. The women were kept in one dirty room in Ship Street for several days, after which they were transferred to Richmond Barracks and then to Kilmainham Gaol. Barrett was released from Kilmainham on 9 May.

Kathleen Barrett continued her work for Ireland after the Rising and like many female members of the Irish Citizen Army subsequently joined Cumann na mBan (she became a member of the Árd Craobh or Central branch). Barrett helped with the Irish National Aid and Volunteer Dependents' Fund (INAAVDF)[2]. In 1918 she campaigned for Sinn Féin in the general election and was also active in the anti-conscription campaign. During the War of Independence she visited wounded Volunteers in hospital and took part in vigils outside Mountjoy Gaol during the hunger strikes and during the executions in 1920 and 1921. She attended many republican funerals, in Dublin, throughout the War of Independence, while also helping to collect for the arms fund. She took the anti-Treaty side during the Civil War and served in 44

Parnell Square, Jenkinson's, Capel Street and other anti-Treaty outposts distributing arms and assisting in whatever way she could. In October 1922 she was sent to London as a courier for the Republican Envoy there, Art O'Brien. She made eight trips in all to London during this period. Her sister Eilish Eady was active in London and when Eady was arrested following the 'round up' in connection with the shooting of Sir Henry Wilson, Barrett went to London to take her place. In March 1923 she was arrested there and sent back to Ireland and was interned in Mountjoy Gaol and the North Dublin Union.

Her activism continued after the formation of the Free State. In 1927 she and others protested at the Abbey Theatre at what they considered the belittling portrayal of the Citizen Army men who fought in 1916 in the production of Seán O'Casey's *The Plough and the Stars*. She was also an active member from its foundation of the Association of the Old Cumann na mBan. She continued throughout this period to raise funds for the IRA and was supportive of republican activities. Kathleen Connolly had married Seamus Barrett in 1911, she died in 1938 and is buried in Glasnevin Cemetery. As with many of the 1916 revolutionaries she was honoured at her funeral by representatives of the Irish Citizen Army, Cumann na mBan and the old IRA who marched in the cortège and her coffin was draped in the Tricolour.

Bridget 'Brigid' Brady (*later Murphy*)
BORN: Dublin, 1896
ORGANISATION: Irish Citizen Army
POSITION DURING EASTER RISING: City Hall

Bridget Brady was a member of the Irish Women Workers Union (IWWU) and a member of the Irish Citizen Army which she joined in 1913. Brady was locked out in 1913 and on advice from James Connolly, went to find work in Belfast for a time where she found a job in a printing works. She was born in Dublin in 1896 to Walter Brady and Catherine 'Kate' Byrne; she was one of eleven Brady siblings baptised in St. Mary's Pro-Cathedral between 1881 and 1896. In 1901 Bridget and her family were living in a three-roomed house on Montgomery Street in Dublin 1. Eleven people: Bridget, her parents Walter and Kate, and seven siblings, as well as a lodger shared these three rooms. Walter Brady and two of his sons, Patrick and Walter, worked as general labourers; these unskilled workers were the lowest paid and most exploited of Dublin workers and formed the backbone of the 1913 Lockout. Children of the working class went to work early to contribute to the family income. In the 1911 census Bridget and her sister Kathleen were working as biscuit packers, most likely in Jacob's Biscuit Factory. When the 1913 Lockout began, Brady volunteered in Liberty Hall with Countess Markievicz, in the 'Stew Kitchen' as she stated in her pension application. She remained active in the Irish Citizen Army and in the Irish Women Workers Union (she appeared in the photo taken of the Irish Women Workers Union outside Liberty Hall in 1913) and eventually went back to work in Jacob's, where she was employed when the Rising broke out.

In her pension statement she described being mobilised about a month before the Rising and was in Liberty Hall on 21 March 1916, when it was raided by the Dublin Metropolitan Police (DMP) looking for weapons. At Easter 1916, she was among those mobilised in Liberty Hall on Sunday night, where the women were engaged in making bandages, collecting cans to make bombs, making first aid outfits and delivering messages. On Monday she was with the group which marched on Dublin Castle but ended up in City Hall. Among her duties at City Hall was to cook and help the wounded. When the garrison at City Hall surrendered she and three other women were among the last down the stairs and the last of the City Hall garrison to surrender. Along with the others she was taken to Ship Street Barracks where she was held for several days, then transferred to Richmond Barracks and subsequently onto Kilmainham Gaol. She was released on 8 May from Kilmainham.

Brady is among the Easter Rising female combatants pictured in a photograph of the Clann na nGaedheal, Cumann na mBan and Irish Citizen Army women taken at a meeting of the INAAVDF held in Mr. and Mrs. Ely O'Carroll's house in Peter's Place, Dublin in the summer of 1916. In September 1917 Brady marched through Dublin city to Glasnevin Cemetery with many Cumann na mBan and Irish Citizen Army women and 30,000 others, in the funeral procession of Thomas Ashe who had died on hunger strike in Mountjoy Gaol. In a tragedy for the family, her brother Christopher Brady, also a member of the Irish Citizen Army who had been in City Hall during the Rising, developed 'lung trouble' while interred in Frongoch in Wales and died soon after his release. It seems Brady took no further active role in the revolutionary activism after 1917. She married Joseph Murphy on 26 December 1938 at the Church of Our Lady of Lourdes (Lower Gloucester Street, Dublin) and had at least one son, Joseph. Bridget Murphy died in 1988, aged ninety-two.

Bridget 'Brigid' Davis (*later O'Duffy*)
BORN: Dublin, 1891
ORGANISATION: Irish Citizen Army (later Cumann na mBan)
POSITION DURING EASTER RISING: City Hall

Bridget Davis was a member of the Irish Citizen Army at the City Hall outpost in 1916. With her best friend, Rosie Hackett, she was active in politics, joining the Irish Citizen Army in 1915 and working in Liberty Hall. She was also a member of the IWWU and participated in the 1913 Lockout. Davis was born in Dublin 1 in 1891, the daughter of Thomas Davis and Bridget Lochead/Loccade and was one of at least eight siblings. Her father was a general labourer and was deceased by 1911 when the family was living in a two-roomed, second class house on Greek Street, Dublin 1. There were two other families in this house with a total of eighteen people living in a six-roomed dwelling. By 1911 Davis was twenty years old and working as a biscuit factory worker, probably in Jacob's, like so many of the other Irish Citizen Army young women who were 'out' in 1916. Like them she participated in the 1913 Lockout as a member of the IWWU and became part of the cultural and political network in Liberty Hall. It was here she met the woman who became her mentor, Dr. Kathleen Lynn.

Brady had been instructed in first aid by Dr. Lynn and was her principle assistant during the Rising. Having been among the Irish Citizen Army members mobilised in Liberty Hall for a month before the Rising, she was then with the Irish Citizen Army contingent, commanded by Seán Connolly, which marched on towards Dublin Castle and City Hall on Easter Monday. Helena Molony stated in her letter of support for Davis' pension application that she 'was posted on the roof of City Hall during Easter Monday, a position of great danger' where she came under fire several times. Molony also wrote that Davis 'acquitted herself with great coolness and courage'.[3] She witnessed the shot that killed Seán Connolly and attended to him as he lay dying. She was arrested on Tuesday and spent several days in the Ship Street Barracks, was then taken to Richmond Barracks and subsequently to Kilmainham Gaol. She was eventually released on the 8 May with many of the other women.

In 1917 Davis was among a group of Irish Citizen Army women, including Molony, Rosie Hackett and Jane 'Jinny' Shanahan who wanted to commemorate the death of James Connolly at Liberty Hall. They made a large banner which read 'James Connolly Murdered, May 12th, 1916' and placed it on the upper floor outside of Liberty of Liberty Hall, barricaded themselves into the building and resisted the police for several hours.[4] She was also among the women who posted copies of the Proclamation around Dublin in 1917. This was part of a vital propaganda role that rebel women played in keeping the republican ideology alive in the immediate aftermath of the Rising, especially as most of the male leadership and membership of the Irish Citizen Army and the Irish Volunteers were interned in England and Wales.

After the Rising Davis remained chief assistant to Dr. Lynn in the reformed Irish Citizen Army and in 1918, as the flu epidemic was sweeping the country to devastating effect, Davis and other Citizen Army women assisted Lynn in administering vaccines to Citizen Army members and their families and nursed victims of the flu in their homes. She left the Irish Citizen Army in 1918, as there was, she said in her pension application, a 'lot of [new] youngsters in the ICA and you could not put up with them'.[5] Instead she joined the Fairview branch of Cumann na mBan and continued her activities. In 1921 she was sent to Co. Longford to assist in nursing wounded members of the flying column of the Ballinalee IRA. In 1919, Davis had become one of the first probationer nurses in St. Ultan's Hospital for Sick Infants. In 1920 she trained as a baby nurse and qualified by 1921. Davis married Patrick 'Paddy' O'Duffy who was also a veteran; he had been interned in Frongoch after the Rising. He was active with 'E' Company of 2nd Dublin Brigade during the War of Independence. When he was wounded Davis was his nurse and they married in 1921. One of their daughters also became a nurse in St. Ultan's. Bridget O'Duffy died in 1954. In her reference letter written in support of O'Duffy's application for the military pension, Dr. Lynn said that she 'was the most devoted helper at all times in the cause'.[6]

Elizabeth 'Bessie' Lynch (*later Kelly*)
BORN: Dublin, 1895
ORGANISATION: Irish Citizen Army
POSITION DURING EASTER RISING: City Hall

Elizabeth 'Bessie' Lynch was born in Dublin on 8 September 1895 to John Lynch and his wife Elizabeth Carroll. In 1911 Bessie Lynch, aged fifteen and a shirt maker, was living with her mother Elizabeth Lynch and her sister Mary (both laundresses) at 41 Mercer Street, Dublin 2. The three women shared one room in a tenement and there were six others families living in the eight-roomed building. Lynch was an early member of the IWWU and appeared in the 1911 photograph of the union women entitled 'Freedom's Martyrs' with Delia Larkin and other 1916 insurgents including Jinny Shanahan, Brigid Brady, Mollie O'Reilly, Brigid Davis, Annie Norgrove and Rosie Hackett. In her pension statement she stated that she was involved in moving guns which were landed during the Howth gun running, taking them to Markievicz' cottage at Three Rock Mountain, Wicklow. Prior to the Rising she was in Liberty Hall, acting in the role of 'personal orderly' to Countess Markievicz (she also worked at her home, Surrey House). Helena Molony wrote that as orderly to Markievicz, Lynch undertook valuable and confidential work. She joined the women's section of the Irish Citizen Army at its formation in 1913 and was among those mobilised for service in the week before Easter Monday. During this time she was involved in attending first aid classes conducted by Dr. Lynn and in making ammunition. Because of her skills as a laundress she was involved in dyeing the khaki uniforms green. She mentioned that she was 'in charge' of Markievicz' home, Surrey House, and was often there when it was raided by the police and military prior to the Rising.[7] In the aftermath of the Rising, Eve Gore-Booth (Markievicz' sister) arranged that a weekly wage continued to be paid to her. Markievicz was hoping that Lynch, whom she said was a 'beautiful laundress', could set herself up in a small business after the Rising.

Lynch spent Easter Sunday night in Liberty Hall and was attached to the garrison which made its way to Dublin Castle. After the insurgents failed to take the Castle, Lynch and the others barricaded themselves into City Hall. After Seán Connolly had been shot dead, she was sent to Liberty Hall for reinforcements and brought some men to City Hall from Liberty Hall. She was there when the garrison decided to surrender and was taken to Ship Street Barracks when she spent the rest of Easter Week. She was then taken to Richmond Barracks and Kilmainham Gaol. She was released on 12 May 1916.

Lynch continued to work within the Irish Citizen Army after the Rising. She was involved in postering copies of the Proclamation around Dublin during the first anniversary of the Rising in 1917. She also hoisted the Tricolour over her house and was arrested and taken to College Street police station, although she did not remain there very long. At the end of 1917, unable to find work, she was released from duty and went to Glasgow. She returned to Dublin and married a Mr. Kelly. She died in 1975.

Kathleen Lynn
BORN: 1874, Mullafarry, near Cong, Co. Mayo
ORGANISATION: Irish Citizen Army
POSITION DURING EASTER RISING: City Hall

Kathleen Lynn was born in 1874 in Mullafarry, Co. Mayo, the second oldest daughter of Robert Lynn, a Church of Ireland clergyman and his wife Catherine (*née* Wynne) of Drumcliffe, Co. Sligo. From an early age she had ambitions to become a doctor and she received her medical degree from the Catholic University medical school in Dublin in 1899. Despite being refused a post at the Adelaide Hospital because of her gender, she became the first female resident at Dublin's Royal Victoria Eye and Ear Hospital in 1910. She also became a fellow of the Royal College of Surgeons in 1909. By 1903 she had set up her own general practice from her home at 9 Belgrave Road, Rathmines. Lynn was a feminist, a socialist and a nationalist. In 1903, influenced by her friends Thomas and Anna Haslam, she became a member of the Irish Women's Suffrage and Local Government Association (IWSLGA) and remained on the executive until 1913. She was also a member of the militant British Women's Social and Political Union (WSPU) and admitted she was quite attracted to the more militant side of suffrage activism. In 1912 Lynn, along with her friend Hanna Sheehy Skeffington, was among those Irish suffragists who campaigned unsuccessfully to have female suffrage included as part of the Third Home Rule Bill. She also became engaged with the national movement through her friendships with Helena Molony and Countess Markievicz (who was a distant cousin). Molony, 'a very clever and attractive girl with a tremendous power of making friends' introduced Lynn to the ideals of advanced nationalism.[8] In 1913, during the Lockout Lynn, having much sympathy with the striking workers, joined Markievicz, Molony and other activists in the soup kitchens in Liberty Hall. Here Lynn was exposed to the extreme poverty of the workers and their families and it was here too that she met her life-long partner Madeleine ffrench-Mullen. She joined the Irish Citizen Army at its formation and became its chief medical officer. Lynn conducted first aid classes in Liberty Hall and it was under her tutelage that many of the women who participated in 1916 learned their first aid skills. She also taught first aid to the women of Cumann na mBan.

In the weeks prior to Easter 1916 Lynn was active in the preparations for the coming insurrection; she was one of the few women with a car and often collected and delivered guns and ammunition, although she did state that it was not until Saturday that she knew where she would be stationed for the Rising. On Easter Monday Lynn and Markievicz went to City Hall in her car which was filled with first aid materials. There the car was unloaded by Bridget Davis, Kathleen Barrett and other Irish Citizen Army women. Lynn, Molony and some of the other women were soon on the roof of City Hall. She remembered that it was a 'beautiful day, the sun was hot', but tragedy soon struck when Seán Connolly was fatally wounded.[9] The beautiful day was soon filled with the sound of bullets but as Nora Connolly O'Brien later recalled the remaining Citizen Army combatants were comforted by the 'quite authoritative manner of Dr. Lynn and... many often told of her calmness... while on the roof of City Hall with bullets smacking all round her she straightened and covered the body of Seán Connolly'.[10]

City Hall was soon surrounded by British soldiers and as Lynn recalled 'the bullets fell like rain... The firing came from all sides and continued till after darkness fell. There was no way of escape'.[11] Soon after, on Easter Tuesday, the City Hall garrison surrendered and Lynn and all the combatants were arrested and marched to Ship Street Barracks, where they remained until the Rising ended. The conditions in Ship Street were grim, the food was bad, the sanitary conditions unhygienic and the blankets they were given were 'crawling with lice'.[12] When the Rising ended the women in Ship Street were taken to Richmond Barracks and then transferred to Kilmainham Gaol. In Kilmainham Lynn shared a cell with Madeleine ffrench-Mullen and Helena Molony. They found Kilmainham a very harrowing experience as they could hear the executions of the leaders taking place. Lynn and eleven other women were then transferred to Mountjoy Gaol and subsequently Lynn was deported to Bath, in England.

Lynn soon returned to Dublin and while she still had her general practice, she found that no hospital would employ her. She continued with her political activities and in 1917 she was elected to the Sinn Féin executive. Along with many of the other women she worked at keeping the memory of the Rising and republican ideology alive. She participated in ceremonies to mark the first anniversary of the Rising, including a march on Sackville Street. She was being watched by the authorities and was on the run between May and October 1918, when she was arrested and sent to Arbour Hill prison. By this time the Spanish flu, which would kill millions worldwide, had come to Dublin and Dr. Lynn was released following the intervention of the Lord

Mayor, Laurence O'Neill. Following her release she helped set up a vaccination scheme to prevent more people getting the flu, and administered vaccines to Citizen Army members, helped by her fellow Citizen Army first aiders. She said that 'In one night that we went to Liberty Hall, the whole of the Citizen Army there – over two hundred of them – were inoculated with this vaccine. Of this number of men, not one developed flu'.[13] They also nursed members who succumbed to the flu. While Lynn was committed to her political activities within Sinn Féin, she and women activists set up the League of Women Delegates (Cumann na dTeachtaire) to 'watch the political movements in Ireland in the interests of Irishwomen'.[14]

In 1919 Lynn along with ffrench-Mullen set up Ireland's first hospital for sick infants, St. Ultan's Hospital for Sick Infants, at Charlemont Street in Dublin 2. The women were horrified at the high infant and maternal mortality rates in Dublin as well as high rates of TB in the city. In St. Ultan's they were committed to research on TB eradication eventually pioneering the BCG vaccination in the hospital with her St. Ultan's colleague, Dr. Dorothy Stopford-Price. Lynn opposed the 1921 Treaty and when she was elected to Dáil Éireann as a Sinn Féin candidate in 1923, she did not take her seat, in common with all the anti-Treaty candidates. She stood again for the Dáil in 1927 but did not retain her seat. She was more involved, especially on matters of public health, in local government and served on the Rathmines Urban District Council until 1930. All her life Lynn remained committed to the right of children to proper health care and education. She promoted the work of Maria Montessori, who visited St. Ultan's in 1934, and established a Montessori ward in the hospital. She was Vice President of *Save the German Children*, an organisation which located homes for German children in Ireland.

Lynn continued to work as a doctor until the spring of 1955 when she was eighty years old. She and ffrench-Mullen were also committed to a healthy outdoor life, relishing the health giving benefits of fresh air. They were involved with An Óige (a youth organisation) and Lynn gave them her cottage in Glenmalure, Co. Wicklow. When Madeleine ffrench-Mullen died in 1944, Lynn wrote in her diary on her return from the funeral to the house they had shared 'the loneliness of coming back, with no MffM to greet me and say what a barren wilderness it had been while I was away'.[15] However, her work continued to keep her busy. Dr. Kathleen Lynn died in September 1955 and was buried with full military honours in Deansgrange Cemetery.

Helena Molony
BORN: Dublin, 1883
ORGANISATION: Irish Citizen Army
POSITION DURING EASTER RISING: City Hall

Helena Molony was born in Dublin in 1883 to Michael Molony, a shopkeeper at Coles Lane, off Henry Street and his wife Catherine (*née* McGrath). Her childhood was not a particularly happy one, as her mother died young and she did not get on with her stepmother. She identified the moment of her political awakening as the day she heard Maud Gonne speak, 'I was a young girl dreaming about Ireland when I saw and heard Maud Gonne speaking by the Custom House in Dublin one August evening in 1903… She electrified me and filled me with some of her own spirit'.[16] She soon joined the cultural, separatist and feminist organisation Inghinidhe na hÉireann, founded by Gonne in 1900.'[17] Molony stated that Inghinidhe 'formed itself into a permanent Society of Irishwomen pledged to fight for the complete separation of Ireland from England, and the re-establishment of her ancient culture. The means decided upon for the achievement of this object was the formation of evening classes for children, for Irish Language, Irish History – Social as well as Political – the restoration of Irish customs to every-day life, Irish games, Dancing and Music'.[18] From the time she joined Inghinidhe Molony was a committed political activist and public speaker. She was soon elected secretary of Inghinidhe and, in 1908, became the editor of their newspaper, *Bean na hÉireann*, a monthly 'woman's paper advocating militancy, separatism and feminism'.[19] Molony said that *Bean na hÉireann* was 'a funny hotch-potch of blood and thunder, high thinking, and home-made bread. We were the object of much good-natured chaff. Friendly newsagents would say "*Bean na hÉireann*? That's the woman's paper that all the young men buy"'.[20] By now Gonne was living mainly in France and Molony, whom she described as 'the most gallant and bravest of my Inghinidhe girls' was largely responsible for both the newspaper and the organisation.[21] Molony was also responsible for introducing Countess Markievicz to Inghinidhe, which proved to be the start of a long activist journey the two would travel together.

Molony was now becoming a well-known figure in Dublin cultural and nationalist circles. As well as her work with Inghinidhe, she began to collaborate with other nationalist activists, male and female. With Markievicz and Bulmer Hobson she helped plan the establishment of the nationalist Boy Scout movement, Na Fianna. Although a feminist, Molony was not supportive of the Irish Women's Franchise

League's ideology of 'Suffrage before all else', believing that nationalism and the fight for Irish freedom took precedence. For Molony feminism was a central part of Irish nationalism believing, as did so many of the Inghinidhe women, that to seek female franchise from the British parliament was 'unworthy and humiliating'.[22]

Molony was a militant activist. In 1911 she was arrested for protesting against the visit of George V when she threw stones at his portrait in a shop window on Grafton Street. She was jailed for this offence but served only a short time as Anna Parnell (sister of Charles Stewart Parnell) paid her fine. Molony had been editing Parnell's history of the Ladies Land League, *The Tale of a Great Sham,* at the time. She began her acting career around this time as well. After appearing to acclaim in several productions by Inghinidhe, she was invited to join the Abbey Theatre where she appeared regularly until the Rising and intermittently for several years thereafter. She often acted opposite her friend Seán Connolly. She played in works by Lady Gregory and Lennox Robinson amongst others. As well as her theatrical career she continued her activism, becoming more involved in the labour movement. 'I was fumbling at the idea of a junction between labour and nationalism', she explained, 'Labour and the Nation were really one'.[23]

When the IWWU was established in 1911 she was at the first meeting. A close colleague and friend of James Connolly, she became manager of the Liberty Hall workers' clothing cooperative (which manufactured cartridge belts prior to the Rising). She was active in the Liberty Hall soup kitchen during the 1913 Lockout and joined the Irish Citizen Army at its formation, becoming secretary of the women's section. She regarded the Citizen Army as more radical than Cumann na mBan and was also critical of that organisation, calling it a 'Ladies Auxiliary', while emphasising the Citizen Army's egalitarianism: 'even before the Russian army had women soldiers, the Citizen Army had them'.[24]

On Easter Monday she went with the Irish Citizen Army garrison to City Hall. She supervised the nine women of the City Hall garrison in establishing a first aid station and the food commissariat. She also witnessed Seán Connolly's death. Along with the rest of the garrison, she was arrested when they surrendered, spent several days in the Ship Street Barracks, was taken to Richmond Barracks and then to Kilmainham Gaol. Molony was one of the handful of women regarded as dangerous so she was not released in the last release of 8 / 9 May 1916. She was, according to a DMP report of December 1916, 'an extremist of some importance'.[25] Instead she was sent to Mountjoy Gaol and then to Aylesbury Gaol in England. She was finally released in December 1916.

On release Molony immediately threw herself back into activism. She aided in the reorganisation of all the republican organisations, serving briefly on the executive of Sinn Féin. She also helped re-establish the IWWU, serving as general secretary until 1918 when Louie Bennett took over, although she did remain an IWWU official for the next two decades. She remained active in the Citizen Army during the War of Independence, working as a courier of arms and messages, training new recruits and continuing with republican propaganda. She assisted Countess Markievicz in her role as Minister of Labour and was a courier for Michael Collins and Liam Mellowes. Like many republican women she served in the Republican Courts; her area was the Rathmines District. She was anti-Treaty and was arrested and imprisoned in Kilmainham Gaol during the Civil War.

After the foundation of the Irish Free State she remained committed to ensuring that the promise of full and equal citizenship for women enshrined in the Proclamation would be achieved. Pressures from her trade union activism meant that she ended her stage career with an acclaimed performance in Lennox Robinson's *Crabbed youth and old age* in November 1922. She remained active in the IWWU and was especially moved by the plight of domestic workers. She was concerned that women in the new Irish Free State retained 'their inferior status, their lower pay for equal work, their exclusion from juries and certain branches of the civil service, their slum dwellings and crowded, cold and unsanitary schools for their children'.[26] She was a member with Maud Gonne of the Women's Prisoners Defence League, and was in the People's Rights Association and the Anti-Partition League. In the Irish Free State, Molony's support for marginalised causes and organisations pushed her further away from the centre of power and influence. Her continuing support for the IRA meant frequent raids on her home. However, her work in the IWWU achieved results and she was prominent in effecting the union's growth to over 5,000 members. She was deeply angered by the second class position of women in Irish society, despite the promises of equality contained in the Proclamation of 1916. She felt the Irish Free State had brought about the:

> sorry travesty of women's emancipation... that women, since (Connolly's) day, [had] that once coveted right to vote but they still have inferior status... lower pay for equal work... exclusion from juries..[27]

She was Irish Trades Union Congress (ITUC) vice president from 1935–36 when the

Conditions of Employment Act was introduced, an act that allowed the displacement of women workers by men. She vehemently opposed this act. She was elected ITUC president in 1937 but ill health affected her ability to continue working. Molony had battled for many years with alcoholism and depression all of which played a part in her retirement from active politics in 1941. She lived with psychiatrist Evelyn O'Brien, with whom she had a close relationship since the 1930s, until her death in 1967. She was remembered as a 'fervent speaker' and 'doughty fighter for the working class'.[28] Molony was interred in the republican plot in Glasnevin Cemetery. President Eamon de Valera said of her at her funeral, 'she was one of the great patriotic women of our time. With James Connolly and Countess Markievicz she worked for Irish freedom, for the Irish worker and for the poor. She stood firmly for the rights of women and their political equality in our society'.[29]

Annie Norgrove (*later Grange*)
BORN: Dublin, 1899
ORGANISATION: Irish Citizen Army
POSITION DURING EASTER RISING: City Hall

In August 2010 Gardaí shut down the North Stand Road due to the discovery of grenades and artillery shells, dating from the revolutionary decade, hidden under the floor of the kitchen at 15 Strandville Place, off North Strand in Dublin. In 1911 a family who would all be active in 1916 was living in this house. These were Alfred George Norgrove (known as George) and his wife Maria, with their children, Emily (aged 13), Annie (aged 11), John (aged 10), Alexandra (aged 8), Frederick (aged 7), Robert (aged 4) and Martha (4 months). Annie Emma Florence Norgrove was born on 10 July 1899 and baptised in the Church of Ireland Church on the North Strand. Unusually the Norgroves were a working class Protestant nationalist family. George Norgrove worked as a gas-fitter and was an active trade unionist. During the 1913 Lockout he became involved in the Irish Citizen Army, helping to assemble a stockpile of bombs in Liberty Hall and in his house during 1915. During the Easter Rising, he served as a lieutenant in the Irish Citizen Army, firstly in the GPO and then in City Hall. His wife Maria and two of his daughters, Annie and Emily, were also involved in trade union politics and in the Rising.

Annie became involved in politics through her family, especially during the

1913 Lockout. She was an early member of the IWWU and joined the women's section of the Irish Citizen Army. She and her sister were active in cultural and political events in Liberty Hall. On the Sunday before the Rising Annie, like many of the other women, was on constant duty in Liberty Hall. There she had trained in first aid with Dr. Lynn and was involved in the practical preparations for the coming fight. She was sent with the contingent led by Seán Connolly to Dublin Castle. When they failed to take Dublin Castle she, like the other women of the Citizen Amy group, helped barricade their position in City Hall on Monday. Annie left a vivid description of her experience in City Hall. She spent most of Monday bringing water to the men stationed on the roof, climbing out and crawling along, keeping her head down out of sight of the British Army snipers stationed on the roofs of the buildings all round. On the roof of City Hall she could see that the 'men's faces [were] blackened from the fumes and smoke of their rifles… their rifles were red hot, now and then one of them would cry out a warning – keep your head down Annie… I heard the warning and just as I ducked a chimney pot smashed in smithereens around me'.[30] She also helped with the wounded and Helena Molony later reported that 'she displayed exceptional bravery…refusing to leave the side of a wounded man [Tommy Coyle] who was propped up on a chair in the Hall and exposed to fire on three sides'.[31] After the insurgents surrendered on late Tuesday afternoon, Annie was marched with the others to Ship Street Barracks where she remained until the following Monday when they were taken to Richmond Barracks and then to Kilmainham Gaol. She was released on 8 May with most of the other women. Annie's father George Norgrove was also arrested and spent time in Frongoch internment camp in Wales. Her sister Emily had also been in City Hall and was arrested, while her mother, Maria, who had served in Jacob's Biscuit Factory, managed to get away before the surrender.

On her release Annie continued her revolutionary activism. She operated occasionally as a courier, moving ammunition around for the Citizen Army and storing arms in her father's house in Strandville Avenue. She was anti-Treaty and took part in the Civil War. She was one of four women with the anti-Treaty garrison at Hughes Hotel in the north inner city. The other three were Marcella Crimmins, Kathleen Macken and Annie Tobin. Her father and her brother Robert were also on the anti-Treaty side during the Civil War. Robert Norgrove fought in Barry's Hotel and the Hammam Hotel on O'Connell Street. Annie helped with cooking at Hayes Hotel and when that fell she retreated to Barry's Hotel where she was ordered home.

Annie Norgrove married William 'Bill' Grange and they had three children. She died in 1976.

Emily Norgrove (*later Hanratty*)
BORN: Dublin, 1897
ORGANISATION: Irish Citizen Army
POSITION DURING EASTER RISING: City Hall

Emily Norgrove was the older sister of Annie Norgrove and the daughter of Alfred George Norgrove and his wife Ellen Maria Carter. She was born in Dublin in 1897 and lived with her family at Strandville Place off the North Stand. On the 1911 census it was noted that this was a small, third-class house with three rooms shared between nine people. Like the rest of her family, Emily became involved in trade union politics, joining the IWWU with her sister Annie. They were involved in the 1913 Lockout, working in the soup kitchen in Liberty Hall. Like Annie, Emily joined the women's section of the Irish Citizen Army when it was set up in 1913. She participated in route marches, drills, first aid classes and was involved in the cultural activities of the Citizen Army and was considered a very popular singer at the Sunday night concerts in Liberty Hall. With Annie she mobilised on Easter Monday and went with the contingent to City Hall. In City Hall she helped with the cooking, attended the wounded and carried arms to the men when they needed them. She was arrested with the rest of the garrison on Tuesday 25 April and spent a week in Ship Street Barracks, before being transferred to Richmond Barracks and later Kilmainham Gaol. Emily described the interrogation all of the women underwent in Kilmainham: 'each of us was brought down and interrogated by Army Officers seated at a long table. We were asked… what we were doing in the garrisons, our answer was first aid when needed, some cooking if necessary, that was all that was asked of us, then we were brought back to our cells'.[32] Emily was released from Kilmainham with the majority of her comrades on 8 May.

Like the rest of the Norgrove family, Emily continued her work with the Irish Citizen Army after her release. She collected funds to help the families of those who had died or were imprisoned and to help re-equip the organisation. She married John Hanratty, also a member of the Irish Citizen Army, in 1920 and they had two children. Like his wife Hanratty had been involved in trade union activism. He was an oven hand in Jacob's Biscuit Factory when the 1913 Lockout began and like thousands of other union workers was locked out of his job. He joined the Citizen Army at its first meeting in Croydon Park, however because of wounds suffered in an accidental discharge of a gun in the drill room in Liberty Hall, he was unable to participate in the Rising. John Hanratty was active during the War of Independence and took the anti-Treaty side during the Civil War. Emily Hanratty took no active part in the Civil War and died in 1977, aged eighty.

Jane 'Jinny' Shanahan
BORN: Dublin, 1891
ORGANISATION: Irish Citizen Army
POSITION DURING EASTER RISING: City Hall

Jane 'Jinny' Shanahan was born in 1891 in Dublin to a Westmeath-born bricklayer's labourer Michael Shanahan and his Wicklow-born wife Margaret (*née* Clancy). In 1911 she was living with her parents and brothers William and Patrick at Dawson Court, near St. Stephen's Green. By that time Shanahan had obtained work in Jacob's Biscuit Factory, where she met another young woman who became a friend and revolutionary comrade, Rosie Hackett.

By 1913 Shanahan was involved in trade union activism. She had become a member of the IWWU and lost her job during the 1913 Lockout. Like many of the locked-out IWWU women she volunteered her services in the Liberty Hall soup kitchen. After the Lockout she remained associated with Liberty Hall and was app-ointed manageress of the co-op shop there, working with Hackett and Helena Molony. This co-op specialised in producing men's working shirts featuring the Red Hand badge crest of the Irish Transport and General Workers Union (ITGWU). Helena Molony stated that Shanahan was in charge of the co-op shop and was responsible for protecting the printing press which was located there. Shanahan joined the women's section of the Irish Citizen Army when it was formed in 1913. Again Molony states that the command of the women's section was largely in Shanahan's hands, and she took part 'in all the Army manoeuvres' and helped 'in the training of recruits'.[33] In the weeks immediately preceding the Rising Shanahan worked long hours and often slept in Liberty Hall, bedding down on a pile of overcoats.

On Easter Monday Shanahan was among the contingent of insurgents sent under the command of Seán Connolly to Dublin Castle. When they failed to take the Castle she and the others retreated to City Hall where they remained for the next twenty-four hours. Shanahan may be the reason why the insurgents held out as long as they did in a seemingly indefensible position. Recalling the events in City Hall she remembered that she encountered some British soldiers advancing up the stairs of City Hall. The soldiers took her to be a civilian and asked if she had been badly treated by the insurgents. 'Oh no sir', she said, 'they treated me well enough but there must be hundreds of them up there in the roof'.[34] Believing then that there were a huge number of insurgents on the roof the British soldiers approached the position more cautiously than they would have had they known the insurgents numbered about twenty men and women. However, the insurgents could not hold out for long and eventually Shanahan and the others surrendered and were marched to Ship Street Barracks where they spent a week in squalid conditions. They were then taken to Richmond Barracks and later Kilmainham Gaol. Shanahan was among those released from Kilmainham on 8 May.

In the aftermath of the Rising Shanahan continued her work in Liberty Hall. She had been instrumental in reorganising the IWWU, which was left in some disarray after Delia Larkin's departure from Ireland in 1915, and continued to be an active member of that union. As with many of the released women, Shanahan worked on the production of republican propaganda material. In 1917 she was involved with the reprinting of the Proclamation and distributed copies of the document around Dublin. She took part in the funeral procession of Thomas Ashe, who had died from force-feeding while on hunger strike in Mountjoy Gaol in September 1917, and helped prepare City Hall to receive his remains. In 1918 she took part in a poster parade in support of the anti-conscription campaign. During the War of Independence Shanahan carried out nursing duties and hid guns for the Irish Republican Army (IRA), while at the same time she received and sent dispatches from her house at Dawson Court. Shanahan opposed the Anglo-Irish Treaty and during the Civil War she ran a hospital at Cullenswood House in Dublin for the anti-Treaty forces. Several attempts were made to arrest her and as a result she had to go 'on the run', staying with friends who were not known to the pro-Treaty forces. After the Civil War she continued her work with the IWWU, appearing on its executive committee in 1931 and in that year she began work as a forewoman at Wm. and M. Taylor's Tobacco Company in Francis Street in Dublin. In 1926 she chaired the IWWU annual convention meeting and she continued on the executive committee until 1936. Jinny Shanahan had been in bad health for some years and in December 1936 she died while a patient at Mercer's Hospital. Her funeral took place on 31 December and her coffin was draped with the Starry Plough, the flag of the Irish Citizen Army. The graveside oration was delivered by her long-time friend and comrade Helena Molony. Molony paid tribute to her work in the 'Labour and National movements' and in the IWWU annual report Shanahan was described as 'an ardent and self-sacrificing supporter of the Labour Movement and a devoted daughter and sister.'[35] She is buried in Glasnevin Cemetery.

Inghinidhe na hÉireann group photo 1905–06. (*Courtesy of Kilmainham Gaol Museum, 13PO-1B54-14*)

Countess Markievicz in the soup kitchen in Liberty Hall during the 1913 Lockout. Many women who were involved in the Rising were radicalised during this period. (*Courtesy of South Dublin Libraries*)

City Hall, Dame Street, Dublin was commandeered by the Irish Citizen Army on Easter Monday, 1916. Several women were stationed here including Dr. Kathleen Lynn. (*Courtesy of Military Archives*)

Fr. Mathew Hall on Church Street, part of the Four Courts garrison. (*Courtesy of Capuchin Archives*)

Destruction on Henry Street after the Rising. On Friday 28 April, the Headquarters battalion, including three women, escaped from the GPO across this street and onto Moore Street. (*Courtesy of Dublin City Library and Archive*)

Marrowbone Lane Distillery (Jameson's) off Cork Street in Dublin, part of the South Dublin Union garrison where 25 women of Cumann na mBan fought during Easter Week 1916. (*Courtesy of Military Archives*)

The Royal College of Surgeons garrison on St. Stephen's Green was commanded by Michael Mallin and Countess Markievicz of the Irish Citizen Army and several women, including Nellie Gifford and Katie Kelly, fought here. (*Courtesy of Military Archives*)

Michael Mallin and Countess Markievicz after the surrender of the Royal College of Surgeons garrison. (*Courtesy of Michael Curran*)

CHANCELLOR DUBLIN   LIBERTY HALL . HEAD-QUARTERS OF CITIZEN ARMY, DUBLIN.

Liberty Hall, Dublin after the Rising. Irish Citizen Army women mobilised here on Easter Monday morning and marched with their male colleagues to various garrison sites in the city. (*Courtesy of Dublin City Library and Archive*)

Richmond Barracks, Inchicore, Dublin. (*Courtesy of National Library of Ireland*)

Richmond Barracks married quarters where the women were held overnight after their arrest on 30 April 1916. (*Courtesy of the Healy Collection*)

Ship Street Barracks, near Dublin Castle. Several women were held here in squalid conditions after their capture on Tuesday 25 April 1916, including the women from City Hall. (*Courtesy of Military Archives*)

Joseph Plunkett's bedroom after a police search conducted after the Rising. His mother, Countess Plunkett did not take part in the Rising but was arrested in her house and taken to Richmond Barracks. (*Courtesy of Kilmainham Gaol Museum, 16PC-1A25-05*)

O'Farrell family photo with Elizabeth O'Farrell on left at back. She accompanied Patrick Pearse when he surrendered to Brigadier General Lowe. (*Courtesy of James Langton*)

MARGARET SKINNIDER
(wearing boy's clothes)

Margaret Skinnider fought in the St. Stephen's Green / Royal College of Surgeons garrison and was wounded in an encounter with British troops on Harcourt Street. (*Courtesy of James Langton*)

Members of Irish Transport and General Workers' Union outside Liberty Hall in 1917. (*Courtesy of Military Archives*)

Members of Cumann na mBan, Irish Citizen Army and Clan na nGael girl scouts at a fund raising event for the Irish National Aid Association and Volunteer Dependents' Fund in the home of Mr. and Mrs. Ely O'Carroll, Peter's Place, Dublin in the summer of 1916. (*Courtesy of Kilmainham Gaol Museum, 18PO-1B53-02*)

Countess Markievicz arriving at Liberty Hall following her release from prison in England, June 1917. (*Courtesy of Kilmainham Gaol Museum, 18PC-1A25-13*)

Cumann na mBan convention held in secret in October 1920 in Whitefriar Street Church, Dublin. Mrs. Pearse is seventh from the left in the row facing the camera with Countess Markievicz beside her. (*Courtesy of Military Archives*)

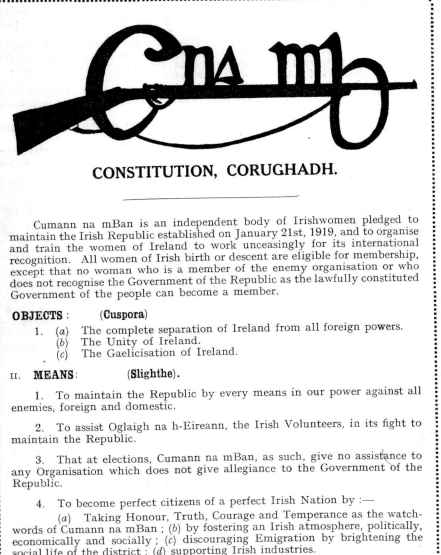

CONSTITUTION, CORUGHADH.

Cumann na mBan is an independent body of Irishwomen pledged to maintain the Irish Republic established on January 21st, 1919, and to organise and train the women of Ireland to work unceasingly for its international recognition. All women of Irish birth or descent are eligible for membership, except that no woman who is a member of the enemy organisation or who does not recognise the Government of the Republic as the lawfully constituted Government of the people can become a member.

OBJECTS :　　**(Cuspora)**

　　1.　(*a*)　The complete separation of Ireland from all foreign powers.
　　　　(*b*)　The Unity of Ireland.
　　　　(*c*)　The Gaelicisation of Ireland.

II.　**MEANS**:　　　**(Slighthe).**

　　1.　To maintain the Republic by every means in our power against all enemies, foreign and domestic.

　　2.　To assist Oglaigh na h-Eireann, the Irish Volunteers, in its fight to maintain the Republic.

　　3.　That at elections, Cumann na mBan, as such, give no assistance to any Organisation which does not give allegiance to the Government of the Republic.

　　4.　To become perfect citizens of a perfect Irish Nation by :—

　　　　(*a*)　Taking Honour, Truth, Courage and Temperance as the watchwords of Cumann na mBan ; (*b*) by fostering an Irish atmosphere, politically, economically and socially ; (*c*) discouraging Emigration by brightening the social life of the district ; (*d*) supporting Irish industries.

　　5.　At all times and in all places to uphold the spirit and the letter of the Cumann na mBan Constitution.

　　6.　The Constitution of Cumann na mBan may not be altered except by a two-third majority vote of a Convention.

First page of Cumann na mBan Constitution, 1919. (*Courtesy of Dublin City Library and Archive*)

1916 Rising veterans of Irish Citizen Army in Liberty Hall in 1966. *(Courtesy of Peter Grange and family)*

THE FOUR COURTS

Máire 'Mary/May/Meg/Maura' Carron
BORN: Dublin, 1897
ORGANISATION: Cumann na mBan (Central [Ard Craobh] branch)
POSITION DURING EASTER RISING: Four Courts

Máire Carron was born in Dublin in 1897. At the time of the 1911 census she was living with her widowed mother Catherine, a French polisher, in No. 64 Dominick Street, but by 1916 they were living in No. 36/37 Nelson Street, near Inns Quay in Dublin. She joined the Central branch, Cumann na mBan in 1915. Carron was ordered to mobilise for duty on Good Friday, 1916 but was eventually sent home on Easter Sunday. She received orders later that evening to mobilise on Easter Monday at Broadstone and from there to the Dominican Priory, Dorset Street, where she stayed the night.

On Tuesday 25 April Carron and her friend Nellie Ennis were asked to deliver messages to the various houses of Volunteers living in Dolphin's Barn, Reginald Street and Cork Street. She also went to Marrowbone Lane Distillery where she received a message from Thomas MacDonagh to be given to Kathleen Clarke at her home. She delivered the message and was then sent to the GPO by Mrs. Clarke to deliver another message to Seán MacDiarmada after which she was sent to Cabra Bridge with medical supplies for the Volunteers stationed there. She returned to the GPO with more dispatches for Patrick Pearse and after delivering them safely she was sent to the Four Courts where she stayed for the remainder of Easter Week. Her friend Nellie Ennis was with her. While in the Courts she tended to the wounded Volunteers and cooked for the garrison and was also requested on numerous occasions to carry dispatches to the surrounding Volunteer outposts. She did this work under heavy fire but carried out her duties successfully.[36] Arrested after the surrender of the Four Courts garrison, Máire and her comrades were taken by lorry to Richmond Barracks on Sunday, 30 April. They were transferred to Kilmainham Gaol the next day.

On her release from Kilmainham on 8 May, Carron rejoined the Central branch of Cumann na mBan and was involved in all the activities necessary to reorganise the branch. She collected information from the families of Volunteers in the Inns Quay area so that they would receive money from the Volunteer Dependents' Fund. Over the next three years she was involved in all the major activities undertaken by Cumann na mBan, including the funeral processions of Irish Volunteers Joe Norton,

Thomas Ashe, Richard Coleman and Pierce McCann. She collected money not just for the Volunteer Dependents' Fund but also for the Volunteer Arms Fund. As the Volunteers had no money to buy weapons the money had to be raised and it fell to Carron and her comrades in Cumann na mBan to do this. They regularly organised concerts and ceilis and were successful in raising substantial amounts of money for the Volunteers. Carron was usually one of the stewards at these events. At this time, she was attached to 'B' Company, 2nd Battalion, Dublin Brigade, Irish Volunteers or IRA, as they were to become known.

Carron was involved in the anti-conscription movement in 1918, preparing field dressings and rations in the home of Count Plunkett, and helped campaign for the 1918 general election. She also carried out propaganda work which usually entailed posting handbills outside the churches around the city; her area of operation was the churches in Church Street, Gardiner Street, Phibsboro and Dominick Street as well as painting Republican slogans around the city. Carron also worked as an intelligence operative for the Volunteers. She became aware that detectives had been sent from Ulster to Dublin. She passed this information to Volunteer Christopher Farrelly who in turn forwarded it to the IRA GHQ. She continued this work throughout the War of Independence, discovering the addresses of Black and Tans and other British agents and worked directly for Farrelly in this regard.

Throughout this period her home in Nelson Street was a safe house and arms dump. The IRA regularly left arms and ammunition there as well as important documents and Carron was always at hand to remove the weapons and documents when they were needed. She would receive word of where and when weapons were needed and would send girls to the location to deliver the arms. When the operation was over, she would receive word that the guns had to be collected and would again arrange this. This work was too risky for the Volunteers to do as they would most likely be searched if stopped by the military and so it had to be carried out by women. Carron also treated IRA men who were wounded in ambushes. Because of her special training in home nursing, her services were always needed. She had undertaken an advanced course in Home Nursing at the Mater Hospital and also at the home of George Gavan Duffy. There was also a first aid station in No. 9 Geraldine Street which was attached to the 2nd Battalion, Dublin Brigade and Carron and her comrades would have to be available to treat any wounded Volunteers. On 23 November 1920 she began work as a shorthand typist in Dáil Éireann.

While it was essential to raise money for the purchase of weapons, it was very difficult to openly purchase them, especially as the War of Independence escalated. Again it fell to Cumann na mBan to provide a way of doing this and Carron and her comrades were very successful in obtaining arms for the IRA. They befriended British soldiers and persuaded them to sell their weapons and ammunition. The women did not purchase the arms directly but instead they would inform the Volunteers of their contact, who would then make the purchase directly. By the end of the War of Independence Carron was promoted to section leader in the Central branch of Cumann na mBan.

Carron opposed the Anglo-Irish Treaty and when the Civil War began she was on duty at Tara Hall, Jenkinson's in Capel Street, and 44 Parnell Square, which was the initial headquarters of the anti-Treaty IRA before they had taken over the Four Courts, and acted as medical orderly to Dr. Seán Geraghty and Dr. Murray. Carron was also one of the Guard of Honour over the remains of Cathal Brugha in the Mater hospital after his death on 7 July, 1922. Carron was not arrested during the Civil War and it seems she took no further part in any republican activity after the Civil War ended. Carron was one of the first civil servants to be appointed by the Irish Government at the formation of the State in 1922 and was attached to the Department of Local Government and Public Health at the Custom House as a shorthand typist, where she worked for forty-two years until her retirement in May 1963. She was also a member of the Old Cumann na mBan Association. Máire Carron never married and died in 1963 aged sixty-six. She is buried in Glasnevin Cemetery.

Ellen 'Nellie' Ennis (*later Costigan*)
BORN: Dublin, 1894
ORGANISATION: Cumann na mBan (Central [Ard Craobh] branch)
POSITION DURING EASTER RISING: Four Courts

Ellen 'Nellie' Ennis was born in Dublin in 1894. Her father Joseph worked as a bookbinder, and the 1911 census shows that he and his wife Ellen were living in No. 12 Dominick Street Lower with their five children, Patrick, Agnes, Ellen, Mary and Joseph. Nellie was working as a bookfolder. She joined the Central branch, Cumann na mBan in 1915. She mobilised with her comrades on Easter Monday at New Road, Broadstone and stayed there all day. That evening, Ennis and her friend Máire Carron were sent to the Dominican Priory, Dorset Street, to report to Sorcha MacMahon who in turn gave them messages to be delivered to houses in Cork Street, Reginald Street and Dolphin's Barn. They carried out their orders successfully.[37]

On Wednesday 26 April, Ennis made her way to the Four Courts and while there she helped cook for the garrison. Arrested on the surrender of the Four Courts garrison, she was taken to Richmond Barracks with her comrades on Sunday 30 April. They were driven to the barracks in a lorry and Fr. Columbas, a Capuchin priest in Church Street, who had stayed with the garrison in the Four Courts, accompanied them to the barracks. On their transfer to Kilmainham Gaol, he visited them every day. Ennis shared a cell in Kilmainham with Máire Carron. They were released on 8 May 1916.

After her release Ennis rejoined Cumann na mBan and took part in the reorganisation of the Central branch. She assisted with the Irish National Aid and all the other duties required, including the distribution of propaganda leaflets outside the churches throughout the city every Sunday, the anti-conscription movement and campaigning for the 1918 general election. Ennis resigned from Cumann na mBan in March 1919. She does not give a reason for doing this in her pension application. She married Michael Costigan but they had no children and he died young. Nellie Costigan died in 1937 and is buried in Glasnevin Cemetery. She was forty-three years old.

Brigid Lyons (*later Lyons Thornton*)
BORN: Sligo, 1898
ORGANISATION: Cumann na mBan
POSITION DURING EASTER RISING: Four Courts

Brigid Lyons was born in 1898 into a staunchly republican family. Her father Patrick Lyons was a farmer and a Fenian and had been active in the land wars in Sligo. Her mother was Margaret Lyons (*née* McGuinness). Originally from Sligo, she went to live with her uncle, Frank McGuinness, in Co. Longford when she was eight years old, as her mother had died in childbirth. Educated at the Convent of Mercy, Longford and the Ursuline Convent, Sligo, Brigid entered University College Galway (UCG) in 1915 to study medicine. Her uncles, Frank and Joseph (Joe), were involved in the nationalist movement and following her father's and her uncles' political ideals, she joined Cumann na mBan soon after its inception in 1914, while still only a teenager. Lyons was also a suffragist, supporting the campaign for the right to vote for women.

On hearing that the Rising had begun she left Longford, travelled to Dublin and took part in the rebellion. She served alongside her uncle, Joe McGuinness, in the Four Courts where she helped to feed the garrison. When the garrison got the order to surrender Lyons described the moment as 'terrible, shattering, chaotic'.[38] She was arrested after the surrender and taken to Richmond Barracks and Kilmainham Gaol, but was released on 9 May. She was eighteen years old. After her release, Lyons returned to Galway to continue her medical studies and also quickly resumed her work with Cumann na mBan. In 1917 she helped set up a branch of Cumann na mBan in Galway and helped campaign for Sinn Féin in the 1918 general election and also raised money for the fund. During the War of Independence she transported weapons for the IRA in Galway and was later transferred to the Longford Brigade IRA, where she helped buy weapons and ammunition for the brigade. She rose to the rank of commandant and she smuggled hand grenades by train to the Longford Brigade, IRA which was under the command of Seán MacEoin, a close family friend. She also carried messages to Michael Collins for MacEoin.

Lyons completed her studies and qualified as a doctor in 1922. She supported the Treaty and helped set up the Irish Army Medical Service in 1922 and became the first woman to be commissioned in the Irish Army. During the Civil War she was the medical officer in charge of Kilmainham Gaol, looking after the anti-Treaty female prisoners being held there, many of whom were her former friends. At this time she suffered a recurrence of childhood tuberculosis and was advised to go to France to recuperate. While in Nice, she met her future husband, Captain Edward Thornton (b. 1899) from Co. Mayo who was also convalescing from tuberculosis. She moved to Leysin Feydey in Switzerland to take advantage of new medical treatments and was soon joined by Edward. In 1926 the couple returned to Ireland and married.

In 1929 Lyons was appointed State Medical Officer in the Department of Maternity and Child Welfare for Co. Dublin. She later helped introduce the BCG vaccination and was part of the scheme to vaccinate children to combat the spread of tuberculosis. Her husband died suddenly in 1947 and she devoted the rest of her life to medicine and the fight for the rights of political prisoners. After retirement she continued to do medical research in Trinity College, Dublin and continued to do voluntary work in the Rotunda Hospital well into her eighties. Brigid Lyons Thornton died in 1987 and is buried beside her husband at Toomore Cemetery in Foxford, Co. Mayo. She was eighty-nine years old.

Kathleen 'Kate' Martin

BORN: Co. Wicklow, 1899
ORGANISATION: Cumann na mBan (Colmcille branch)
POSITION DURING EASTER RISING: Four Courts/Church Street

According to the 1901 census Kathleen Martin was born in Co. Wicklow in 1899 and was living in No. 10 Marlboro Terrace, Arklow, Co. Wicklow. From the 1911 census it seems that she was studying in Dublin to be a teacher as there is an entry for her name at an address in No. 23 North Eccles Street, Dublin. Also noted at this address was Louise Gavan Duffy, who was training to be a teacher at this time and who later served in the GPO during the Easter Rising. Martin is noted as being able to speak Irish and English.

She was a member of the Colmcille branch, Cumann na mBan which was set up in 1916. According to Eilís Ní Riain's witness statement, Martin served with Ní Riain at the first aid station in the Fr. Mathew Hall during Easter Week. Each of the young women was given a white arm band and was attached to the hospital staff and over the week the girls were thrown into the centre of activity as the numbers of those wounded in the fighting increased daily.

Martin was arrested after the surrender of the Four Courts garrison and taken to Richmond Barracks. She was transferred to Kilmainham Gaol and released on either 8 or 9 May. There is no record for a pension for Martin and the information that is known comes from Eilís Ní Riain's witness statement and the Cumann na mBan membership roll.

Bríd S. Martin

BORN: Co. Wicklow
ORGANISATION: Cumann na mBan (Colmcille branch)
Position during Easter Rising: Four Courts/Church Street

While there is no further information for Bríd S. Martin other than her name as a member of the Four Courts garrison, it is known that she was a member of the Colmcille branch of Cumann na mBan. It is possible that she was related to Kathleen Martin, likely her sister or cousin, who was also out in 1916 as a member of the Colmcille branch of Cumann na mBan. There is no pension application for Bríd Martin.

Florence 'Flossie' Meade (*later Griffin*)
BORN: Dublin, 1891
ORGANISATION: Cumann na mBan (Central [Ard Craobh] branch)
POSITION DURING EASTER RISING: Hibernian Bank/GPO
and the Four Courts

Florence 'Flossie' Meade was born in Dublin in 1891. Her family moved house quite a few times. In 1901 they were living in No. 168 St. Joseph's Place North, Inns Quay. In 1911 they were living in No. 68 Cabra Park, Phibsboro and at the time of the Rising the family was living in No. 112 Cabra Park. Her father was Peter Meade, a salesman, born in Kilkenny and her mother was Margaret Meade (*née* Woods) originally from Co. Westmeath. Also at home in 1911 were her brothers William, Walter and Henry who were members of the 1st Battalion, Dublin Brigade, Irish Volunteers. Meade was a fluent Irish speaker and a member of the Gaelic League. She joined the Central branch (Ard Craobh) Cumann na mBan in 1914.

On Easter Saturday she removed explosives from a property on the North Circular Road to the Kissane house on Hardwicke Street. On Easter Monday together with Mrs. Kissane and Mary and Louisa O'Sullivan, Meade transferred rifles that she had hidden in her bedroom to Mrs. Kissane's house in Hardwicke Street, Dublin 1. On receiving her mobilisation orders, she went to the home of Michael Flanagan on Primrose Street. With no information forthcoming she went home. Rather than wait for orders, on Tuesday 25 April she made her way to the Hibernian Bank on Sackville Street where she found some of her comrades from the Central branch. They stayed there for a while before going to the GPO after which they were requested to go to the Four Courts.

While in the Four Courts Meade carried out secretarial duties for Commandant Edward 'Ned' Daly. During the week she also carried dispatches, weapons and explosives between the various outposts surrounding the courts. Arrested after the surrender of the Four Courts garrison on Saturday 29 April, she was taken prisoner to Richmond Barracks and later transferred to Kilmainham Gaol. According to her pension file she was released on 10 May.

Meade married Gerald Griffin soon after her release from prison. They had three daughters. Her husband had also been involved in the Rising as a member of the 1st Battalion, Dublin Brigade, Irish Volunteers. Her brothers William, Henry and Walter Meade had also participated in the Rising. After her marriage she resigned from

Cumann na mBan. Although no longer a member of the Cumann na mBan, during the War of Independence her home was regularly used by the IRA as a safe house for holding weapons and ammunition. Florence Griffin died in 1984 and was buried in St. Fintan's cemetery in Sutton. She was ninety-three years old.

Caroline 'Carrie' Mitchell (*later McLoughlin*)
BORN: Dublin, 1884
ORGANISATION: Cumann na mBan (Central [Ard Craobh] branch)
POSITION DURING EASTER RISING: GPO/Imperial Hotel and the Four Courts

Caroline 'Carrie' Mitchell was born in Dublin in 1884. At the time of the 1911 census she was living in No. 8 North Leinster Street, Arran Quay in Dublin and worked as a clerk. She was the daughter of Thomas, a carpenter, and his wife Mary. Her brother Patrick, also a clerk, was also involved in the Rising as a member of the Irish Volunteers. It is unclear when she joined Cumann na mBan, however she was a member of the Central branch prior to 1916. She took part in the Easter Rising, reporting for duty on Tuesday 25 April at the GPO. She was sent to the Imperial Hotel, opposite the GPO, and stayed with the garrison there until Wednesday. That morning Mitchell was ordered to get first aid supplies and although she was able to get out of the building and get the supplies, she could not make her way back in as she could not pass a barricade that had been erected in Sackville Street. On Thursday she went with her supplies to the Four Courts.[39] She cycled there and got through the streets easily as she was wearing her Red Cross armlet. Having made her way into the Courts she remained with the garrison until the surrender on Saturday 29 April. She was arrested and taken with her comrades to Richmond Barracks, accompanied by Fr. Columbas. When they reached the barracks, Fr. Columbas was shocked to discover that the women were to be held there. He protested against this as the barracks was full of soldiers, there were no women present and he feared for their safety. As a result of his protests the women were removed to Kilmainham Gaol the next day, 1 May.

Mitchell was released with her comrades on 9 May. She rejoined Cumann na mBan after her release but according to her pension file she resigned in March 1917. No reason is given for her resignation. She married William McLoughlin in 1919 and lived in Wicklow. By 1936 she was living in Brighton and later lived in London.

Pauline Morkan (*later Keating*)
BORN: Dublin, 1893
ORGANISATION: Cumann na mBan (Central [Ard Craobh] branch)
POSITION DURING EASTER RISING: Hibernian Bank/
Four Courts

Mary Pauline Morkan was born in 1893 to Michael and Mary Morkan. Michael Morkan worked as a publican. At the time of the 1911 census Pauline Morkan was living at number 43 Arran Quay, Dublin and worked as a draper's assistant. She joined the Central Cumann na mBan in 1915 and took part in the funeral of O'Donovan Rossa in August 1915.[40]

When the Rising began Morkan initially went to the Volunteer garrison in the Hibernian Bank on Sackville Street but was soon sent to aid Ned Daly's garrison in the Church Street/Four Courts area where she and her comrades, Florence Meade and Máire Carron amongst others, cooked for the Volunteers in the Four Courts. Arrested after the surrender with some of her colleagues who did not manage to escape, they were taken to Richmond Barracks. Morkan remembered that they were treated well by the British soldiers while in the barracks. She was later transferred to Kilmainham Gaol where she shared a cell with three other women and was released after nine days. As a result of her involvement in the Rising, Morkan lost her job in Brown Thomas.

Morkan continued her work with Cumann na mBan in the aftermath of the Rising and collected and distributed money for the INAAVDF. She left Cumann na mBan in March 1919 and the following year she married Irish Volunteer Edward Keating; they had served together in the Four Courts during the Rising. Pauline Keating died in 1973, aged eighty-one, and is buried in Mount Jerome Cemetery.

Mary O'Sullivan *(later O'Carroll)* – Pictured
Louisa O'Sullivan *(later Pollard)*
BORN: Cork City (1882 and 1893)
ORGANISATION: Cumann na mBan (Fairview branch)
POSITION DURING EASTER RISING: Reis' Chambers/
Hibernian Bank/Four Courts

Mary and Louisa O'Sullivan were born in Cork city to John O'Sullivan, a tea mixer and Margaret O'Sullivan (*née* Cox). Mary, the older of the two sisters, was born in 1882 and Louisa, nine years later in 1893. It is unclear when the family moved to Dublin but they are noted as living in the city by 1901. According to the 1911 census they were living at No. 13 Arranmore Avenue, North Circular Road. Mary was working as a stationer while Louisa was working as a seamstress. The sisters first joined the Fairview (Caitlín Ní hUallacháin) branch, Cumann na mBan in 1914 but were transferred to the Central branch on Good Friday 1916. By that time, the family had moved to No. 23 Arranmore Avenue, North Circular Road. The week prior to the Rising the sisters and their comrades made first aid dressings and prepared other medical supplies. They also learned how to clean and maintain weapons. Their home in Arranmore Avenue was a regular arms dump for the 1st Battalion, Dublin Brigade, Irish Volunteers.

On Easter Monday Mary and Louisa mobilised with some of their comrades from the Central branch at New Road, Broadstone after which they were sent to retrieve ammunition from Oak Lodge on the North Circular Road and bring it to the Volunteers stationed at Cabra Bridge. They also brought food for the men. They stayed with the garrison and later that night they made several journeys to their home to get revolvers, rifles and ammunition which were being stored there. They also retrieved weapons from Meade family home in Cabra Park and brought them to the Volunteers in Kissane home in Hardwicke Street.[42]

On Tuesday 25 April, they made their way to Foley's Typewriting premises, owned by the family of fellow Cumann na mBan members Brigid Foley and her sister Nora, which was located above Reis' Chambers on Sackville Street and there found some of their colleagues. They were in the Hibernian Bank for a short time but soon made their way to the Four Courts, which was under the command of Ned Daly, after receiving a request from James Connolly to do so. Pauline Morkan and Florence Meade accompanied them to the courts. They reached the building safely and while there they tended to men wounded in the fighting. The Four Courts garrisons surrendered on Saturday 29 April, but the women were held in the building overnight, Mary, Louisa, Florence Meade and Pauline Morkan amongst them. The next day, Sunday 30 April, they were taken with their male comrades to Richmond Barracks. They were transferred to Kilmainham Gaol on 1 May and held until 10 May.

According to Mary, on their release from Kilmainham a priest took the women and their comrades to Hogan's public house on James' Street in the hope of getting them shelter for the night. However when they arrived they found that the military had taken over the premises. Forced to find somewhere else to stay, they were accompanied by a British sergeant to a home in Gardiner Street, where the Farrells, relatives of fellow Cumann na mBan member Brigid Lyons, lived. They arrived safely and stayed the night.

Their brother Seán O'Sullivan, a captain in the Irish Volunteers, had also participated in the Rising. He was tried and sentenced to death after the Rising but this sentence was commuted to life imprisonment. Mary did not rejoin Cumann na mBan after the Rising. According to her statement for her pension application, the reason she did not or could not rejoin was because 'I had too much trouble at home'. She did not elaborate or give any more details as to what this meant. It could be a number of things, she was the eldest child in the family and it is quite possible that her responsibilities increased due to an illness or death of her mother. She later married Patrick O'Carroll and they had one daughter. Mary O'Carroll died in 1960 aged seventy-eight and is buried in Glasnevin Cemetery.

Unlike Mary, Louisa did rejoin the Central branch and helped with the reorganisation of the branch and with collecting money for the INAAVDF. She was assigned to collect money in the North Strand and Rutland Street. However, Louisa did not remain an active member of Cumann na mBan and resigned from the organisation at the end of 1917. Like Mary, she did not give any reason in her pension application for her resignation. It is possible that she resigned due to her marriage to Frank Pollard, a member of the Irish Volunteers. She took no further part in any Republican activities. Louisa Pollard died in 1986 aged ninety-three.

Kathleen 'Kitty' Fleming

ORGANISATION: Cumann na mBan (Central [Ard Craobh] branch)
POSITION DURING EASTER RISING: Reis' Chambers/Hibernian
Bank/Four Courts

There are no records available giving any further information on Kathleen Fleming other than the Organisation Rolls of Cumann na mBan which identify her as a member of the Central branch, Cumann na mBan.

Margaret 'Maggie' McLoughlin

ORGANISATION: Cumann na mBan (Central [Ard Craobh] branch)
POSITION DURING EASTER RISING: Reis' Chambers/Hibernian
Bank/Four Courts

There are no records available giving any further information on Margaret 'Maggie' McLoughlin other than the Organisation Rolls of Cumann na mBan which identify her as a member of the Central branch, Cumann na mBan.

THE GPO

Winifred 'Winnie' Carney (*later McBride*)
BORN: Bangor, Co. Down, 1887
ORGANISATION: Cumann na mBan and Irish Citizen Army
POSITION DURING EASTER RISING: GPO/Moore Street

Winifred Carney was born on 4 December 1887 at Fisher's Hill, Bangor, Co. Down. She was the youngest child of three sons and three daughters of Alfred Carney, a commercial traveller, and Sarah Carney (*née* Cassidy). Her father was a Protestant and her mother a Catholic. She went to the CBS in Donegall Street, Belfast, where she became a junior teacher. In her early twenties she became involved in the Gaelic League and the feminist and trade union movements with her friend Marie Johnson, wife of Thomas Johnson, later leader of the Irish Labour Party. In 1912 she became Secretary of the Irish Textile Workers' Union based at 50 York Street, Belfast, which functioned as the women's section of the ITGWU and was led by James Connolly, who became a close friend. During the 1913 Lockout Carney was active in fund raising and relief efforts for the Dublin workers. She was present at the founding of Cumann na mBan in Wynn's Hotel, Dublin on 2 April 1914 and was President of the Belfast branch of that organisation. As well as training in first aid, the Belfast branch also had regular rifle training and Carney was a crack shot, regularly getting the best results in rifle practice. She was also a member of the Irish Citizen Army and became personal secretary to James Connolly, who trusted her with dispatches, instructions and plans for the Rising. On 14 April 1916, Carney received a telegram from Connolly, asking her to come to Dublin immediately. She did and for the next week she typed dispatches and mobilisation orders in Liberty Hall.

On Easter Monday, Carney marched with Connolly and the Irish Citizen Army to the GPO, armed with a typewriter and a gun. During the Rising she acted as Connolly's secretary and, even after most of the women had been evacuated from the GPO on the orders of Patrick Pearse, she refused to leave. Three women remained with the headquarters staff: Carney, Julia Grenan and Elizabeth O'Farrell. The three women accompanied the garrison when they evacuated the GPO on Friday 28 April to their new headquarters at No. 16 Moore Street. Carney remained by Connolly's side throughout, typing dispatches, dressing his wounds and attending to the other wounded men. After the surrender she was interned first in Richmond Barracks, then Kilmainham Gaol, Mountjoy Gaol and, from July, in Aylesbury Prison in England. She was finally released 24 December 1916.

In autumn 1917 she was the Belfast delegate to the Cumann na mBan convention and was appointed president of the Belfast branch. In 1918 she was briefly imprisoned in Armagh and Lewes (England) prisons. She visited IRA prisoners in Belfast Gaol and was party to a plan for a jail break. In the General Election of 1918 she stood for Sinn Féin in Belfast's Victoria division, advocating a workers' republic, but was unsuccessful. She resigned from the Cumann na mBan executive around 1919, but continued as Belfast secretary of the Irish Republican Prisoners' Dependents Fund (1920 – 1922). She became a member of the revived Socialist Party of Ireland in 1920 and attended the annual convention of the Independent Labour Party in Glasgow in April 1920. In 1922 the 'B Specials' raided her home and on finding what they considered seditious documents, Carney was imprisoned in Armagh Prison for eighteen days and fined 40 shillings. She was anti-Treaty and during the Civil War sheltered republicans such as Countess Markievicz and Austin Stack in her home in Belfast.

In 1924 she joined the Court Ward branch of the Northern Ireland Labour Party (NILP) and was active in the party's radical wing promoting republican socialism. She continued to work for the ITGWU in Belfast and Dublin until September 1928, when she married George McBride (1898 – 1988). McBride was a Protestant, a textile engineer, staunch socialist and NILP member who had joined the UVF in 1913 and fought in the British Army (1914 – 1918). In about 1934 Carney joined the small Belfast Socialist Party, but her health was deteriorating and she took little active part in politics. She died on 21 November 1943 in Belfast and was buried in Milltown Cemetery, Belfast. Winifred Carney always kept faith with Connolly's ideal of a workers' republic although she did realise that not many of the other revolutionaries shared this ideal. As an acquaintance Murtagh Morgan said, 'her idea was the Connolly idea of the Republic... she did not agree with the new Free State government... she....stuck with the Connolly line and maintained it right up to her death'.[43]

Brigid 'Bríd/Bridget' Foley (*later Martin*)
BORN: Cork, 1887
ORGANISATION: Cumann na mBan (Central branch)
POSITION DURING EASTER RISING: GPO/Hibernian
Bank, Skeltons Sackville Street, Church Street

Brigid Foley was born in 1887 at Knockmonlea, between Youghal and Killeagh, in Co. Cork. She was one of thirteen siblings and was the daughter of farmer Richard Ó Foghludha (Foley) and his wife, Margaret 'Peg' Long, both Irish speakers. In the 1901 census Brigid is recorded as a 'scholar', aged fourteen, living at home in Knockmonlea with her parents and siblings. In 1902, aged fifteen, she moved to Dublin to further her studies. She lived with her brothers and sisters at No. 5 Cabra Road, Dublin and with her siblings Kate, Nora, Micheál and Risteárd she joined the Keating branch of the Gaelic League. The 1911 census shows Brigid and her siblings still residing on the Cabra Road. Showing an early indication of their political thinking, they completed the census form in Irish. Brigid was employed as a commercial clerk. Her brother Risteárd, who wrote under the pen name Fiachra Éilgeach, was a noted journalist, editor and Gaelic scholar who wrote for *An Claidheamh Soluis* among other literary journals and newspapers.

Foley was a member of the Central branch of Cumann na mBan from 1915. She was a very active member of the organisation and was quickly recruited to carry guns and dispatches for the Volunteers. The Foley family had a typing business in Reis' Chambers on Sackville Street and their office was used regularly for meetings by Seán MacDiarmada and his comrades. She typed many messages for MacDiarmada, Éamonn Ceannt and Diarmaid Lynch and was sent with these messages around the country as a trusted and able dispatch carrier. In her witness statement she said that Seán MacDiarmada told her to 'always have a nightie and a toothbrush ready as you never know when you may be sent with a dispatch'.[44]

On 17 April 1916 she was sent to her native Cork with dispatches from MacDiarmada to Tómas MacCurtain, O/C Cork Brigade Irish Volunteers and Terence MacSwiney, vice O/C. On Wednesday 19 April she made the journey to Cork again. On the evening of Easter Sunday 1916 she and her sister took a taxi to Cork carrying a sealed message from the Military Council for Tómas MacCurtain confirming MacNeill's countermanding order and postponing mobilisation until noon on Monday. Arriving in Dublin that evening, Foley made her way to the GPO to report to MacDiarmada, who then sent her home. She returned to the GPO the next day, Tuesday, and MacDiarmada sent her to the Hibernian Bank with a dispatch for Captain Thomas Weafer, Commanding Officer of the garrison. Foley's sister Nora was also there. Foley was sent to her office in Reis' Chambers which had been taken over by the Volunteers and over the next few hours she was sent back and forth between these outposts and the GPO carrying dispatches. That evening Weafer gave orders to the Foley sisters and Maeve Lawless to go to Skeltons, a former tailor shop in Lower Sackville Street, and set up a first aid station. They reached Skeltons and prepared the building as best they could, gathering food supplies from the nearby Dublin Bread Company (DBC). The women stayed in Skeltons for one day. In that time they only treated one casualty, Ernest Kavanagh, the political cartoonist who had been fatally wounded by a British soldier while trying to enter Liberty Hall. He died soon after. On Wednesday evening they returned to the Hibernian Bank. On Thursday, Foley, with her sisters Nora and Kate made their way to Church Street in the hope of seeing their brother Micheál who was fighting with the Four Courts garrison. They remained in Church Street for the night and were sent home with a number of women on Friday. When they returned home on Saturday they found that their house had been raided by the military.

On Monday 1 May, Foley and fellow Cumann na mBan member Effie Taaffe went to the hospitals throughout the city looking for wounded Volunteers and brought messages to their families. The next day she was arrested at her home on the Cabra Road and taken to Ship Street Barracks. Within twenty four hours Foley and her fellow prisoners were marched from Ship Street to Richmond Barracks and then transferred to Kilmainham Gaol; she remembered that the gaol was filthy.[45] With little or no furniture at first, they were forced to sleep on the floor. The sanitary conditions were basic with no privacy. The women had to request to use the facilities and were accompanied by two soldiers to the lavatory. The soldiers stood guard but there was no door and in some cases the soldiers did not act in an honourable fashion. Rather than go through such humiliation, many women including Foley refused to use the facilities in the gaol, which in turn affected their health. In her case her health was affected permanently.

On the night of Sunday 7 May the women were called together. After their names had been called out they were told they were free to go. Foley's name was not called and she was returned to her cell. Alone and afraid she refused to sleep and instead prayed all night, hiding behind the door. According to Foley, some of the soldiers were frequently drunk.[46] This was verified by the Capuchin priests from Church Street, who insisted on staying in the prison on at least one occasion to ensure the safety of the women there. More women were released over the next few days until only twelve women remained, including Foley, Countess Markievicz, Marie Perolz and Countess Plunkett.

In all twelve women remained in Kilmainham and were later transferred to Mountjoy Gaol and were held there for six weeks. Their treatment in Mountjoy was much better than the treatment they received in Kilmainham. They had proper bathroom facilities and could associate freely with each other. Foley's sister Nora visited her regularly while she was in Mountjoy. While there, Foley and her comrades were asked to sign a form agreeing to move to Oxford or Reading in England.[47] Failure to sign would mean imprisonment in England. Refusing to sign, they were transported to Lewes Gaol in England soon after. While in Lewes they were treated well. In late August Foley and Marie Perolz were released and returned to Ireland. One thing however remained with Foley from her time in prison and that was the fact that the bread they received was terrible. She organised what became known as the '25 Drives'.[48] Money was raised in order to send good quality bread to the men interned in Frongoch. Every week twenty loaves of bread and 6lbs of butter were sent to the camp for the prisoners and this continued until their release in December 1916. As a result of the British bombardment of Sackville Street during the Rising, their family business was gone. But the sisters were not out of business too long as they found new premises on Bachelor's Walk. Foley and her family resumed their activities with the republican movement.

Foley soon became involved in the activities undertaken by Cumann na mBan, including working for the INAAVDF, organising events to raise money and the anti-conscription campaign in 1918. She married James Joseph Martin in June 1918 and moved to Leeson Park. Foley was present in the Mansion House at the opening of Dáil Éireann on 21 January 1919. By now the sisters had moved their business and rented offices at No. 15 College Green. Once again they put their offices at the disposal of both the Dáil and the IRA. Dispatches were sent to and delivered from their offices and many prominent IRA men would regularly go there. As the War of Independence escalated Foley and her family came under scrutiny from the authorities and their premises were raided regularly by the Black and Tans, who left a reminder on the wall after one raid which read 'Do not work for Dáil Éireann or ??? By Order of the Black and Tans'.[49] During such raids their machinery and stock were often destroyed.

At this time very few people, let alone women, owned a car. Foley was one of the few to have such a luxury. Realising its value to the IRA she made the car available to them. She would receive word that it was needed and would leave the keys in the car. As well as providing her offices and car to the IRA, her home on Leeson Park was open to men on the run. In February 1921, her home was raided by the Auxiliaries under the command of Major King who had a notorious reputation in relation to his treatment of IRA men who were held in his custody. They came to arrest her husband who, unlike Foley, was not active in the republican movement. Recalling the raid, Foley stated that King asked her if she was a Sinn Féiner and when she said that she was, told her 'Do you know that I could put you against the wall and shoot you for that?'.[50] Her husband was away at the time but on his return the following evening he was arrested and taken to Dublin Castle. An Auxiliary, John Reynolds, was present with King when her husband was arrested. Reynolds told Foley that he would make sure that her husband would be fine, that he would look after him.

Her husband was released days later and, wishing to thank Reynolds for keeping his word, she brought him cigarettes. They began to talk, during which time Foley came to realise that Reynolds could be of use to the IRA. She reported her findings to Michael Collins who in turn suggested that she arrange a meeting with Reynolds at her office. The meeting took place and she asked Reynolds if he would be willing to pass on information regarding the Auxiliaries in return for payment. Reynolds agreed and proved to be a very valuable agent for the IRA. With information he provided the IRA were able to plan numerous ambushes on the Crown forces.[51]

Foley did not take part in the Civil War. Although she did receive medals for her contribution to the Rising and the War of Independence, she did not initially apply for a pension. She stated in her witness statement that she never applied for a military pension 'on principle'.[52] However due to a change in her financial circumstances she was forced to make an application and was awarded a pension in 1956.[53] Brigid and her husband eventually returned to live in Cork. She died in Cork in June 1970 and is buried in Killeagh Cemetery.

Julia 'Sheila/Sighle' Grenan
BORN: Dublin, 1883
ORGANISATION: Cumann na mBan
POSITION DURING EASTER RISING: GPO

Julia Grenan was born in 1883 in Dublin, the daughter of Patrick Grenan and Elizabeth Kenny. In the 1901 census she was living with her father (a widower) and her siblings Patrick and Mark. Her father was a joiner and the family shared a two-roomed flat in a tenement house at No. 25 Lombard Street, Dublin. In 1911 she was recorded as a visitor in the home of her life long companion Elizabeth O'Farrell at Hastings Street, Ringsend. Here Grenan was recorded as a dressmaker and prior to the Rising she was working as a furrier in one of the big Dublin stores. Grenan and O'Farrell had met at school where they were educated by the Sisters of Mercy. They shared similar political interests and strong nationalist and feminist beliefs. Along with O'Farrell, Grenan joined Inghinidhe na hÉireann sometime around 1906 and both were also members of the suffrage organisation, the Irish Women's Franchise League (IWFL). They supported the striking workers during the 1913 Lockout and worked in the soup kitchen in Liberty Hall. There they got to know Countess Markievicz and worked with her to prevent recruitment into the British Army. When Cumann na mBan was established in 1914, Inghinidhe na hÉireann amalgamated into the organisation and was set up as a distinct branch. Grenan and O'Farrell were members of this Inghinidhe branch on its formation.

On Easter Sunday 1916, Markievicz accompanied Grenan to Liberty Hall and told James Connolly she and O'Farrell could be trusted completely. With an insurrection planned for the following day, they were assigned to the Irish Citizen Army. Grenan was sent to Dundalk and Carrickmacross with dispatches. On returning to Dublin, she reported for duty to the General Post Office and performed nursing and courier duties over the next few days. She and O'Farrell also delivered ammunition from the GPO to the garrison in the College of Surgeons by hiding it under their clothes. After James Connolly's ankle was shattered by a bullet on 27 April, O'Farrell and Grenan volunteered to care for him and stayed in the GPO as it was shelled by British artillery. With the building in flames, they, along with Connolly's secretary, Winifred Carney, were the only three women who refused to leave until the final evacuation on the evening of Friday 28 April. They retreated with the garrison to Moore

Street, where O'Farrell and Grenan nursed the wounded. While O'Farrell was chosen to deliver the news of the surrender to the other garrisons, Grenan surrendered in Moore Street with the other insurgents and was arrested.

Having spent a miserable night outside in the cold at the Rotunda Hospital, she was marched with the other insurgents to Richmond Barracks. She and Winifred Carney had to support the partially disabled Seán MacDiarmada, who was now without his walking stick. As they marched towards the Barracks the insurgents could hear 'a mass of howling women [the separation women] from the back streets who called us filthy names and shrieked curses at us'.[54] When they arrived in Richmond Barracks they found horrendous conditions, overcrowding, unsanitary hygiene arrangements and little or no food or water. Having already spent a night out in the cold at the Rotunda the conditions at Richmond Barracks did little to help MacDiarmada, Grenan or the other prisoners. Along with the other women Grenan was later transferred to Kilmainham Gaol. While in Kilmainham she recalled hearing the shots fired at the executions. She was released on the 8/9 May 1916.

After the Rising both Grenan and O'Farrell continued to work for the Republican cause. They were involved in fund raising for the INAAVDF and carried dispatches for the IRA during the War of Independence. In 1922 they both supported the anti-Treaty side. Living together at 27 Lower Mount Street, Dublin, they remained hostile to the Free State and, during and after the Civil War, collected funds for the families of anti-Treaty prisoners. They regularly attended republican functions and in 1933 resigned from Cumann na mBan when that organisation voted to rescind its oath of allegiance to the first and second Dáils. Both women supported the 1956–62 IRA border campaign. Grenan was a member of Mná na Poblachta, a breakaway group from Cumann na mBan, led by Mary McSwiney which was committed to 'pure republicanism'. She was one of the many women who were committed to achieving the promise of equality for women, promised in the Proclamation of 1916, who then objected strenuously to the 1937 Constitution, particularly the position of women in the home as contained in Articles 41.1 and 41.1.1. She wrote several letters to newspapers attacking this Constitution. After Independence Grenan was employed in the Irish Hospital Sweepstakes and also worked as a furrier. She lived at Lower Mount Street with O'Farrell until O'Farrell's death in 1957. In common with many anti-Treaty comrades, neither Grenan nor O'Farrell applied for a military pension for their activities during the Rising or the War of Independence, as O'Farrell said 'all governments since 1921 had betrayed the Republic'.[55] Grenan, O'Farrell and many other women of Cumann na mBan never recognised the legitimacy of the State set up in 1922. Julia Grenan died in 1972 and is buried with Elizabeth O'Farrell at Glasnevin Cemetery.

Anne 'Annie' Higgins/O'Higgins
BORN: Dublin, 1897
ORGANISATION: Cumann na mBan
POSITION DURING EASTER RISING: GPO

Annie G. O'Higgins was a composer, musician and music teacher, born in Dublin around 1897. Her parents were John Higgins, a cooper, and Elizabeth Higgins. In 1901 the family lived in Rathmines and by 1911 they were living at St. Kevin's Terrace, off Bride Street in the south city centre. Anne Higgins qualified as a piano teacher with the Municipal School of Music in 1916 and worked there for many years as a music teacher. She was a talented composer and invented a new method of teaching harmony. In 1934 the *Irish Times* reported that 'Miss Anne Higgins, whose new suite of Irish airs for full orchestra, will be broadcast from Dublin next Tuesday, [was] the instructor in Harmony and Counterpoint at the Municipal School of Music, and has been for the past ten years assistant lecturer under the Department of Education, at their summer school course for music teachers'.[56]

By 1916 she was a music teacher in Carrickmacross, Co. Monaghan and a member of the Central branch of Cumann na mBan. She was stationed in the GPO during the Rising, where she served as a courier. On Thursday of Easter Week she was sent north to deliver messages by Patrick Pearse. She cycled to Drogheda and then got a train to Carrickmacross. She delivered her messages to Carrickmacross, Bailieboro, Kilnaleck, Ballinagh and Cavan that day but when she arrived in Kingscourt, Co. Cavan she was arrested and imprisoned in Armagh Gaol. After the surrender she was transported to Richmond Barracks and then to Kilmainham Gaol. While imprisoned she put music to the words of a poem by nationalist poet Ethna Carbery, *There's a Green Glen in Éireann,* later printed by the Gaelic Press, Dublin. She was moved from Kilmainham Gaol to Mountjoy Gaol where she remained until June 1916. After her release she lost her job in Carrickmacross, but she continued to work both as a music teacher in Dublin and as an activist within the revolutionary movement there.

In her witness statement Eilís Bean Uí Chonaill (Ní Riain) mentioned that in 1920 O'Higgins had offices at 14 North Frederick Street where the offices of the Ministry of Labour of the first Dáil were also covertly located. Uí Chonaill spoke of her delight when, on going to these offices to help the Minister for Labour, Countess Markievicz and her officials, she met the neighbouring tenant, Miss O'Higgins: 'I recognised her as a Cumann na mBan member… who had taken part in the Rising… The recognition was mutual and, when I talked over the coincidence of our occupying the same house, she said she would do all she could to help us. Our relief at having her as a co-tenant instead of a doubtful stranger was great and the fact that she had a number of young pupils calling throughout the day was a further help to us'.[57] Her mother, Mrs. Lily O'Higgins, also supported the IRA. Her house at Sherrard Street was used as a safe house in which guns and documents were kept. She also looked after IRA men on the run including Dick Barrett, Charlie Hurley and Charlie Price.

In 1922 Annie Higgins supported the anti-Treaty side and was later a member of Sinn Féin. She continued to work as a music teacher but tragically died in a fire in 1935. At that time O'Higgins and her mother Lily lived at No. 16 Parnell Square which also housed the headquarters of Sinn Féin. On Sunday, 18 August 1935 the building caught fire, one of the largest fires seen in Dublin that year. Several residents were rescued from the building but O'Higgins and her mother lived at the top and were overcome by smoke. It was apparent that O'Higgins was trying to drag her bedridden mother to safety as both were found lying on the floor near the window. Anne O'Higgins was about thirty-seven years old when she died. The *Irish Press* noted that 'both women embodied the secrecy, loyalty and courage that so helped Ireland's active service units'.[58]

Martha Kelly (*later Murphy*)
BORN: Dublin, 1897
ORGANISATION: Irish Citizen Army
POSITION DURING EASTER RISING: GPO

Martha Kelly was born in 1897 in Kilmainham, Dublin to Hugh Kelly, a general labourer, and his wife Bridget Cullen. Kelly was a member of the Irish Citizen Army from 1913 and trained in first aid in Liberty Hall under Dr. Kathleen Lynn. She was in Liberty Hall prior to the Rising 'attending to the guard and making up first aid outfits'.[59]

On Easter Monday she went to the GPO with a contingent led by George Oman of the Irish Citizen Army and stayed there preparing food and doing other duties. On Tuesday she left with a small party and was stationed in the Imperial Hotel on Sackville Street (O'Connell Street) for the rest of the week. She helped with food preparation and was also engaged in first aid activities, nursing among others Noel Lemass, younger brother of the future Taoiseach, Seán Lemass. After the surrender she was arrested at the Pro-Cathedral on Marlborough Street and taken to Richmond Barracks and later transferred to Kilmainham Gaol. She was released on 22 May. After the Rising Kelly lost both her home and her job in the Metropolitan Laundry and received aid from the INAAVDF.

In 1917 she found work in J.J. Walsh's shop in Blessington Street, located near Mountjoy Gaol. Because of its proximity to the prison Kelly, working with a sympathetic warder in the prison, regularly received and sent messages from republican prisoners there which she would then pass on to the IRA. Martha Kelly married Michael Murphy in 1918. Captain Michael Murphy was O/C of 'A' Company, 2nd Battalion, Dublin Brigade, Irish Volunteers. After her marriage she continued to be active and during the War of Independence she carried dispatches to and from the 2nd Battalion to IRA GHQ, while making her house available to men on the run. She housed Frank Teeling, a member of Michael Collins' Squad who participated in the assassinations of fourteen suspected British agents on 21 November 1920. Teeling was wounded and captured during the assassinations and was later imprisoned in Kilmainham Gaol. Awaiting trial, he, along with Simon Donnelly and Ernie O'Malley, successfully escaped on 14 February 1921. The men had to go on the run and Teeling was hidden in Kelly's house for 'a long time'. Teeling stated in his support letter to her pension application that the house always contained 'six loaded 45 Revs' (revolvers) for use of 'herself, husband and myself'.[60] Her house was raided on the night Teeling left it but the guns had been moved earlier by her husband.

Her husband was arrested during an attack on the Custom House on 25 May 1921. Kelly continued her activities and 'dispatches continued to be left in the house, and arms and ammunition were left in the house and removed to the dump as before... This continued up to the ceasefire'.[61] By now Kelly was a trusted member of Cumann na mBan and worked very closely with the IRA. She was entrusted with the key of the 2nd Battalion's arms dump and was responsible for the custody and security of the weapons. Kelly opposed the Treaty and on the outbreak of the Civil

War she reported to Barry's Hotel, headquarters of the Dublin Brigade, anti-Treaty IRA, where she assisted in food preparation and first aid. She carried messages from her husband, who was also stationed in Barry's Hotel, to Cathal Brugha, stationed in the Hammam Hotel. And throughout the war, her home was used as an arms dump for the anti-Treaty forces. In 1922, she kept the arms captured during the raid on the Anglo-American Oil Company in her house. She and Murphy had sixteen children (eight sons and eight daughters). When she died in 1943 she was only forty-six years old. Both Michael and Martha Murphy were awarded 1916 medals, War of Independence medals for active service and military service pensions and both appear in the 1936 photograph of survivors of the 1916 Garrison, a copy of which hangs in the GPO.

Catherine 'Kathleen' Ryan (*later Treston*)
BORN: Dublin, 1890
ORGANISATION: Cumann na mBan
POSITION DURING EASTER RISING: GPO

Catherine Ryan was born in Dublin in 1890 to Francis 'Frank' Ryan and Mary Mercer and was baptised at St. Agatha's Church. In 1901 the family and their children Sarah, Thomasina, Catherine and Frank were living at No. 22 Ballybough Road, Dublin. Frank senior and Frank junior were both working as carpenters, while the girls were still in school. In 1908 Catherine Ryan married William Treston, the son of James and Kate Treston of Bayview Avenue off the North Strand Road, Dublin. James Treston was also a carpenter and this may be how William and Catherine met each other. William Treston did not follow his father into carpentry, rather he is recorded as a qualified dentist in 1901, although as he was only seventeen at the time, it is likely he was a dental technician or assistant rather than a dentist. By 1911, the couple had two daughters, Rachel and Frances Muriel. The couple and their children were then living with Catherine's mother Mary (widowed), her sister Sarah Mercer and Catherine's sisters Sarah and Thomasina Ryan at No. 7 Ballybough Road. Thomasina Ryan would later marry Seán McGarry, who was a captain in the Volunteers, and served in the GPO during the Rising, acting as aide-de-camp to Tom Clarke.

By 1916 Treston was active in Cumann na mBan and she joined the outpost in the GPO once the Rising began. In her witness statement Cumann na mBan member Aoife de Burca mentioned seeing Treston in the GPO providing nursing care for the insurgents even though she 'had only maternity training'.[62] It is unclear when Treston was arrested but on capture she was taken first to Ship Street Barracks, later transferred to Richmond Barracks and then Kilmainham Gaol. While she was imprisoned in Kilmainham Gaol she, in common with many of the women, suffered ill treatment. Kathleen Lynn noted that in Ship Street Barracks 'an officer told a soldier to prod Nurse Treston for not at once falling into line saying he had seen her shoot six police'.[63] Catherine Treston (or Nurse Treston as she is often referred to) is pictured in the photograph of the revolutionary women taken in the garden of Mr. and Mrs. Ely O'Carroll's house in Peter's Place, Dublin in the summer of 1916 at a meeting of the Irish National Aid and Volunteer Dependents' Fund (INAAVDF). She continued her activities during the War of Independence, during which time she acted as a courier, occasionally delivering letters to and from Michael Collins. Catherine Treston died before she could apply for a military pension but she is on the 1966 Roll of Honour which lists many who participated in the Easter Rising. She died in 1928.

MARROWBONE LANE DISTILLERY

Mary 'May' Byrne *(later Doyle)*
BORN: Dublin, 1898
ORGANISATION: Cumann na mBan (Inghinidhe branch)
POSITION DURING EASTER RISING: Marrowbone
Lane Distillery

Mary 'May' Byrne was born in 1898 and joined the Inghinidhe branch, Cumann na mBan in 1915. At the time of the Easter Rising she was living in her family home at 16 Susan Terrace, Donore Avenue. Byrne was responsible for mobilising many of the women on Easter Monday who then proceeded to Cleaver Hall and served with members of the 4th Battalion, Dublin Brigade, Irish Volunteers, who took over Jameson's Distillery in nearby Marrowbone Lane.[64] She remained with the garrison throughout the week, during which time she was promoted to the rank of Section-Commander by Rose McNamara, O/C of the women in Marrowbone Lane. When the garrison surrendered on 30 April, she was arrested and taken to Richmond Barracks. The women were held there for one day before being transferred to Kilmainham Gaol. She was released with her colleagues from the Inghinidhe branch on the night of 8 May.

On her release Byrne rejoined her branch in late May/early June 1916 and helped in the reorganisation of the movement which included collecting money for the Irish National Aid and Volunteer Dependents' Fund. Each branch of Cumann na mBan was given certain areas in which they were to collect money and her area covered Bridgefoot Street and St. Augustine Street. Every Sunday morning the women would go house to house collecting money, often not finishing their work until at least 2 pm. In April 1917 Byrne was elected 2nd Lieutenant of the Inghinidhe branch and as a result of her promotion her workload increased. She was now responsible for overseeing drilling and training of the branch. Like her comrades she took part in the many funerals of Volunteers that occurred over the coming years.

She also took part in Lá na mBan (Women's Day) on 9 June 1918. This day was organised as an anti-conscription protest, with Cumann na mBan women leading the parade to City Hall. Byrne was also present at the protest meeting held in September 1918 in Foster Place in which she and her colleagues were batoned by the police.[65] During the 1918 General Election Byrne was in charge of the first aid station at the polling station in Donnybrook. Around this time she began her work with Volunteer Seán O'Sullivan who worked in the Volunteer munitions factory in Parnell Street. She would regularly hold weapons and ammunition for him at her home. Much of these munitions came from the British Army in Island Bridge barracks. In April 1919, she was elected 1st Lieutenant of the Inghinidhe branch. As a result she was responsible for arranging drill practice and all aspects of training the women, including first aid. As 1st Lieutenant she also had to attend special training lectures held for officers, especially in the preparation of field dressing, and her home in Susan Terrace was used as an examination depot for Cumann na mBan.

During the War of Independence she had many areas of responsibility. For example when the campaign began to intensify and ambushes on the Crown forces became more frequent, she had to ensure that at least two Cumann na mBan women were in position at the first aid station at No. 5 South Frederick Street. If any Volunteers were wounded in action, Byrne would have to arrange for the wounded man to be taken to a safe house and cared for. Propaganda work was essential to the success of the IRA's campaign against the British and this work was carried out most effectively by women like Byrne who as officers arranged for the distribution of leaflets and bill-posting which was carried out on a weekly basis.

In October 1920 Byrne was elected captain of the Inghinidhe branch of Cumann na mBan, a post which she held until January 1922. Towards the end of the War of Independence an order was issued from the District Council, Cumann na mBan that every branch was to supply food parcels to IRA men imprisoned in Mountjoy Gaol with each branch responsible for one week at a time. This was known as 'Prisoners Week'. Byrne resigned from Cumann na mBan on 26 January 1922, shortly after the Treaty was ratified by the Dáil. She did not take part in the Irish Civil War.

Annie Cooney (*later O'Brien*)[66]
– Pictured Centre
Elizabeth 'Lily' Cooney (*later Curran*)
– Pictured Right
Eileen Cooney (*later Harbourne*)
– Pictured Left
BORN: Dublin (1896, 1898 and 1900)
ORGANISATION: Cumann na mBan
(Inghinidhe branch)
POSITION DURING EASTER RISING:
Marrowbone Lane Distillery

The three Cooney sisters Annie (born 1896), Elizabeth (Lily, born 1898) and Eileen (born 1900) came from a staunch republican home, the daughters of Michael and Mary Cooney. According to the 1901 census the family was living at No. 48 Bow Lane but by 1911 they were living in No. 16A Basin Street Upper, quite close to Marrowbone Lane. Michael Cooney worked as an engine driver in 1901 and an electrical engineer (probably on the trains) in 1911. All three sisters were fluent Irish speakers and in 1911 Annie was working as a seamstress, while Lily and Eileen were attending school.

It was through Christopher Byrne that the girls joined the republican movement. Byrne, a lieutenant in 'F' Company, 4th Battalion, Dublin Brigade, Irish Volunteers, was living with the family. Volunteers such as Con Colbert, captain of 'F' Company, would visit him there. A friendship developed between Annie and Colbert and he suggested she should join Cumann na mBan. Annie joined the Inghinidhe branch in August 1915, immediately after the funeral of O'Donovan Rossa at which she had sold commemoration booklets. Lily and Eileen followed in Annie's footsteps and also joined the Inghinidhe branch in late 1915. Because of their friendship with Colbert and Byrne the Cooney home was used by the 4th Battalion to store arms. Prior to the Rising a large quantity of guns and ammunition was stored there and later distributed to the company. As a result of this activity the girls were aware that a big operation was planned and a few weeks prior to the Rising Colbert asked Annie to make signalling flags for the Volunteers.

Using her expertise as a seamstress Annie made her own Cumann na mBan uniform, basing it on Con Colbert's Volunteer uniform and finished it just before Easter Sunday. At 10p.m. on Easter Sunday night the girls received a dispatch from Colbert to Christy Byrne about the mobilisation for the next day. On Easter Monday the sisters made their way to Cleaver's Hall in Donore Avenue where they met their comrades from the Inghinidhe branch. Eventually they received their orders and under the leadership of Rose McNamara they marched to meet the Volunteers and made their way to Marrowbone Lane Distillery. After gaining entry to the building, the women were divided into sections and Annie, Lily and Eileen made their way to the barley loft where a Volunteer sniper was in position.

Throughout the week the women cooked for the Volunteers and tended the wounded, although compared to other outposts there were relatively few casualties amongst this garrison. When the order to surrender came on Sunday 30 April, the men told the women to leave and gave them their arms to hide. The women however refused and all twenty-two marched off with their comrades to Ross Road, near St. Patrick's Park where the military were waiting. Soon after, they were all marched to Richmond Barracks, flanked on either side by armed soldiers; the women singing marching songs all the way. On arriving at the Barracks they were brought to a large square after which the women were separated from the men.

The next day, 1 May, the Cooneys were transferred to Kilmainham Gaol. Wardresses from Mountjoy Gaol were brought over to Kilmainham to search them. Describing the conditions in Kilmainham, Annie stated that, at first, they were put three to a cell on the ground floor in the old west wing. Annie shared a cell with Margaret 'Loo' Kennedy and Agnes MacNamee. Despite having three women to a cell there were only two beds, so the women had to take it in turns to sleep. They protested at their treatment and after a few days they were put two to a cell. They were allowed to exercise for one hour a day and they were fed by the soldiers on duty, but were given no cutlery.[67] The women were allowed to attend mass in the chapel in the gaol the following Sunday 7 May. They sat on the balcony in the chapel and, while there, the Cooney sisters saw Éamonn Ceannt, Seán Heuston, Michael Mallin and their good friend, Con Colbert. Ceannt, Mallin, Heuston and Colbert were executed the next morning, 8 May and the Cooneys heard the gunshots. Later that evening Annie and her sisters and most of the women were released, accompanied by Fr. McCarthy, James' St. Church.

After their release the girls rejoined Cumann na mBan and helped reorganise the Inghinidhe branch. They raised money for the INAAVDF by collecting money at local churches and holding flag days, ceilis and concerts. They attended lectures in first aid and home nursing. These lectures were given by Dr. Kathleen Lynn and Dr.

Geraghty and were held in No. 6 Harcourt Street. They took part in most, if not all, of the major events involving Cumann na mBan including demonstrations outside Mountjoy Gaol, acting as stewards, keeping order during the hunger strike in 1917 and at the funeral of Thomas Ashe. The sisters were usually together at these events. They acted as stewards on 9 June, Lá na mBan, in which thousands of women from Dublin signed the anti-conscription pledge in City Hall. They were also present at a protest meeting in Foster Place in September 1918, which was organised by Cumann na mBan to protest against women being held in prison in England; there were only women speakers present at the meeting. The sisters were also members of the Inchicore branch of the Gaelic League. This branch was set up after the release of the Volunteers from Frongoch in December 1916 and members of both Cumann na mBan and the Volunteers would regularly meet at Emmet Hall, the home of executed leader Michael Mallin. In late 1918 Christy Byrne received word that the building was going to be attacked by the military from nearby Richmond Barracks. Lily Cooney was ordered to retrieve weapons for the Volunteers and Lily, Annie and Eileen with other members of Cumann na mBan stationed themselves in the building with the Volunteers waiting for the attack which did not materialise. In December that year the Spanish Flu epidemic swept through the country and the Cooney sisters nursed people living in the Dublin tenements and also in St. Ultan's Hospital.

Prior to the Rising the Inghinidhe branch was divided into two sections, but on reorganisation in 1917 it was divided into four sections with two squads in each. Lily was appointed squad leader, a position she held up to the truce. In 1919, Annie Cooney was appointed Adjutant of the Inghinidhe branch and held that rank until the truce in July 1921. During the War of Independence their family home was used to store weapons. The IRA had a munitions factory in a bicycle shop in Parnell Street and ammunition was regularly brought from there to the Cooney home. Their father worked as a fitter in Dolphin's Barn Brick Factory and would bring the ammunition from his home and hide it in the brickworks. If their father was not available to transfer the ammunition and bomb cases, Annie, Lily and Eileen would bring them instead. Despite being raided numerous times by the military, the arms store in the brickworks was never discovered. All the while, the sisters were also collecting money for the IRA Arms Fund.

As the War of Independence escalated in 1920, ambushes against the military increased dramatically. The events surrounding what became known as Bloody Sunday sent shock waves through the British establishment. At 9 a.m. on the morning of 21 November, members of Michael Collins' Squad and other IRA men assassinated British secret service men in their lodgings around the city. On the preceding Saturday night, 20 November, the Cooney sisters were told by Christy Byrne to be ready at 6 a.m. the next morning at University Church, St.Stephen's Green and to wait there until met by him and two other men. Their job was to take the weapons from the men and get them to safety. That morning the sisters waited. In order not to draw attention to themselves, they went into the church in turns, two would go in while one waited outside keeping watch for the men. The girls heard the shooting and waited in a laneway between the church and the corner of Harcourt Street. After collecting the guns they made their way home.

The sisters, particularly Lily, also gathered intelligence for the IRA. She was responsible for locating and the subsequent arrest of an informer who was supplying photographs of prominent IRA men, including Dick McKee and Peadar Clancy who were both murdered by the Crown forces in Dublin Castle on Bloody Sunday. Lily gave the IRA a description of the informer and where he could be found. He was arrested and tried by the IRA and deported. On Saturday 2 February 1921 the Cooney home was raided by the military. Soldiers arrived in two lorries. Eileen Cooney and Christy Byrne were in the house and both were held under guard. Annie arrived home, was searched and a letter was discovered. When she tried to explain away the letter, Annie was accused of lying and was arrested and taken to the Bridewell station. On her arrival there she was placed with five other girls who had been arrested during similar raids. The following Monday Annie was brought to Mountjoy Gaol and placed with the other female political prisoners. Three weeks later she was taken to Dublin Castle and interrogated. She was charged with spying on the authorities. During the search on her home a map was discovered noting the addresses of British agents living in Dublin. Annie was tried on 27 April at the North Dublin Union. She was found guilty and sentenced to six months imprisonment. The sentence was reduced to four months and having served three months already she was released on 27 May. On release she rejoined her comrades in the Inghinidhe branch.

Annie's arrest did not deter Lily or Eileen and they continued with their activities. Christy Byrne was still living with the family and he asked the sisters to help with the planned escape of Frank Teeling, Ernie O'Malley and Simon Donnelly from Kilmainham Gaol. Members of Cumann na mBan would take it in turns to accompany members of the IRA to the Gaol and wait at the side gate for the escapees. Lily and Eileen went with Seán Harbourne (Eileen's future husband) and Andy Healy. Pretending to be courting couples they went three or four nights in a row and the sisters were present on the night that the Volunteers arrested some soldiers who were returning to the gaol with their girlfriends. On the night of 14 February the men succeeded in escaping from Kilmainham Gaol, the sisters saw them leave and once they were sure the men were safely away they went home.

After the raid on their home in February, Christy Byrne left as he knew the military would return for him. In April their house was again raided. Unfortunately for Byrne, who had not been at the house for weeks, he visited that night and was arrested and taken firstly to Richmond Barracks, then Collinstown and finally Kilmainham Gaol. It was around this time that Lily and Eileen (who was now a section commander in the Inghinidhe branch) became responsible for communications between IRA prisoners in Collinstown and Kilmainham Gaol and the IRA on the outside. Through a friendly soldier in Collinstown, the sisters regularly brought dispatches to and from the prison. During the Truce, mid-1921, Annie became engaged to IRA man Denis O'Brien, whom she met in 1916. He was O/C 'C' Company, 4th Battalion.

The Cooney sisters opposed the Treaty. Cumann na mBan was the first of the republican organisations to hold a convention on the issue of acceptance or rejection of the Treaty. The Convention was held on 5 February 1922 in the Mansion House and every branch from around the country was represented by two delegates. Lily Cooney was appointed to represent the Inghinidhe branch. Cumann na mBan voted to reject the Treaty.

Prior to the outbreak of the Civil War on 28 June 1922, Annie and Eileen were in Kildare. They received word that a fight was inevitable and decided to return to Dublin; it took them two days to get home. By the time they arrived in Dublin, the Civil War had begun. They immediately went to No. 27 Dawson Street, Cumann na mBan headquarters, and received their orders. Annie, Lily and Eileen were sent to the dispensary in South Earl Street, a Cumann na mBan first aid post attached to the 4th Battalion who had once again taken over Marrowbone Lane Distillery. While there, they commandeered supplies for the garrison. On 30 June, Annie and Lily tried to make their way to the anti-Treaty headquarters in the Four Courts but they failed to get near the building and returned to the dispensary. Paddy O'Brien, brother of Denis O'Brien who had been O/C of the garrison, was wounded during the fighting and the sisters visited him at his home in Pim Street. He sent them to the Courts with a dispatch for the men not to surrender, but when they got there it was too late; the garrison had already surrendered and was taken prisoner to Jameson's Distillery in nearby Smithfield. Annie and Lily went to the distillery and saw the men through the windows, including Annie's fiancé. The men gave the sisters messages to give to their families and were given a dispatch from Joe McKelvey to give to Oscar Traynor, O/C of the Dublin Brigade who had his headquarters in the Hammam Hotel in O'Connell Street. They got to the hotel and delivered the message after which they returned to Jameson's and took whatever equipment they could from the men. Eileen had by this time joined her sisters. They had been asked to get weapons for Ernie O'Malley who had escaped from Jameson's. They carried out their task successfully, cycling through the city with their cargo, under constant fire from the pro-Treaty forces.

During the Civil War Annie and Eileen were attached to the 2nd Battalion Active Service Unit (ASU) to carry weapons and ammunition to and from operations against the pro-Treaty forces. Like so many of their comrades in Cumann na mBan the sisters took part in the funerals of IRA men killed in action, including the funeral of Cathal Brugha and Paddy O'Brien. In the meantime those IRA men who had been arrested at the Four Courts were now being held in Mountjoy Gaol. The sisters were in regular contact with the men and just like in the War of Independence, their experience in communications between the prisoners and the IRA outside was put to full use. In July they received a letter from the prisoners requesting their help for an attempted escape. They were asked to smuggle weapons and ammunition into the prison. Over the next two months they were successful in smuggling into the prison eight Webley revolvers and ammunition. Each week they made a soda cake, wrapping one gun in oiled silk and placing it in the mixture before baking it. Another parcel of butter and jam was made to accompany the cake. They simply placed the bullets in the butter. They then brought the parcels to the prison and handed them in at the gate. In all, they did this eight times and were never discovered. They also managed to smuggle an army uniform into the gaol. The escape attempt took place in October but it did not succeed.

As the Civil War continued Cumann na mBan continued to raise funds for IRA men in prison. They tried to raise money through raffles and jumble sales and functions but more often than not they had to use their own money to help those in distress. Eileen was appointed official courier to Joe O'Connor, O/C 3rd Battalion,

Dublin Brigade and would collect and deliver all his communications. Lily also took part in the burning of the offices of Pathé's Gazette in Abbey Street and as the Civil War continued she was put in charge of communications to and from Portlaoise Prison and later the Curragh Camp, in particular Tintown No. 2. Throughout the Civil War their family home was raided by the pro-Treaty forces, looking for their younger brother Thomas who was a member of the anti-Treaty IRA. The sisters managed to evade capture during the Civil War. After the end of hostilities in 1923 they continued to provide assistance to the IRA, locating safe houses for men on the run and giving money and clothing to republicans released from prison. The sisters campaigned for republican candidates in the general election later that year.

It is unclear when Lily and Eileen left Cumann na mBan. Annie remained a member until 1926. She later married Denis O'Brien, while Eileen married Seán Harbourne, both IRA men. Lily married Michael Curran sometime after 1936. Annie O'Brien died in 1959. Her husband, a Garda detective sergeant, was murdered outside their house in 1942. Annie O'Brien was a founder member of the Association of Old Cumann na mBan and served on the executive. She was sixty-three years old when she died and is buried in Mount Jerome Cemetery. Lily Curran died in 1980 aged eighty-two and is buried in Mount Jerome Cemetery. She had worked with the Irish Press from its foundation, becoming one of the first women photographic printers in the art department. Eileen Harbourne died in 1982, also aged eighty-two, and is buried in Cruagh Cemetery in Rathfarnham, Dublin.[68]

Marcella Cosgrove
BORN: Dublin, 1873
ORGANISATION: Cumann na mBan (Inghinidhe branch)
POSITION DURING EASTER RISING: Marrowbone Lane

Marcella Cosgrove was born in Dublin in 1873 to Bartholomew Cosgrove and Mary Whittaker. In the 1901 census Cosgrove is recorded as a housekeeper and could speak both English and Irish. She shared a flat at Georges Quay with her brother Thomas, a cover maker, and her sister Annie, a book folder. In 1911 she was living on her own in Tara Street, and signed her name in Irish, Marsála Ní Coisghraighe. Cosgrove was a pupil of William 'Willie' Rooney, a nationalist, poet and journalist who, in 1892, set up the Celtic Literary Society. From a young age she was an advocate of women's rights and Ireland's rights as a nation and was a supporter of the Ladies' Land League, which had been set up in 1880 by Anna Parnell. Cosgrove joined Inghinidhe na hÉireann in 1905. This organisation had been set up by Maud Gonne McBride in 1900, a sister society of the Celtic Literary Society, which women were, initially, not allowed to join. Inghinidhe was based solely in Dublin and encouraged women to campaign for their rights not just as women but Irish women and was very active in the promotion of the idea of independence for Ireland. The organisation promoted the development and purchase of Irish goods and insisted that its members wear clothes made from Irish materials. The women of Inghinidhe were very proactive in their communities. They set up a school in Dublin's inner city to help educate some of the poorest children in the city and also helped provide daily meals for the poor children in the Liberties. Cosgrove was immersed in this work.

In April 1914, when Cumann na mBan was established, she was a founding member and, with many of her colleagues from Inghinidhe, formed the Inghinidhe na hÉireann branch which, up to the aftermath of the Easter Rising, was the only branch based on the south side of the city. As it was the only branch of Cumann na mBan on the south side at the time, they were attached to both the 3rd and 4th Battalions of the Irish Volunteers. Cosgrove was elected Quartermaster of the branch.[69] During the Rising she served in Marrowbone Lane Distillery, and as Quartermaster it was her responsibility to ensure that there were enough supplies to sustain the garrison. Following the surrender she and her comrades were taken to Richmond Barracks and then Kilmainham Gaol. They were released on 9 May. Following her release from Kilmainham Gaol, Cosgrove rejoined Cumann na mBan and was involved in the reorganisation of the Inghinidhe branch.

At this time, Cosgrove lived at No. 3 George's Quay with Julia Maher, a fellow member of Cumann na mBan. Maher ran a sweet shop next door to No. 3 and, during the War of Independence, Maher's shop and their house were often raided by the Black and Tans. Like many of the women involved in the Nationalist movement, Cosgrove opposed the Anglo-Irish Treaty and during the Civil War she served with the anti-Treaty IRA in the United Services Club, St. Stephen's Green. She continued to be involved in national and cultural issues and, as a past pupil of Willie Rooney, became a member of the old Celtic Literary Society. Marcella Cosgrove died in 1938 and is buried in Glasnevin Cemetery. She was sixty-three years old. Her niece, who declined a state funeral for her aunt, said Cosgrove 'did what she did for Ireland and would not have wished to have such an acknowledgment'.[70] Cosgrove's Inghinidhe na hÉireann brooch is in the collection of the Allen Library Dublin and her Cumann na mBan brooch is in the collection of the National Museum of Ireland.

Bridget Hegarty (*later Harmon***)**
BORN: Dublin, 1897
ORGANISATION: Cumann na mBan (Inghinidhe branch)
POSITION DURING EASTER RISING: Marrowbone Lane Distillery

Bridget Hegarty was born in Dublin in 1897. In 1901 she and her family, father Bartholomew (an engine driver in a brewery), mother Mary Ann (*née* Moran) and siblings, Anne, Patrick, Bartholomew and James all lived in No. 94 Rialto Buildings, Rialto, along with her grandmother Anne Moran. All seven members of the Hegarty family were sharing a three-roomed house. In the 1911 census she was recorded as being fourteen years old and still in school.

Hegarty did not state when she joined the Inghinidhe branch, Cumann na mBan but it can be assumed that it was most likely around September 1915 as this is when the organisation saw an increase in membership in the aftermath of the funeral of O'Donovan Rossa in August that year. She mobilised with her comrades at Emerald Square on Easter Monday, 1916 and from there proceeded to Marrowbone Lane Distillery. While there she cooked and tended to those wounded and was arrested on the surrender of the garrison on Sunday 30 April. She was held in Richmond Barracks overnight and transferred to Kilmainham Gaol the next day, and was released with her comrades on 8 May.[71]

She rejoined the Inghinidhe branch and was involved in the reorganisation, carrying out work for the Irish National Aid and Volunteer Dependents' Fund and attending parades and funerals. She took part in the funeral of Thomas Ashe in September 1917. Hegarty resigned from Cumann na mBan in March 1918. In her pension application she did not give any reason for doing so. She did not take part in any further activities in connection with the Republican movement. She married Joseph Harmon, had a son and a daughter and later lived on Raphoe Road, Crumlin, Dublin. Bridget Harmon died in 1970 and is buried in Mount Jerome cemetery. She was seventy-three years old.

Josephine 'Josie' Kelly (*later Greene*)
BORN: Dublin, 1895
ORGANISATION: Cumann na mBan (Inghinidhe branch)
POSITION DURING EASTER RISING: Marrowbone Lane Distillery

Josephine Kelly was born in Dublin in 1895. In 1901 the Kelly family was living at No. 10 Rialto Buildings. John Kelly, originally from Co. Longford, was a tailor and his wife Elizabeth, from Co. Meath, was a tailoress. Obviously the family travelled around for work in the early years of the marriage as two children, James and Lizzie, were born in England while two other children, Mary and Catherine, were born in Co. Louth. The three youngest children, John, Josephine and Gertrude, were all born in Dublin. At the time of the 1911 census she was living at No. 76 Donore Avenue, with her widowed mother Elizabeth and five siblings.

Kelly was working as a shop assistant and joined the Inghinidhe branch Cumann na mBan in 1914. According to her pension file, Josephine was responsible for recruiting at least six other girls from her neighbourhood into the branch. From the beginning Josephine demonstrated a keen interest in learning first aid. She regularly attended all classes provided by Cumann na mBan on first aid, qualifying and receiving a certificate for her training. Three weeks prior to the Rising, she attended a first aid meeting and was asked by Éamonn Ceannt, O/C 4th Battalion to purchase first aid supplies and every evening after that she and her comrades prepared field dressings and other medical equipment.

Kelly mobilised with her comrades at Cleaver Hall, Donore Avenue on Easter Monday morning and proceeded to make their way to Marrowbone Lane Distillery. Throughout the week she was in charge of first aid. She was arrested after the surrender and taken to Richmond Barracks and later Kilmainham Gaol and was released with her comrades on 8 May. As a result of her involvement in the Rising Kelly lost her job and had to find work elsewhere, which at the time was quite difficult.[72] Rather than stay idle she continued with her studies in first aid, taking exams and also rejoined the Inghinidhe branch. She did not participate in the public parades and funerals with her colleagues, preferring instead to remain in the background collecting and distributing money for the Irish National Aid and Volunteer Dependents' Fund and less public work on the anti-conscription campaign. As she was known to the authorities Kelly felt it was better for both her and the organisation if she was not seen to be directly involved with them. Her expertise in first aid was required elsewhere and she had to be on hand, ready to treat wounded men at a moment's notice.

Once the War of Independence began Kelly was ready at all times to carry out this work. Her home, 'Mar Lodge', Donore Avenue, which she shared with her mother, was always available to treat wounded Volunteers who could not risk going to hospital for fear of arrest. Not only did she treat the men successfully, but her home was also used as an arms dump by the 4th Battalion who would regularly leave guns and ammunition there, and if she was not present, they would leave their weapons in outhouses at the rear of her home. Very often, late at night she would then have to find a safe location to store them. While doing this work Kelly was regularly called on by the Volunteers to arrange for safe houses for men who were recovering from their wounds or for those on the run.[73]

On Bloody Sunday, 21 November 1920 Kelly, like many of her comrades in the Inghinidhe branch, had a role to play. Not only was she responsible for bringing weapons to the Volunteers for use in the operation, but after the shootings, Volunteer Paddy Lambe came to her looking for help to get out of the city and she assisted him. She continued to assist the IRA in this manner up to the end of the War of Independence, but did not take part in the Civil War. She later married and lived in Kimmage. Josephine Kelly died on 11 June 1968 aged seventy-three.

Margaret 'Loo' Kennedy
BORN: Dublin, 1892
ORGANISATION: Cumann na mBan (Inghinidhe branch)
POSITION DURING EASTER RISING: Marrowbone Lane Distillery

Margaret 'Loo' Kennedy was born in Dublin in 1892 and lived at No. 117 Donore Terrace, South Circular Road all her life. In the 1911 census she was living there with her parents Patrick (born in Kildare), her mother Mary (born in Carlow) and her sisters Catherine, Mary and Teresa. She was educated by the Sisters of Charity at Basin Lane, Dublin. Her sister Teresa was working as a milliner, Catherine a clerk and Mary worked in drapery sales, while Margaret was not employed.

Kennedy joined the Inghinidhe branch of Cumann na mBan in August/September 1915 just after the funeral of O'Donovan Rossa. The branch held their meetings in No. 6 Harcourt Street every Thursday night and had lessons in first aid, signalling, Morse code and 'Dispatch Memorising'. She described their training in her witness statement: 'In Camden Street we were trained and exercised in drill, figure marching, stretcher-drill, signalling and rifle practice with a little rook rifle. We also went on route marches regularly on our own initiative in order to train the girls in marching and in taking control. We had two instructors from the Fianna for drill, signalling and rifle practice'.[74] The Inghinidhe branch differed to the other branches of Cumann na mBan in that they were governed by officers rather than a committee. Similar to the organisation of the Irish Volunteers they elected their officers and were the first branch to do so. At the time of the Easter Rising, Eileen Walsh was Commandant of Inghinidhe, while Rose McNamara was Vice-Commandant. Marcella Cosgrove was elected Quartermaster. Because they were the only branch on the south side of the city, the Inghinidhe branch was attached to both the 3rd and 4th Battalions of the Dublin Brigade, Irish Volunteers and was made up of two sections, one attached to each battalion.

Kennedy and her comrades took part in the Dublin parade on St. Patrick's Day, 17 March 1916, which was one of a series of well-organised parades which served as a show of strength for the advanced nationalist movement. These were huge events in which members of Cumann na mBan and Irish Volunteers all around the country paraded in open formation, and were very successful publicity events, similar to the funeral of O'Donovan Rossa the previous year. Three weeks prior to the Rising, Cumann na mBan were requested to make field dressings for the Irish Volunteers.[75] The Inghinidhe branch went to Volunteer headquarters at No. 2 Dawson Street and every night in the weeks leading up the Rising they were busy making all the necessary first aid equipment. While there they were told to be ready for manoeuvres which would take place on Easter Sunday. However due to Eoin MacNeill's countermanding order cancelling the events for the Sunday, Kennedy and her comrades waited for further instructions.

Kennedy mobilised at 10 a.m. on Easter Monday at Cleaver Hall in Donore Avenue. The hall was being used by the Gaelic League at the time. With at least eight other women she was sent to the home of Sheila O'Hanlon, fellow Inghinidhe member, in Camac Place, Dolphin's Barn to collect first aid equipment and other essential material. After obtaining the equipment she and her comrades returned to Emerald Square and marched off behind members of 'A' Company, 4th Battalion, Irish Volunteers and made their way to Marrowbone Lane Distillery. The Distillery was an outpost attached to the command of Éamonn Ceannt, O/C 4th Battalion, who had his main command in the South Dublin Union, (now St. James's Hospital). The distillery overlooked the Union and the task of the Volunteers stationed there was to cover the Union from surprise attack from the military. Kennedy was positioned in the loft of the distillery with the Cooney sisters.

Throughout the week, Kennedy and her comrades cooked and looked after the garrison. The women refused to leave the garrison when the order to surrender came on Sunday 30 April, and marched behind their comrades to the place of surrender on the Ross Road, via the Coombe. Despite the failure of the rebellion, the women kept the men's spirits up by singing songs. On the way Kennedy picked up a rifle and carried it to the Ross Road, but had to give it up once there. They were soon marched off to Richmond Barracks, once again singing along the way. Once they reached the Barracks the women were separated from the men and placed in two rooms in the married quarters of the Barracks and transferred to Kilmainham Gaol the next day. Kennedy remembered that she had no complaints about her treatment in Kilmainham. She was released from Kilmainham on the evening of 8 May. She immediately rejoined the Inghinidhe branch, helped in the reorganisation of the branch and participated in all the activities at the time, collecting funds and investigating cases for the INAAVDF. The women would meet at the beginning of each week to discuss the cases and would again meet at the end of the week and sort out the money which had been collected. Also at this time the branch held two parades weekly.

Kennedy rose quickly through the ranks of the Inghinidhe branch and in September 1917 she was elected captain. She was a strict disciplinarian, demanding dedication from her colleagues, and was also very efficient. The following year, in September 1918, she was also appointed Secretary to the Dublin District Council, Cumann na mBan.[76] As Secretary she had to inspect all the Dublin branches of Cumann na mBan. She was O/C in charge of the women for Lá na mBan 1918, in which thousands of women signed the anti-conscription pledge in City Hall on 9 June. During the 1918 General Election she was responsible for setting up first aid stations around the city on polling day. Kathleen Clarke, widow of Tom Clarke, executed leader of the Rising, had been imprisoned in England at this time. She was eventually released and Kennedy arranged that all branches of Cumann na mBan be represented at her homecoming. She organised stewards to be present, all women, at Westland Row train station, which was completely surrounded by crowds of people. Members of the Central branch were based at the train station itself and the other women kept the crowds back, keeping the road clear. Once Clarke was out of the station the Central branch formed an advance guard and led the procession while the other women fell in behind. In 1919, Kennedy was elected Commandant, Dublin City Cumann na mBan and held that rank until the position was abolished in October 1921. She was then responsible for the activities of all the Dublin branches of Cumann na mBan. She organised training for the women, parades, and established a network of safe houses throughout the city for the Volunteers.

During the War of Independence she was responsible for establishing first aid posts throughout the city, working directly with the officers of the IRA. She was elected onto the executive of Cumann na mBan in 1920 and remained there until October 1921.[77] As a member of the Executive, Kennedy had to attend meetings every Monday at which they decided the policy of Cumann na mBan throughout the whole country. Each member was allocated a county to look after and Kennedy was in charge of Sligo and had to inspect the Cumann na mBan branches there and also in Tullamore, Co. Offaly. Every Sunday she held lectures in Parnell Square for the officers of each Cumann na mBan branch. There they received lectures in training, drill and signalling and they would in turn train each of their branches. At this time she was also responsible for distributing propaganda material for the IRA. Every Saturday she would receive parcels of material and would arrange for their distribution around the city that night and early Sunday morning. In 1920 she was sent to England by the Cumann na mBan executive in response to a proclamation issued by the British government that women were not to harbour wanted men.

Kennedy opposed the Anglo-Irish Treaty. At this time she had rejoined the Inghinidhe branch and by January 1922 she was once again captain and also Secretary to the Dublin District Council. She was a steward at the convention held by Cumann na mBan in February 1922 to discuss the merits of accepting or rejecting the Treaty. At the outbreak of the Civil War in June 1922, she was appointed O/C in charge of the Cumann na mBan hospital that had been set up in Tara Hall, Gloucester Street. She had between 200 and 300 women under her command and would send them to other anti-Treaty outposts as they were needed. The women remained in the hospital until they were forced to evacuate on 7 July. Kennedy was asked to organise the Guard of Honour for the funeral of Cathal Brugha, anti-Treaty, who had been mortally wounded during the fighting in O'Connell Street. She provided members of Cumann na mBan to act as stewards and organised them to march in Brugha's funeral procession.

Sadly this scene would be repeated many times by the women during the Civil War. Shortly after Brugha's death, the women were requested to do the same for Harry Boland, also anti-Treaty, who was fatally wounded in the Grand Hotel in Skerries later that month.[78]

Kennedy managed to evade arrest during this time but her health began to suffer and from September 1922 she became less involved with Cumann na mBan. She resigned as Secretary of the District Council and left Dublin in October 1922. Despite the fact that she was not as active, a warrant was issued for her arrest and pro-Treaty forces raided the homes of many of her comrades in the Inghinidhe branch looking for her. As a result she did not return to Dublin until Christmas Day 1923, well after the Civil War had ended. Kennedy continued to be active in politics in the years that followed. She joined Fianna Fáil and was appointed a Senator by Taoiseach Eamon de Valera in 1938. She remained a member of the Seanad until 1948. She was President of the Old Cumann na mBan and first Chairman of the United Conference of the Old IRA and kindred associations, and was later its Honorary President. Margaret 'Loo' Kennedy died in 1953 and was buried with full military honours in Deansgrange Cemetery. She was sixty-one years old.[79]

Catherine 'Katie' Liston [80]
BORN: Dublin, 1885
Mary Liston
BORN: Dublin, 1895/1896
ORGANISATION: Cumann na mBan (Inghinidhe branch)
POSITION DURING EASTER RISING: Marrowbone Lane Distillery

The Liston sisters were members of the Inghinidhe branch, Cumann na mBan. There are no records of the sisters' involvement other than Rose McNamara's witness statement recording that they were part of the Marrowbone Lane garrison.[81] According to the 1901 census the family lived at No. 27 Inchicore Square, New Kilmainham. Their father Michael was from Co. Tipperary and worked as a railway engine driver and is noted in the census as speaking Irish and English. His wife Mary and their children were born in Dublin. According to the 1911 census all their children, from their eldest son Patrick to their youngest child Margarete, who was eleven years old, could speak Irish. Catherine (Kate) was born in 1885 while Mary was born in 1895/96. According to the 1901 census, Catherine was working as a monitoress.

Their younger brother Michael, born in 1897, was a member of the 4th Battalion, Dublin Brigade, Irish Volunteers. He fought in Marrowbone Lane Distillery during the Easter Rising and was wounded during the fighting.[82] Catherine, Mary and Michael were arrested after the surrender on Sunday 30 April and imprisoned in Richmond Barracks. The sisters were transferred to Kilmainham Gaol with their comrades on 1 May and were both released soon after. There is no further mention of the Liston sisters in any documentation regarding their involvement in the War of Independence or Civil War.

Josephine 'Josie' McGowan
BORN: Dublin, 1898
ORGANISATION: Cumann na mBan (Inghinidhe branch)
POSITION DURING EASTER RISING: Marrowbone Lane Distillery

Josephine 'Josie' McGowan was born in Dolphin's Barn, Dublin in 1898, and was the youngest of four children. She was the only daughter of Charles McGowan (a car driver), and his wife Margaret. She had three older brothers, Charles, Claude and France [sic]. All six members of the family lived in one room in a tenement house on the South Circular Road. As a young girl she was a member of the Gaelic League and also a member of the Inghinidhe branch of Cumann na mBan. Two of Josie's brothers, Charles and Claude, were members of the Irish Volunteers. Charles was a member of the 3rd Battalion, Dublin Brigade while Claude was a member of the 2nd Battalion. As a member of the Inghinidhe branch, McGowan was attached to the Marrowbone Lane garrison during the Easter Rising and was among the twenty-two women from that garrison who were arrested and held in Richmond Barracks and Kilmainham Gaol after the surrender. After her release from prison she rejoined her comrades in Cumann na mBan and was involved in helping with their many activities at the time.

Josie McGowan died on 29 September 1918, the death certificate stated that she died of pneumonia, however, according to family history she was injured in a baton charge and on being taken to the Dublin Mountains to be treated she died. Both of these stories may actually reveal the truth behind her death. According to the pension application of Priscilla Kavanagh (*née* Quigley), who had served with McGowan in Marrowbone Lane Distillery during the Rising, members of Cumann na mBan, including the Inghinidhe branch, were involved in a protest meeting at

Foster Place.[83] The women were campaigning against the ill treatment of female prisoners Kathleen Clarke, Countess Markievicz, and Maud Gonne McBride, incarcerated in English Gaols and the manner in which republican prisoners in general were being treated in prison by the authorities. Speakers at the meeting included Helena Molony and Hanna Sheehy Skeffington. According to Kavanagh, the women were surrounded by the police who, while observing the situation, broke up the meeting with a violent baton charge. Some of the women were arrested. As a member of the Inghinidhe branch McGowan would have been present. According to her family she received severe blows to her head during the baton charge and was taken to the Inghinidhe branch first aid station in Ticknock, Co. Dublin. Newspapers at the time verify the story of the protest meeting and the rough treatment the women received.

Josie McGowan was only 20 years old at the time of her death. She was buried in a pauper's grave in Glasnevin Cemetery. Her father Charles died seven days later and was buried with his daughter. Today their grave is marked with a headstone erected by their family. Josie McGowan received posthumous medals for her contribution in the Easter Rising and the War of Independence, the latter medal has the 'Comhrac' (Fighting or Active Service) bar.

Rose McNamara
BORN: Dublin, 1885
ORGANISATION: Cumann na mBan (Inghinidhe branch)
POSITION DURING EASTER RISING: Marrowbone Lane Distillery

Rose Ann McNamara was born in Dublin in 1885, the daughter of Benjamin McNamara and his wife Johanna (*née* Mangan). She was baptised in St. Mary's Pro-Cathedral in September 1885. In 1901 she was still at school and living with her widowed mother, Johanna, a shopkeeper, at Charles Street, Dublin. She joined Inghinidhe na hÉireann in 1906, when she was introduced to the organisation by Marie Perolz, whose sister was married to McNamara's brother. She later joined the Inghinidhe branch of Cumann na mBan when it was established in 1914. The Inghinidhe branch was the first to organise itself on military lines similar to those of the Irish Volunteers. This meant that the branch had a Commandant (Eileen Walsh), Vice-Commandant (Rose McNamara), Quartermaster (Marcella Cosgrove) and Section Commander (May Byrne).

Prior to the Rising the women were engaged in preparing first aid kits in No. 2 Dawson Street. As Vice-Commandant, McNamara was responsible for organising her comrades and mobilised with twenty-four members of the Inghinidhe branch at Weaver's Hall, Cork Street on Easter Monday. This section was to be attached to the Marrowbone Lane garrison. After the surrender they refused to leave the men and twenty-two were arrested. They kept up the morale of the men by singing all the way to Richmond Barracks.[84] They were later taken to Kilmainham Gaol. The Inghinidhe women were a lively bunch as during their exercise period in the gaol they began to Irish dance and when threatened that they would be kept in their cells they proceeded to dance in their cells. She and the other women were released on 9 May.

McNamara rejoined Cumann na mBan and was involved collecting and distributing money for the Irish National Aid and Volunteer Dependents' Fund and in 1917 helped reorganise the Inghinidhe branch. She was appointed 1st Lieutenant. Cumann na mBan assisted in the lying-in-state of Volunteer Thomas Ashe who had died as a result of force-feeding in Mountjoy Gaol in September 1917. They acted as stewards and were responsible for controlling the crowds gathered outside the prison. This was a role McNamara and her comrades would play all too often over the coming years. In 1918 she and many members of Cumann na mBan marched in the funeral cortège of Volunteer Richard Coleman.[85]

During the War of Independence McNamara also took part in the vigils outside Mountjoy during the hunger strikes. In 1919 she was promoted to captain of the Inghinidhe branch. With the escalation of the conflict, ambushes against the Crown forces became more frequent. A vital role played by Cumann na mBan was the administration of first aid to wounded Volunteers. First aid stations were set up throughout the city, there were at least three such stations on the south side covering the 3rd Battalion area. As captain, McNamara would receive word from the IRA of an impending ambush and would make sure the women were ready to deal with casualties or take arms. She was at this time a member of the District Council of Cumann na mBan and on more than one occasion as a result of her position she had to participate in courts-martial.

McNamara opposed the Treaty and on the outbreak of the Civil War on 28 June 1922 she assisted the anti-Treaty forces, delivering messages to different anti-Treaty outposts in the city and to the relatives of anti-Treaty IRA men around the country after which she returned to Dublin and was stationed with the anti-Treaty

IRA garrison in the United Services Club, St. Stephen's Green. She evaded arrest throughout the Civil War during which time she continued to assist the anti-Treaty forces by collecting funds and delivering parcels for republicans in prison, carrying out propaganda work and later campaigning for the general election in 1923. She continued her involvement with Cumann na mBan and was executive member of the Association of Old Cumann na mBan. Rose McNamara never married. She died in 1957 and is buried in Glasnevin Cemetery. She was seventy-two years old.

Roseanna 'Rose' Mullally (*later Farrelly*)
BORN: Co. Dublin, 1893
ORGANISATION: Cumann na mBan (Inghinidhe branch)
POSITION DURING EASTER RISING: Marrowbone Lane Distillery

Roseanna 'Rosie' Mullally was born in 1893. At the time of the 1911 census Mullally was living with her family at No. 24 Oldbawn, Tallaght where her father was a farm labourer. Her father John was born in Kildare. Her mother Bridget and her ten siblings were all born in Dublin. Mullally joined the Inghinidhe branch, Cumann na mBan in 1915 and was present at the funeral of Jeremiah O'Donovan Rossa, the veteran Fenian, at Glasnevin Cemetery in August 1915.[86] This funeral was extremely important in terms of propaganda value for the nationalist movement and all nationalist/republican organisations took part, including Cumann na mBan who walked in the procession. This work would, in the coming years, become all too familiar for the women of Cumann na mBan.

Mullally mobilised for action on Easter Monday and served with her comrades of the Inghinidhe branch in Marrowbone Lane Distillery. Arrested after the surrender on Sunday 30 April she was taken to Richmond Barracks and transferred to Kilmainham Gaol on 1 May. She was released with her comrades on 8 May.

Mullally rejoined her branch and was involved in the task of reorganising the movement. This work entailed collecting and distributing funds for the Irish National Aid and Volunteer Dependents' Fund. She and her colleagues were allocated certain areas in Dublin city, and would then go house to house collecting money to be used for the dependents of those imprisoned. She resigned from Cumann na mBan at the end of 1917 or early 1918. Mullally gave no reason in her pension file as to why she resigned but it is quite possible that she resigned as she got married to Mr. Farrelly. Rose Farrelly died in 1984. She was ninety-nine years old.

Kathleen Murphy
BORN: probably Dublin, 1887
ORGANISATION: Cumann na mBan (Inghinidhe branch)
POSITION DURING EASTER RISING: Marrowbone Lane Distillery

Kathleen Murphy was born in 1887. At the time of the Rising she was married to Seamus Murphy who was a Captain in the 4th Battalion, Dublin Brigade, Irish Volunteers and later O/C of the Marrowbone Lane garrison during the Easter Rising. They lived at No. 7 St. Mary's Terrace, Rathfarnham and had married in 1915. She was not a member of Cumann na mBan at the time of the Rising but she was attached to them and served with the Inghinidhe branch in Marrowbone Lane alongside her husband. Although not a member of the organisation Murphy would regularly deliver messages for Patrick Pearse and Eoin MacNeill from her home, hiding the messages in a basket of eggs.[87]

Murphy became involved in the Rising when she went to view the mobilisation of the Volunteers and Cumann na mBan at Emerald Square. Her husband Seamus asked her to get supplies of ammunition from their home in Rathfarnham and bring them to him. Murphy completed this task and made her way to the distillery that evening and stayed with the garrison for the remainder of the week. Throughout the week she was in charge of cooking and feeding the garrison while also assisting the men on night duty. This entailed three women on duty with the men, staying awake through the night, in order to let the men get some sleep. The girls would wake them at intervals throughout the night.

When the garrison surrendered on Sunday 30 April, Murphy refused to leave and remained with her husband, taking with her two revolvers and some ammunition which she refused to hand over to the soldiers when she reached Richmond Barracks. She managed to hold onto them until she was taken to Kilmainham Gaol the next day. As a result of her behaviour, she was not released from Kilmainham until 12 May as she was seen to be an extremist by the authorities.[88] She managed to speak to Con Colbert before he was executed and brought his last messages to his family when she was released. In the meantime her husband Seamus and many of his comrades were sent from Richmond Barracks to Knutsford Prison in England and later to Frongoch internment camp in Wales. After her release from prison Murphy became very ill. She was in the early stages of pregnancy and went to Loughrea, Co. Galway to recuperate. She gave birth to twins in December 1916 and once fully recovered she made her way to England to visit the prisons where the men were being held, bringing parcels and messages from home. On her return from England in January 1917 Murphy came back to Dublin and set up home with her young children in St. Enda's, Rathfarnham, which had been the home of Patrick Pearse.

By August 1917 Murphy, with her husband Seamus and young family returned to Galway where she joined Cumann na mBan. While there she would regularly deliver dispatches to the various IRA units throughout the county. With the onset of the War of Independence in 1919 it became too dangerous for her husband to remain at home, so he had to go on the run. In the meantime, Murphy tended to wounded Volunteers and continued to deliver dispatches and in one such incident in early 1920, when she was bringing a dispatch from Volunteer Jimmy Flynn, a prisoner in Galway Gaol, she was arrested.[89] She quickly ate the dispatch which was written on vellum. The only way she could do this was to eat it with a bag of sweets, which she managed to do, but as a result was sick for a week after. Soon after this incident Murphy was ordered to leave Galway by the RIC (Royal Irish Constabulary).

Kathleen and Seamus Murphy returned to Dublin at the end of 1920 where she immediately offered her services to the republican movement. Lily O'Brennan, who had served with her in Marrowbone Lane in 1916, would frequently call on her to help wounded Volunteers and to help during the Belfast boycott,[90] which was being implemented by O'Brennan. Murphy was one of twelve women who paraded around the streets of Dublin wearing a sandwich board highlighting the plight of the Catholic population in Belfast during the pogroms there. Between May and November 1921, she was in charge of the Dáil Publicity Department which was based at her home in 73 Rathgar Road. She was living there under an assumed name, that of Mrs. Cathleen Millar, along with her husband Seamus and their three children.[91]

Murphy did not take part in the Civil War. After hostilities ended the family remained in Dublin where her husband became the Chairman of the Assistance Commissioners. She had five daughters and two sons and died in 1946. She was fifty-nine years old and was buried, with full military honours, in Glasnevin Cemetery.

Lily O'Brennan
BORN: Dublin, 1878
ORGANISATION: Cumann na mBan (Inghinidhe/Central branch)
POSITION DURING EASTER RISING: Marrowbone Lane Distillery

Lily O'Brennan was born in Dublin in 1878, the third daughter of Francis Brennan, auctioneer, and his wife, Elizabeth. She was born into a strongly nationalist family, indeed it is alleged that her father, Francis, was a Fenian. She became a teacher, writer and playwright. In 1912, she wrote a play, *May Eve in Stephen's Green* and produced it with Máire Nic Shiubhlaigh in Fr. Mathew Hall where it received good reviews. She was present at the inaugural meeting of Cumann na mBan and joined it as a member of the Central branch. In the weeks leading up to the Rising she and her sister Áine, wife of Éamonn Ceannt, Commandant of the 4th Battalion, Dublin Brigade, Irish Volunteers, were engaged in preparing for the events to come.[92] During Easter Week she served with the Marrowbone Lane garrison. She was arrested and held in Kilmainham Gaol and was released on 8 May, the day her brother-in-law, Éamonn Ceannt, was executed in the gaol. She continued to be involved in the Republican movement and was a clerk for the National Aid Association which later amalgamated with the Irish Volunteer Dependents' Fund, becoming the Irish National Aid and Volunteer Dependents' Fund. She also worked at this time locating the graves of Volunteers killed during the Rising and marking them. A member of Sinn Féin, she was co-opted onto its executive committee as well as being a member of the executive of Cumann na mBan. In 1917 she toured Co. Longford and Co. Wicklow in a recruitment drive for Cumann na mBan.

During the War of Independence O'Brennan was a district judge in the Republican courts, while also working for the Dáil's Department of Labour. With Eilís Ní Riain, she was responsible for ensuring the safety of wounded Volunteers and on receiving word of an impending raid it was their job to get the men away to another hospital, usually late at night. In 1920 she was also in charge of an employment bureau for the IRA, set up by Cathal Brugha, then Minister for Defence. She was attached to Dáil Eireann Labour Department during the War of Independence, set up a working department under Countess Markievicz, then Minister for Labour, (around March 1920) and was engaged in publicity work, especially foreign publicity. She resigned from the Cumann na mBan executive in June 1921. She oversaw support for the

Belfast boycott in Dublin and during the Treaty negotiations in London she was private secretary to Arthur Griffith. She opposed the Treaty and became secretary to Erskine Childers.

During the Civil War O'Brennan carried dispatches between the Sinn Féin offices in 23 Suffolk Street and the Four Courts. She also helped set up a hospital in Suffolk Street, sheltered wanted anti-Treaty IRA men and also helped with anti-Treaty propaganda. She was asked by Childers to meet him in Cork where he was carrying out his propaganda work. She was arrested in October 1922 and was imprisoned in Mountjoy Prison, Kilmainham Gaol and the North Dublin Union. While in Kilmainham she helped organise the 7th anniversary commemorations of the Rising. She helped keep up the spirits of the imprisoned women and a fellow inmate described her as 'rather diminutive and full of humour'.[93] After she was moved to the North Dublin Union she took part in an abortive escape attempt, and was finally released in July 1923 and resumed her work with her anti-Treaty colleagues, helping campaign in the general election that year. Throughout all of this activity she also carried out work for the White Cross.[94] In later life O'Brennan wrote plays and short stories for adults and children in both English and Irish, and was a founding member of the Catholic Writers' Guild. She also wrote an account of the War of Independence entitled *Leading a Dog's Life in Ireland*. She died in 1948, aged seventy and is buried in Deansgrange Cemetery.[95] Her papers are held at the UCD archives.

Margaret 'Cissie' O'Flaherty (*later Timmons*)
BORN: Dublin, 1896
ORGANISATION: Cumann na mBan (Inghinidhe branch)
POSITION DURING EASTER RISING: Marrowbone Lane Distillery

Margaret Mary O'Flaherty was born in 1896 and was one of eight children born to James and Mary O'Flaherty. At the time of the 1901 census Margaret was living with her family in No. 20 Bow Lane West, Dublin. James and Mary O'Flaherty were originally from Wicklow. James O'Flaherty was a worker on the railway and he lived with his wife, children and four lodgers at No. 20. By 1911, the O'Flahertys were living in No. 22 Rialto and the entire family signed the census in Irish as Ó Flaithbheartaigh or Máighréad Ní Fhlaithbheartaigh in Margaret's case. This was a sign of their growing nationalism and attachment to the Irish language.

O'Flaherty joined the Inghinidhe branch of Cumann na mBan in 1914 and took part in the Easter Rising, serving with her comrades in Marrowbone Lane Distillery during Easter Week. Her three brothers, William, Martin and James, were members of the Irish Volunteers and also took part in the fighting. When the garrison surrendered, O'Flaherty was arrested and taken to Richmond Barracks and later Kilmainham Gaol. She was released with the majority of her comrades from the Inghinidhe branch on 8 May.[96]

She rejoined Cumann na mBan but eventually had to resign from the Inghinidhe branch in order to care for her sick father. Although she did not take part in the War of Independence, she and her sister were active participants in the Irish Civil War, taking the anti-Treaty side in the conflict. In the aftermath of the battle of the Four Courts on 30 June 1922, her sister was instrumental in getting both Seán Lemass and Ernie O'Malley (anti-Treaty IRA) out of Dublin city after both men had escaped from custody in Jameson's Distillery, Smithfield. Lemass made his way to her sister's house at 103 Rialto Cottages, Rialto after which O'Flaherty arranged to get the men away safely to Dún Laoghaire. She married Joseph Timmons in 1925 and lived with her family in Crumlin and Terenure. Margaret Timmons died in 1982. She was eighty-six years old.

Sheila O'Hanlon (*later Lynch*)
BORN: Dublin, 1895
ORGANISATION: Cumann na mBan (Inghinidhe branch)
POSITION DURING EASTER RISING: Marrowbone
Lane Distillery

Sheila O'Hanlon was born in Dublin in 1895, the daughter of James and Rose O'Hanlon. She was christened Julia but later changed her name to the Irish spelling of Sheila. She lived with her family in No. 7 Camac Place, Dolphin's Barn. Her father was a commercial clerk and in the 1911 census her occupation was noted as dressmaker. She and her sister Mollie joined the Inghinidhe branch, Cumann na mBan in 1915. Prior to the Easter Rising O'Hanlon provided accommodation in her home for Volunteers who had come from England and also held rifles there. On Easter Monday she was ordered by Éamonn Ceannt to mobilise her own squad, six women in all, at Cleaver's Hall, after which she brought first aid supplies from her home in Camac Place to the Marrowbone Lane Distillery where she served throughout the Rising, holding the rank of Squad Commander.[97] Arrested after the surrender, O'Hanlon was held with her comrades in Richmond Barracks and later Kilmainham Gaol. She was released on 8 May.

O'Hanlon immediately rejoined the Inghinidhe branch, still holding the rank of Squad Commander and helped in its reorganisation. She collected money for the Prisoners' Dependents' Fund with responsibility for collections in Inchicore, South Circular Road and New Street. She also took part in all public parades and demonstrations including the funeral of Thomas Ashe in September 1917 and the anti-conscription demonstrations in 1918. Like most members of Cumann na mBan, O'Hanlon helped campaign for Sinn Féin in the 1918 General Election. Members of the Inghinidhe branch carried out all the pre-election work in No. 6 Harcourt Street.[98] During the election, Cumann na mBan established first aid stations through-out the city. O'Hanlon was on duty at the first aid station in both Ballyboden and Camden Street.

During the War of Independence she was chosen to carry out 'special duties' for Margaret 'Loo' Kennedy, Commandant of the Inghinidhe branch. This work entailed taking messages to officers of the District Council, Cumann na mBan relating to meetings and mobilisations. While carrying out this work O'Hanlon was regularly stopped and searched by the military, but nothing was ever found on her.[99] She was later attached to the IRA Intelligence Unit, Dublin Brigade carrying out surveillance on suspected spies. Women were vital in storing and transporting weapons and ammunition for the IRA. On one occasion O'Hanlon was requested to bring a machine gun to Nassau Street. The gun was too big to be taken in one go and she successfully dismantled the weapon and in three separate journeys brought the gun to its destination safely. While this work was carried out by women to great effect, it was in the field of propaganda that they were to prove themselves experts. Thanks to the women the *Irish Bulletin*, the daily republican newssheet, was delivered, without fail, throughout the country and around the world, highlighting the conditions in Ireland which were not being reported in the mainstream media. O'Hanlon and her comrades would regularly carry out this work at night while also posting republican handbills and writing republican slogans on walls in prominent places all over the city. Throughout this time her home in Camac Place was regularly raided by the Crown forces, but she was never arrested.

When the Anglo-Irish Treaty was signed O'Hanlon, with most of her comrades in the Inghinidhe branch, refused to accept it and fought with the anti-Treaty forces in the Civil War. During the fighting in Dublin between 28 June and 5 July 1922 she served in the Minerva Hotel and later in Tara Hall, Gloucester Street administering first aid to wounded anti-Treaty men. She also delivered dispatches between Oscar Traynor's headquarters in 'The Block' on O'Connell Street and Tom Derrig, a member of the anti-Treaty IRA Executive who was based in Fleming's Hotel in Bray. After Cathal Brugha was fatally wounded in the fighting, O'Hanlon was a member of the Guard of Honour on duty with his remains in the Mater Hospital and also took part in the procession at his funeral on 10 July. Although the main battle for Dublin was over in a short time, the anti-Treaty forces were still very active and between July 1922 and October 1923, O'Hanlon worked as a courier attached to the anti-Treaty IRA GHQ and from 1923 she worked directly for Frank Aiken who, on the death of Liam Lynch in April 1923, became Chief of Staff of the anti-Treaty forces. O'Hanlon was arrested by the pro-Treaty forces in October 1923 while delivering dispatches. She was taken to the North Dublin Union (NDU) but still had on her person the dispatches she was meant to deliver.[100]

After her release it seems O'Hanlon did not take part in any further republican activities. She married Gilbert Lynch, a member of the Irish Volunteers and a veteran of the Rising in 1924/25 and lived in Crumlin. Gilbert Lynch was a former president of the Irish Trade Union Council and, up to his retirement in 1957, national organiser of the Amalgamated Transport and General Workers' Union. In 1927 he was elected Fianna Fáil TD for Galway and took part in the negotiations which resulted in the decision of the Fianna Fáil Party to enter Dáil Éireann. He and his wife Sheila had three sons and two daughters. Sheila Lynch died in 1970 aged seventy-five.

Josephine 'Josie' O'Keeffe/O'Keefe (*later McNamara*)
BORN: Dublin, 1897
ORGANISATION: Cumann na mBan (Inghinidhe branch)
POSITION DURING EASTER RISING: Marrowbone Lane Distillery

Josephine 'Josie' O'Keeffe was born in Dublin in 1897 and lived with her family in No. 11 South Brown Street. She was the daughter of Andrew O'Keefe, a general labourer, and his wife Mary. From a young age O'Keeffe showed a keen interest in all aspects of Irish culture and heritage and was a member of the Gaelic League. In the 1911 census it is noted that she was fluent in both Irish and English, while she and her younger sister Emily were successful Irish dancers and won medals for their dancing in the Irish Feiseanna held in the Fr. Mathew Hall, Church Street. At the time of the census O'Keeffe's occupation was noted as silk weaver, not an uncommon trade considering the area in which she lived. South Brown Street was right in the heart of the weaving trade in the Liberties of Dublin. There is no doubt that it was through her work as a weaver that O'Keeffe became politically active. This most likely happened during the 1913 Lockout when many weavers, both men and women, most notably Michael Mallin, a fellow silk weaver and member of the Irish Citizen Army (ICA), were involved in the Lockout. Many of these strikers later took part in the Easter Rising.

O'Keeffe and her sister Emily, who was two years younger, joined the Inghinidhe branch, Cumann na mBan in 1915. They mobilised on Easter Monday and marched with the Volunteers from Emerald Square to the Marrowbone Lane Distillery where they stayed for the entire week. The sisters were arrested after the surrender and held in Richmond Barracks and Kilmainham Gaol. They were both released on 8 May.[101] O'Keeffe immediately rejoined the Inghinidhe branch and with her comrades who had also fought in the Rising set about reorganising the branch. They would regularly send parcels of food to the Volunteers imprisoned in England and when they were released in December 1916 and into mid-1917, O'Keeffe and her comrades helped care for them on their return. She took part in all the major parades, demonstrations, protests and funerals that followed, including the funeral of Thomas Ashe in September 1917 and Lá na mBan, the anti-conscription protest held at City Hall on 9 June 1918. She collected and distributed money for the Irish National Aid and Volunteer Dependents' Fund, campaigned for Sinn Féin candidates in the 1918 general election and was on duty on voting day. She was also one of the women batoned by the police during the protest meeting in Foster Place in 1918.[102]

During the War of Independence O'Keeffe's responsibilities increased. She was appointed by the officers of the Inghinidhe branch to attend the monthly District Council meeting. In April 1920 she was appointed 2nd Lieutenant of the Inghinidhe branch, a post she held until October 1921 when she was appointed 1st Lieutenant of the branch. She regularly tended to wounded Volunteers from the country brigades who were recovering in hospital in Dublin. Because these men were not known to the authorities in Dublin it was easier for the women to bring them food and receive letters from them. She was also in regular contact with Volunteers who were imprisoned in Mountjoy Gaol and Kilmainham Gaol. She was privy to the plans of an attempted escape of IRA men from Mountjoy. The plan was to break out of the gaol by cutting the bars on the cell windows. O'Keeffe successfully smuggled into the gaol the hacksaws necessary for the job, but in the end the escape did not take place. She regularly brought parcels of food and other home comforts to Volunteers who were imprisoned in Kilmainham Gaol, most notably Simon Donnelly, O/C 'C' Company, 3rd Battalion, IRA, and Intelligence Officer of the company.

After his escape from Kilmainham in February 1921, Donnelly enlisted O'Keeffe to carry out intelligence work for him. She was in charge of a number of girls who would collect information regarding the movement of the military but more importantly the home addresses of suspected spies or informers. The young women would report back to her and in turn O'Keeffe would report their findings to Captain Margaret 'Loo' Kennedy who would forward the information to Donnelly. Throughout all this time her home in South Brown Street was an arms dump and safe house regularly used by members of both the 3rd and 4th Battalion IRA.[103] Although she was still working as a silk weaver, she had to be always on hand to take the weapons away to safety after an ambush had taken place while also being prepared to treat any wounded men. At a moment's notice she would have to leave her place of work to carry out her orders. It seems her employers were understanding. She managed to evade capture until April 1921. While attending a football match in Crumlin she was arrested by the Auxiliaries who had seen her alerting members of the IRA that the Auxiliaries were coming to the ground. Her quick thinking ensured that the Volunteers got away but O'Keeffe did not know what her fate might be. She was taken as a hostage by the Auxiliaries who drove her around the city for hours in a caged lorry, after which time she was brought to the North Dublin Union (NDU). She was released later that evening.

In October 1921, during the Truce, O'Keeffe was appointed to the rank of 1st Lieutenant in the Inghinidhe branch.[104] When the Anglo-Irish Treaty was signed in December 1921, like most of her comrades, she could not accept the agreement. Cumann na mBan was the first of the republican bodies to hold a convention to discuss the issue of accepting or rejecting the Treaty. She was one of the delegates appointed to attend the Convention which was held in the Mansion House in February 1922. Cumann na mBan voted overwhelmingly to reject the Treaty. There were of course many members who voted to accept the Treaty and like other organisations, Cumann na mBan split into pro-Treaty and anti-Treaty factions. In the months preceding the Civil War, rallies were held all over the country by those for and against the Treaty. At one such pro-Treaty rally at College Green in March 1922 O'Keeffe, together with Brigid O'Mullane and a number of other women, jumped up on the platform and managed to remove the Tricolour before getting away through the crowds with their trophy.

In May she was responsible for bringing arms and bombs to the anti-Treaty IRA who had taken over the Ballast Office, Westmoreland Street. This building was evacuated before the Civil War began. When Civil War finally did break out on 28 June 1922 O'Keeffe and her sister Emily were already serving with the anti-Treaty IRA in Norton's Distillery in Newmarket. O'Keeffe was appointed O/C in charge of the women there.[105] The building was evacuated on the evening of 30 June after which she made her way to Tara Hall in Gloucester Street, one of the Headquarters of the anti-Treaty forces, and while there helped build a barricade to prevent the pro-Treaty forces gaining entry. Sadly during the Civil War it was the responsibility of Cumann na mBan to bury their fallen comrades. O'Keeffe was one of those ordered to act as Guard of Honour at the funeral of Cathal Brugha on 10 July, 1922.

O'Keeffe continued to assist the 3rd Battalion anti-Treaty IRA, her home was still being used as an arms dump, despite the fact that those on the pro-Treaty side knew of its existence. She would also bring guns to be used in the gun salute at republican funerals. In September 1922 she was appointed to the rank of Captain of the Inghinidhe branch in place of Loo Kennedy. The Civil War was by this time intensifying, with the anti-Treaty forces reverting to the guerrilla tactics that had served the IRA so well against the British during the War of Independence. They attacked bridges, transport networks and military barracks all over the country. One such attack took place in late 1922 on Wellington (Griffith) Barracks, South Circular Road. O'Keeffe supplied the weapons for the ambush and in the aftermath of the attack, Volunteer James Spain, anti-Treaty, who lived only a short distance from the barracks, was killed by members of the pro-Treaty forces. O'Keeffe was in charge of the funeral arrangements.

On 6 February 1923, O'Keeffe's home in South Brown Street was raided by the National Army. Despite the efforts of the raiding party, nothing was found that might incriminate either Josephine or her sister Emily. There were plenty of arms and ammunition in the house, but the sisters had hidden them so well they were not discovered. O'Keeffe was imprisoned in Mountjoy Gaol and released after six or seven weeks. After her release she did not play any further active part in the republican movement. She later married John McNamara who had been a member of the South Galway Brigade and later, North Clare Brigade IRA. She and John set up home in Galway and had four sons and one daughter. Josephine McNamara died in 1966, shortly after she had attended the ceremony to rename Galway railway station in honour of Éamonn Ceannt.[106] She was seventy-one years old.

Emily O'Keeffe/O'Keefe (*later Hendley*)
BORN: Dublin, 1899
ORGANISATION: Cumann na mBan (Inghinidhe branch)
POSITION DURING EASTER RISING: Marrowbone Lane Distillery

Emily O'Keeffe was born in 1899 in Dublin and was the younger sister of Josephine O'Keeffe. The two sisters shared an interest in Irish culture and heritage. They were fluent Irish speakers, members of the Gaelic League and won medals for Irish dancing. They joined the Inghinidhe branch, Cumann na mBan in 1915 and served together during the Easter Rising with the Volunteers of the 4th Battalion, Dublin Brigade in Marrowbone Lane Distillery. The sisters had been mobilised by fellow Inghinidhe branch member Rose Mullally on Easter Monday morning. While in the Distillery, O'Keeffe cooked for the garrison and on the surrender of the garrison on Sunday 30 April, Emily was arrested with her sister and taken to Richmond Barracks and later Kilmainham Gaol.[107] She was released with her comrades from the Inghinidhe branch on the evening of 8 May.

On their release from Kilmainham the sisters rejoined the Inghinidhe branch and took part in all activities required in rebuilding the organisation in the aftermath of the Rising. Emily O'Keeffe took part in all parades and public displays including the funeral of Thomas Ashe in September 1917, the anti-conscription demonstrations, Lá na mBan on 9 June 1918 in City Hall and was also present at the protest meeting in Foster Place where the women were batoned by the police.[108] She was appointed Squad Leader and later towards the end of the War of Independence, she was appointed Section Commander. Almost from the beginning of the War of Independence, her family home in South Brown Street was used as an arms dump by 'C' Company, 3rd Battalion, Dublin Brigade IRA. O'Keeffe and her sister Josie held rifles, revolvers and bombs for the Battalion. A regular visitor to their home was Paddy O'Flanagan, Commandant of the 3rd Battalion who, prior to an ambush, would call on them requesting weapons. Although Josie O'Keeffe was in overall charge of the dump, if she was not present it fell to Emily to give out what was needed to the IRA. During the war Emily regularly carried out propaganda work, distributing leaflets and posting republican material. In late 1920 she delivered parcels of food to Volunteers who were being held prisoner in Beggar's Bush Barracks.[109] Every day for over a week she went to the barracks with food for the men.

O'Keeffe and her sister Josie both took the anti-Treaty side during the Irish

Civil War. They continued to provide their home as an arms dump for the republicans and in May 1922, she brought revolvers and ammunition from her home to the anti-Treaty garrison in the Ballast Office which was located on the corner of Westmoreland Street and Aston Quay. When the Civil War began on 28 June 1922 the sisters served with the anti-Treaty garrison, under the command of Albert Rutherford, 3rd Battalion, Dublin Brigade, in Norton's Malt House in Newmarket, a short distance from their home on South Brown Street. While there, O'Keeffe cooked for the men and was ordered by Rutherford to go to a house on nearby South Circular Road and remove weapons being held there, which she successfully did. The sisters remained in Norton's until 2 July when the garrison decided to leave the building and take up positions elsewhere in the city where the fighting was intensifying. After the main battle for Dublin city ended on 5 July the anti-Treaty IRA resorted to the guerrilla tactics that had served them so well during the War of Independence. Roads, railways and bridges were targeted in order to hamper the movement of the pro-Treaty forces. In August 1922 a number of bridges around the city were to be blown up by the anti-Treaty IRA. This action became known as 'The Night of the Bridges' and O'Keeffe participated in this event, bringing weapons to the men who were involved.[110]

Although their family home was well known to the pro-Treaty forces as an arms dump, it was not raided by them until 6 February 1923. Josie was arrested in this raid but Emily evaded capture. Despite the fact that there were weapons in the house the raiding party failed to locate them. Once O'Keeffe was certain that the soldiers had left she successfully removed the weapons to another location. With her sister now in prison Emily continued to assist the anti-Treaty forces as before, supplying and removing weapons for them as needed. Sadly one task O'Keeffe was required to do more frequently as the Civil War escalated was to supply arms to Albert Rutherford to be used in the gun salute at the funerals of anti-Treaty IRA men who died in the conflict. After each funeral she would remove the weapons to safety. She managed to evade capture during the Civil War. Once the conflict ended it seems so too did her involvement in the republican movement. She later married James Hendley and they had a son and a daughter. Emily Hendley died in 1983 aged a eighty-four and is buried in Mount Jerome Cemetery.

Agnes MacNamee/McNamee
BORN: Dublin, 1899
ORGANISATION: Cumann na mBan (Inghinidhe branch)
POSITION DURING EASTER RISING: Marrowbone Lane Distillery

Agnes McNamee was born in Dublin in 1899 to James and Agnes McNamee. In the 1911 census the family was living in Emerald Square in the south inner city. James McNamee was a teacher, originally from Westmeath. MacNamee joined Cumann na mBan in 1915, serving with the Inghinidhe branch. James Kevin McNamee, Agnes' brother, was also involved in the Rising as a member of Na Fianna and fought with the garrison in Marrowbone Lane during the Rising.[111] He was active as a member of the IRA during the War of Independence. He used his position as an employee with the Irish Agricultural Wholesale Society to assist Liam Mellows, IRA Director of Purchases, with the purchasing and provision of munitions and war materials to the IRA.

McNamee is mentioned in the Organisation Rolls for Cumann na mBan and the witness statement of Rose McNamara states that she was a member of the Inghinidhe branch, stationed at Marrowbone Lane Distillery during the Rising. There is one further mention of Agnes in the witness statement of Annie and Lily Cooney. In that statement Annie recalled that she shared a cell with Agnes when they were brought to Kilmainham Gaol on 1 May 1916. Annie Cooney said that the 'were put three in a cell, the majority on the ground floor. They were dreadful, filthy places, not having been used for years before that. We got two paillasses – which the soldiers called biscuits – between every three prisoners. Miss Lou Kennedy and Agnes McNamee – since dead – were with me. We took turns at night on the paillasses, not sleeping very much, of course'.[112] After the Rising, McNamee worked as a shop assistant and stayed involved in Cumann na mBan.[113] She was arrested in May 1919 for refusing to pay a fine 'inflicted on her for the crime of collecting money for the Irish Language Fund' without a permit from the British Government.[114] Her fine was double that of others because her name appeared in Irish on the charge sheet. She served seven days in Mountjoy Gaol for refusal to pay the fine. She got ill in prison and was continuously under doctor's care after that. She, her commanding officer Rose McNamara wrote, enjoyed good health until her prison experience in 1919, and despite bad health continued with her Cumann na mBan activism until her death. Agnes McNamee died in 1922, aged 22. Her mother, Agnes, applied for a Dependents' Allowance based on her daughter's service, which had adversely affected her health. The allowance was refused as it was decided 'death due to disease not attributable to service'.[115]

Maria Quigley (*later Clince*)
BORN: Dublin, 1897
ORGANISATION: Cumann na mBan (Inghinidhe branch)
POSITION DURING EASTER RISING: Marrowbone Lane Distillery

Maria Quigley was born in Dublin in 1897. In the 1901 census, Quigley and her family, including her younger sister Priscilla, were living in 35 Darley's Buildings, Merchant's Quay. Her father Patrick, a labourer, was from Co. Carlow and her mother Priscilla was from Dublin. At the time of the Rising the family had moved to 15 Wolseley Street, South Circular Road. Quigley and her sister Priscilla both joined the Inghinidhe branch, Cumann na mBan in 1915. Three weeks prior to the Rising, Cumann na mBan spent their time preparing field dressings and other first aid equipment for the Volunteers. The sisters mobilised on Easter Monday morning and made their way to Marrowbone Lane Distillery where they served for the entire week. Both were taken to Richmond Barracks after the surrender and then transferred to Kilmainham Gaol with their comrades on 1 May and held there until their release on 8 May.[116]

After her release Quigley rejoined the Inghinidhe branch and helped in the reorganisation of the movement, carrying out work for the Irish National Aid and Volunteers Dependents' Fund. She was promoted to Section Commander of Inghinidhe, a post which she held until 1918. It was at this time, 1917, that she was chosen to work for Simon Donnelly, Captain of 'C' Company, 3rd Battalion, Dublin Brigade. Éamon de Valera, Commandant of the 3rd Battalion during Easter Week, was still in prison in Lewes Gaol, England. While there he wrote dispatches and memos on tiny pieces of paper and managed to have them smuggled out of the prison and sent to Donnelly who in turn gave these documents to Quigley to transcribe for use as propaganda against the British authorities.

Quigley was present at Lá na mBan, the anti-conscription parade on the 9 June 1918 and was also present at the protest meeting in Foster Place where the police baton charged the women, mostly members of Cumann na mBan who were protesting at the treatment of prisoners in Holloway Gaol. In 1918 she was promoted to the rank of adjutant of the Inghinidhe branch and with this promotion her responsibilities within the branch increased.[117] As adjutant, she was responsible for giving lectures in first aid to other branches and once a week for two months she gave lectures to the Dundrum branch. During the 1918 general election she was on duty at the polling station in Glencullen, Co. Dublin.

Maria Quigley resigned from Cumann na mBan in March 1920, after which she married James Clince and moved to Gorey, Co. Wexford. She did not take part in the Civil War. Maria Clince died in 1969, aged seventy-two, and is buried in St. Michael's Cemetery, Gorey.

Priscilla 'Sheila' Quigley (*later Kavanagh*)
BORN: Dublin, 1899
ORGANISATION: Cumann na mBan (Inghinidhe branch)
POSITION DURING EASTER RISING: Marrowbone Lane Distillery

Priscilla Quigley was born in Dublin in 1899 and was the younger sister of Maria Quigley. The two sisters joined the Inghinidhe branch, Cumann na mBan in 1915 and on Easter Monday both mobilised with their comrades from the Inghinidhe branch and served with the garrison in Marrowbone Lane Distillery where Priscilla treated wounded Volunteers and cooked for the garrison. Quigley was arrested after the surrender and was taken to Richmond Barracks and later to Kilmainham Gaol. According to their pension applications, while in Kilmainham both sisters refused to sign a form pledging to refrain from future involvement in similar organisations.[118] Their refusal delayed their release which according to the sisters happened on the 11 May rather than 8 May when the majority of the Inghinidhe branch were released.

After her release from prison Quigley rejoined the Inghinidhe branch and took part in its reorganisation and was promoted to Squad Leader soon after rejoining.[119] She took part in many of the events associated with the reorganisation including collecting and distributing funds for the Prisoners' Dependents' Fund, the funeral of Thomas Ashe in 1917 and the anti-conscription campaign. The night prior to the general election of 1918 she arranged for a first aid station to be set up in Ticknock and on the day of the election she was on duty at the first aid post in Donnybrook.[120] She continued her first aid training and, on passing the exam with honours, was selected by the Cumann na mBan executive to attend the Mater Hospital for special training. Every day for two months she went to the accident ward and witnessed severe injuries and how to treat them. This training would come in very useful over the next few years when she had to be on hand to treat Volunteers wounded in battle. As a result of her training Quigley then gave lectures in first aid to the Central branch, Cumann na mBan.

Quigley was promoted to Section Commander of the Inghinidhe branch and in October 1920 she was again promoted, this time to the rank of 1st Lieutenant.[121] With her promotion her responsibilities increased. By now the War of Independence was escalating. She was responsible for distributing republican propaganda material. Leaflets and dispatches were brought to her home in Wolseley Street every Saturday night and she oversaw their distribution. Throughout this time her home was used as an arms dump, dispatch centre and a safe house for IRA men on the run. In April 1921 Quigley was sent around the country to give lectures and special training in first aid, Morse code, signalling and organisation. This work took her to Longford, Newtowncashel, Clough and Rathclyne and she even gave the Newtowncashel IRA Flying Column instructions in field dressing.

On her return to Dublin she resumed her duties, giving first aid lectures every Friday to the Inghinidhe branch. Together with May Byrne, she supervised the first aid station in South Frederick Street, ensuring that girls were available to treat men from the 3rd Battalion who might be wounded in an ambush. Throughout the War of Independence she regularly treated wounded Volunteers at her home. On one occasion she treated Volunteer John Burke, 4th Battalion Dublin Brigade, keeping him in her home for six weeks, and she was quite confident in her ability to treat severe cases. For example, in July 1921 Volunteer Jack McCabe was brought to her having been shot in the thigh.[122] The doctor present wished to amputate his leg. As soon as this was reported to Quigley she immediately removed McCabe by cab to St. Vincent's Hospital, and arranged for another doctor to treat him. In doing so she saved McCabe's leg and he made a full recovery. Due to differences with the Inghinidhe branch, Quigley resigned from the organisation in October 1921.[123] Despite her resignation, her home was still available to the 3rd and 4th Battalion IRA as a safe house and arms dump.

On the outbreak of the Civil War on 28 June 1922 Quigley rejoined her comrades in Cumann na mBan and presented herself for duty. She first served in Tara Hall, Gloucester Street and later the Minerva Hotel where she treated wounded anti-Treaty IRA men.[124] Between this time and 3 July she also carried messages between the anti-Treaty outposts in Tara Hall and the Hammam Hotel on O'Connell Street.

Quigley was not arrested after the fighting in Dublin ended and continued to support the republicans. On 22 December 1922 she, through her quick-thinking, was responsible for saving many of the members of the 3rd Battalion from capture. The pro-Treaty forces carried out a raid on Fitzpatrick's on Wexford Street during which they found lists containing the names and addresses of the staff officers of the 3rd Battalion. Quigley went to all the houses of the men to let them know it was not safe to be there while also removing any weapons or other material from their premises. She carried out her work successfully and even housed two of the men, Captain Paddy White and Paddy Dunne. Quigley evaded arrest during the Civil War and did not take part in any further republican activities. She married Liam Kavanagh and died in 1973 and is buried in Mount Jerome Cemetery. She was seventy-four years old.

Katie Byrne
Member of the Inghinidhe branch of Cumann na mBan, imprisoned in Richmond Barracks and Kilmainham Gaol. There is no record of Katie Byrne after 1916.[125]

Bridy Kenny
Member of the Inghinidhe branch of Cumann na mBan, imprisoned in Richmond Barracks and Kilmainham Gaol. There is no record of Bridy Kenny after 1916.[126]

Kathleen 'Katie' Maher
Although not a member of the Inghinidhe branch in 1916, Kathleen Maher is on the organisation rolls from April 1920 – March 1921.[127]

Josephine (Spicer) Spencer
No information other than Rose McNamara's witness statement recording Josephine Spicer as a member of the Inghinidhe branch who served in Marrowbone Lane Distillery during the Easter Rising.[128]

ST. STEPHEN'S GREEN/ROYAL COLLEGE
OF SURGEONS

Madeleine ffrench-Mullen
BORN: Malta, 1880
ORGANISATION: Irish Citizen Army
POSITION DURING EASTER RISING: St. Stephen's Green/Royal
College of Surgeons

Madeleine ffrench-Mullen was born in 1880 in Malta, the eldest child of St. Laurence ffrench-Mullen, a Royal Navy surgeon. While still a child she moved, with her family, back to Ireland and lived in Dundrum, Co. Dublin. Like her brother, Douglas ffrench-Mullen, she became active in nationalist politics and the Gaelic revival movement and she joined Maud Gonne's Inghinidhe na hÉireann in the early 1900s. In her diaries Rosamond Jacob described ffrench-Mullen as 'a very pleasant bright girl'.[129] She was one of the original contributors to *Bean na hÉireann*, the journal of Inghinidhe na hÉireann, editing the children's column. For the majority of the period 1900–1911, she lived in Brussels and Leipzig but on her return to Dublin in 1911 she resumed her political activities.

In July 1911 the newly crowned king, George V, and his wife Mary visited Ireland. As a tribute to them the authorities sought to collect signatures of welcome of as many 'Irish Marys' as possible. Inghinidhe na hÉireann gathered a counter set of signatures denouncing the monarchy and colonisation and ffrench-Mullen became involved in this 'anti-welcome campaign'. During the 1913 Lockout, she served in the Liberty Hall soup kitchen, where she met her lifelong partner Dr. Kathleen Lynn. She joined the Irish Citizen Army at its formation in 1913.

ffrench-Mullen served with the Citizen Army at St. Stephen's Green Park and the Royal College of Surgeons during the Rising. She was in charge of the first aid station set up in the park and assisted with food provisions.[130] She also commandeered vehicles for the battalion and removed civilians from the area. A member of the Irish Citizen Army garrison at the Royal College of Surgeons, Frank Robbins, said that ffrench-Mullen, who was appointed 'doctor' to the garrison once they moved to the College of Surgeons, did her job 'very efficiently'.[131] She tended to the wounded in the College, including Margaret Skinnider, who suffered three bullet wounds. At the surrender she was arrested, interned in Richmond Barracks, Kilmainham Gaol and finally Mountjoy Gaol.

After her release in June 1916, ffrench-Mullen worked with Belgian refugees from the war in Europe.[132] She was also involved in the Connolly Cooperative society which provided work for those who had fought in the Easter Rising and had become unemployed because of their activities in 1916. In Liberty Hall she was involved in setting up a small shirt factory to provide work for the young Citizen Army women who had no work. She also became involved in republican propaganda and at Easter 1917 she drove to various places in Dublin to publically read the Proclamation with Citizen Army member, Maeve Cavanagh. She was active during the War of Independence and was arrested on a charge of 'keeping a military patrol under surveillance' and was briefly interned in Dublin's Bridewell prison. In 1918 she campaigned with Dr. Lynn and others for better treatment for three women imprisoned in Holloway Prison (Countess Markievicz, Kathleen Clarke and Maud Gonne McBride).

In 1919 she and Lynn established St. Ultan's Hospital for Sick Infants, the first hospital for infants in Ireland.[133] The women were appalled by the high rates of infant mortality in Dublin which had increased during an outbreak of flu and tuberculosis that year. They established the hospital at 37 Charlemont Street, beginning with two cots, about £70 and two infant patients. It was a highly successful venture, aided by their ceaseless fundraising and by support from their wide range of friends and supporters. ffrench-Mullen was secretary of the hospital until her death. She lived with Lynn at 9 Belgrave Road, and she remained active in politics and social causes for the rest of her life. In 1920 she was elected to Rathmines District Council for Harold's Cross. At the Sinn Féin Ard Fheis in October 1926, she argued for social and economic improvements, calling for Sinn Féin to support the provision of school meals, house-building programmes and educational improvements. In 1935, she was one of the founders of the Joint Committee of Women's Societies and Social Workers. This was an umbrella organisation for women's groups who worked together on issues concerning women and children. Among its demands were to have women police, women jurors, legal adoption and better conditions for women in prison and in children's institutions. ffrench-Mullen was also very involved in campaigning for social housing for Dubliners who were still living in dreadful conditions in tenements all over the city.

Madeleine ffrench-Mullen died in 1944 and is buried in Glasnevin Cemetery.[134] The coffin, draped with the Tricolour, was escorted by Irish Citizen Army veterans who were her comrades in 1916. William Oman, a comrade from the Citizen Army, gave the graveside oration. On her the headstone is inscribed 'Also their gifted elder daughter MADELEINE FFRENCH-MULLEN, F.C.C.S. – Whose indomitable courage and ability – Carried Teac Ultain (Infant Hospital) successfully through – Its first 23 years 1919 to 1944'. According to her partner, Kathleen Lynn, she 'hated exploitation, want and greed. From her childhood she tried to play her part in every movement for the social welfare and betterment of people'.[135] The Michael Scott-designed ffrench-Mullen House on Charlemont Street, Dublin was built in 1944 to provide social housing in the city and was named in her honour.

Mary 'May' Gahan (*later O'Carroll*)
BORN: Dublin, 1898
ORGANISATION: Cumann na mBan
POSITION DURING EASTER RISING: St. Stephen's Green/
Royal College of Surgeons, GPO and Imperial Hotel

Mary 'May' Gahan was born in Dublin in 1898, the daughter of Robert Gahan and Mary Murray. In 1911 the family, May, her five siblings, including Joseph and Mathew 'Mattie', who would also take part in the Easter Rising, and her parents were living in a one-roomed home in a house shared with four other families. Robert Gahan was a general labourer, his son Joseph was a factory book boy, while the rest of the children were still at school. In 1912 May's brothers, Joe and Mattie, joined the Irish National Guard which was a youth organisation for the sons and daughters of the working class. Later it became an adjunct of the Irish Citizen Army. Their motto was 'The Guard Dies but Never Surrenders'. There was a female section of the Guard which May joined.

By her early teens she had joined Inghinidhe na hÉireann and as a member of this organisation she was involved in cultural productions and participated in several Abbey Theatre plays. By 1914 she was a member of the Inghinidhe branch of Cumann na mBan.[136] During Easter Week, Gahan was attached to the Stephen's Green/Royal College of Surgeons garrison. She served as a courier during the week, ultimately ending up in the GPO. James Connolly sent her to report to Frank Thornton who was stationed at the Imperial Hotel, Sackville Street. Her brothers Mattie and Joe both served with the Irish Volunteers in the GPO and North King Street area. After the Rising she was arrested in Marlborough Street and taken to Richmond Barracks and then to Kilmainham Gaol; she remembered being pelted by 'bottles and horse dung as she walked to Kilmainham'.[137] She was released from Kilmainham on 8 May.

Gahan was active during the War of Independence. She stated in her pension application that she collected for the INAAVDF and was involved in gun running. She was also involved in the anti-conscription campaigns and as a result of her involvement in these activities she was arrested and imprisoned for two months. In May 1917 she married John O'Carroll, a member of the Irish Volunteers. Together they opened a Milk Bar on Gregg Lane (now Cathal Brugha Street). As John Kenny, Quartermaster of the 1st Battalion, Dublin Brigade said in his witness statement, 'The place (the Milk Bar) was a rendezvous for republicans, not to mention the gun smugglers. The place was afterwards razed to the ground by the Black and Tans. The O'Carrolls, who barricaded the place and fought back, were injured, but escaped'.[138] Also called the Republican Bar it was a centre for republican activity, although ironically, it was also frequented by British soldiers. Ordered by Peadar Clancy, vice O/C of the Dublin Brigade IRA, to get arms and ammunition, O'Carroll purchased guns from the soldiers who frequented the bar, even acquiring a machine gun from a soldier stationed at Ship Street Barracks. The gun was lowered over the wall of the Barracks and taken away in a pram by Gahan. She was, like so many Cumann na mBan women, opposed to the Anglo-Irish Treaty. During the Civil War she worked with the anti-Treaty IRA and was arrested in May 1923 and imprisoned in Kilmainham Gaol and the North Dublin Union.[139] She went on hunger strike several times while imprisoned and was finally released in November 1923. She and her husband John and their two children left Ireland in 1924. After a time in England, South Africa and New Zealand, they finally settled in Australia in 1929, where she had eight more children. She died in Sydney in 1988.

Helen 'Nellie' Gifford (*later Donnelly*)
BORN: Dublin, 1880
ORGANISATION: Irish Citizen Army
POSITION DURING EASTER RISING: St. Stephen's Green/Royal College of Surgeons

Helen Ruth 'Nellie' Gifford was born in 1880 at 26 Cabra Parade, Phibsborough, Dublin, the fifth of twelve children of Frederick Gifford, a solicitor and his wife, Isabella Burton.[140] While her brothers were never politically active, her five sisters were all active in nationalist politics, most prominently Grace (who married Joseph Plunkett in Kilmainham Gaol the night before his execution) and Sydney, a journalist and broadcaster who used the pen name 'John Brennan'. As a young woman Nellie Gifford trained as a domestic economy instructor and worked for several years in rural areas of Co. Meath. Frequently staying in labourers' cottages, she became conscious of the desperate living conditions of the landless rural poor, and was an enthusiastic supporter of the cattle-driving campaign of the radical land agitator and nationalist MP Laurence Ginnell. Educating her sisters on the land issue, she in turn was influenced by their emerging nationalism and feminism. Her sisters Sydney and Muriel were members of Inghinidhe na hÉireann and the suffrage organisation, the Irish Women's Franchise League, while the eldest of the sisters, Katherine, was active in Cumann na mBan after the Rising.[141]

On returning home to Dublin around 1910, Gifford became involved in the Irish Women's Franchise League. She was also a supporter of the trade union movement and was active during the 1913 Lockout. On 31 August 1913, she accompanied James Larkin when, disguised as an elderly clergyman, he checked into the Imperial Hotel on Sackville Street and addressed a crowd of striking workers from a balcony, an address which precipitated the 'Bloody Sunday' police baton charge. She joined the Irish Citizen Army soon after its inception and she used her domestic training to give lessons on camp cookery in Liberty Hall. Prior to the Easter Rising she ran an employment bureau for the members of the Irish Volunteers and the Citizen Army. This was part of a drive against 'economic conscription' in Ireland – the plan was to provide work for members of the Irish Volunteers and Citizen Army so they would not feel the need to join up for the steady wage offered by the armed forces. The Bureau also helped find work for Volunteers who had come from England to avoid conscription.[142]

During the Rising Gifford served with the Irish Citizen Army at St. Stephen's Green and the Royal College of Surgeons, where she supervised the garrison's food stores and the 'kitchen', overseeing the cooking and delivery of rations to her comrades in the college and outlying posts. Contending with a serious shortage of food during the week, she organised for food to be commandeered from local shops and bread vans and couriered from other garrisons. Obviously her training served her well, as despite food shortages at the College of Surgeons, Countess Markievicz later wrote that Gifford 'produced a quantity of oatmeal from somewhere and made pot after pot of the most delicious porridge which kept us going'.[143] Gifford also helped with ammunition supplies. She and other women made the trips to the outpost at Jacob's Biscuit Factory to get extra supplies. As the fighting was drawing to a close Gifford chose not to escape but to remain to the end. She later explained why, writing that 'the Republic promised us equality without sex distinctions, so we were all adjudged soldiers, women and men, whether we worked as dispatch carriers or Red Cross units'.[144] Arrested at the surrender, she was held prisoner in Richmond Barracks and Kilmainham Gaol.

She was one of twelve women detained after the release of most of the other women prisoners from Kilmainham on 8 May. She was transferred to Mountjoy Gaol and released on 4 June. Her sisters, Grace and Muriel, were married to two of the signatories of the Proclamation, Joseph Plunkett and Thomas MacDonagh respectively, both of whom were executed. On her release, Gifford went to England and then to the USA. By early 1917 she was touring the country with several other women veterans of 1916, lecturing and raising awareness of the Rising throughout America. In 1918 in America she married Joseph Donnelly from Omagh, Co. Tyrone. The marriage did not last and she and her husband separated. In 1921 she returned to Ireland with their year-old daughter Maeve.

Gifford later worked as a broadcaster and journalist, broadcasting children's stories on Radio 2RN (later Radio Éireann) and wrote pieces for the *Irish Press* and other newspapers. She was devoted to preserving the historical record of the independence movement and she organised a small exhibition of 1916 memorabilia in 1932, afterwards campaigning for a permanent exhibition of Irish nationalist history. As secretary of the 1916 research committee, she collected a substantial body of material about nationalist organisations, the Easter Rising and the War of Independence. This collection formed the basis of the present National Museum of Ireland collection of 1916 artefacts at Collins Barracks. She was a secretary of the Old IRA Association, an early member of the Old Dublin Society (mid-1930s) and a founding member of the Kilmainham Gaol Restoration Society (c.1960).[145] She died on 23 June 1971 at the Gascoigne Nursing Home in Dublin aged ninety-one.

Bridget 'Brigid'/'Bridie' Goff

BORN: Dublin, 1889
ORGANISATION: Irish Citizen Army
POSITION DURING EASTER RISING: St. Stephen's Green/Royal College
of Surgeons

Bridget Goff was born in Dublin on 26 February 1889, one of eight children born to John Goff and Elizabeth Murphy between 1876 and 1896. John Goff was originally from Elphin in Roscommon and married Elizabeth Murphy in Dublin in 1874. In the 1901 census John Goff was recorded as an insurance clerk, living on Lisburn Street, Dublin. In 1911, Bridget was living with her mother Elizabeth (a widow), her sister Kate (a factory girl) and her brother John (a van driver) in a two-roomed flat at 13 Henrietta Street, Dublin 1. Her mother had given birth to 11 children in all, but only four were still living in 1911. In 1911, Bridget had a job 'serving wine' and later she worked for Countess Markievicz at her home in Surrey House, Rathmines.

She was involved in the soup kitchen in Liberty Hall during the 1913 Lockout and she joined the Irish Citizen Army in 1914. On the Sunday before the Easter Rising, Palm Sunday, Goff participated in a route march but, rather than stay with her comrades in Liberty Hall that night, she chose to stay at Surrey House.[146] She returned to Liberty Hall on Monday morning with Nora Connolly, where she began getting the rations together for the Irish Citizen Army. With the others she marched to St. Stephen's Green. By Tuesday, the garrison had evacuated the park for the safety of the Royal College of Surgeons and Goff remained in the College until the surrender. In St. Stephen's Green she worked at the first aid station which was located in the summer house and is said to have entertained all the women with jokes to keep their minds off their situation. After the surrender she was arrested and was led away to Richmond Barracks and then Kilmainham Gaol. She was released on 8 May 1916. Eva Gore-Booth, sister of Countess Markievicz (Goff's employer), made sure that she was given a month's wages to tide her over. After her release she volunteered to work on collecting funds for the INAAVDF. She was also active during the War of Independence. She did not marry and worked as a domestic worker until her health gave out. She then lived with her sister, Catherine (Kate) O'Keeffe. Bridget Goff died in 1952 and is buried in Mount Jerome Cemetery. She was sixty-three years old.

Roseanna 'Rosie' Hackett
BORN: Dublin, 1893
ORGANISATION: Irish Citizen Army (later Cumann na mBan)
POSITION DURING EASTER RISING: St. Stephen's Green/Royal
College of Surgeons

Roseanna 'Rosie' Hackett was born in Dublin in 1893 to John Hackett and his wife Roseanna Dunne. Soon after the birth of their second daughter Christina (1894), John Hackett died, which left the young widow in precarious circumstances. By 1901 the family was living in a two-roomed tenement in Bolton Street with Mrs. Hackett's siblings John, James and Catherine Dunne and a lodger. In 1906 Roseanna Hackett was re-married to Patrick Gray and by 1911 the Gray family was living in a four-roomed house at Old Abbey Street. Rosie Hackett was then seventeen years old and working as a packer in Jacob's Biscuit Factory, where she was involved in trade union activities, joining the ITGWU and later the IWWU.

In 1913 Hackett was one of the many Jacob's workers who came out on strike during the Lockout. She herself wrote that as a result of the 'big strike' she became attached to Liberty Hall, and she was to remain attached for the rest of her life.[147] When the strike ended she was not given her job back as she was considered a 'disruptive element'. She joined the women's section of the Irish Citizen Army as soon as it was formed in 1913, and worked with Helena Molony in the cooperative workroom and shop in Liberty Hall. She was in the shop when it was raided by the Dublin Metropolitan Police on 21 March 1916, following the publication of the *Gael* newspaper's inflammatory St. Patrick's Day issue. Hackett stood her ground as the police tried to gain entry to the premises. Not only were there copies of the *Gael* in the building but more importantly, rifles and ammunition were stored there also. 'The little girl in charge', as the *Workers' Republic* called her when reporting on the incident, kept the police at bay until James Connolly, who had been summoned, came down brandishing a gun and told the police to 'drop those papers or I'll drop you'.[148] After that incident a permanent guard was kept on Liberty Hall until the Rising.

In the weeks before the Rising, Hackett attended first aid classes organised in Liberty Hall by Dr. Kathleen Lynn. She went on Citizen Army route marches and worked in the small shop in Liberty Hall. She was on the final route march on Sunday 23 April and was ordered that evening to remain with the other Citizen Army members in Liberty Hall until further notice. She knew something big was coming 'as some time before the Rising, Connolly told us we would have to buck up and get ready, that the day was coming.'[149] On Easter Sunday, she was kept busy running back and forth between Connolly and the print room in Liberty Hall, with papers containing drafts of the Proclamation. Later that night she delivered 2,500 copies of the final printed Proclamation to Helena Molony in the co-op shop.

The next morning, Easter Monday, Hackett was informed by Dr. Lynn that she would be with Madeleine ffrench-Mullen. She recalled, 'Wherever Miss French [sic] Mullen would go, I was to be next to her. The white coat, which I got, was down to my heels, and I had to shorten it. I remember Plunkett and some other men were laughing at the coat touching the ground'.[150] At roughly 11.50 a.m., Commandant Michael Mallin, ffrench-Mullen, Hackett and the rest of this Citizen Army contingent left Liberty Hall and set off to St. Stephen's Green. When they reached the park, they cleared out the civilians, locked the gates and dug trenches, while Hackett helped ffrench-Mullen and several other women (including Nora O'Daly, May Moore, Bridget Murtagh and Bridget Goff) set up the first aid station at a small lodge, the summer house, located at the south-west corner of the Green. On Tuesday the insurgents abandoned the militarily insecure Green and took up position in the Royal College of Surgeons where they remained until the surrender. Hackett was among those who made it to the College and resumed her first aid duties with ffrench-Mullen. The College came under a sustained barrage of gunfire from the British military who had taken over the Shelbourne Hotel and other prominent buildings in the area.

Hackett came close to death at least once. She remembered that on one occasion she 'was lying down on one of the beds... The men were trying out some rifles they had found in the College. The people upstairs sent for me to go for a cup of tea... I had only left the bed, when a man, named Murray, casually threw himself down on it and, whatever way it happened, this bullet hit him in the face. We attended him there for the whole week. He was then brought to Vincent's Hospital where he died after a week. They remarked that had I not got up when told to go for the tea, I would have got it through the brain, judging by the way the bullet hit this man'.[151] When the order to surrender came on Sunday 30 April, Hackett noted the deep despair that was felt by the insurgents. She saw Markievicz 'sitting on the stairs, with her head in her hands' and while Mallin shook hands with all of the contingent there, he looked 'terribly pale [and] his face was drawn and haggard'.[152] Hackett was arrested along with the others, taken first to Dublin Castle, then on to Richmond Barracks, before being imprisoned in Kilmainham Goal. As they were marched away from the College, Irish Citizen Army captain, William Partridge, reportedly ordered Hackett and the other women around her to proudly hold their 'heads erect' as they were marched past a hostile crowd that had gathered outside. She was released on 8 May with most of the other female detainees.

After her release Hackett resumed her activities as a member of the Citizen Army and worked from Liberty Hall, once the building, which had been ruined by bombardment during the Rising, was restored. On the first anniversary of the Rising in 1917 she was among the women who organised the printing and distribution of the Proclamation throughout the city. The women organised themselves into parties and posted the Proclamation in prominent locations all over Dublin city. On 12 May 1917, the first anniversary of Connolly's death, Hackett with Helena Molony, Jinny Shanahan and Bridget Davis hung a banner emblazoned with the words 'James Connolly Murdered 12th May 1916' from the top floor of Liberty Hall. The women barricaded themselves in a room and held off a large police contingent, which had arrived to remove the banner, for several hours. Hackett later claimed it took '400 police' to break down the barricade and get the banner down. She also resumed her trade union work and was elected clerk of the IWWU.

In 1918 when the ITGWU revised its rules and allowed women members into the organisation she became the full-time official, No. 1 branch, of the newly formed women's section of the ITGWU. She remained a member of the Citizen Army until 1918/19 when like many of the other women she joined Cumann na mBan, in her case she joined the Fairview branch. During the War of Independence her room in Liberty Hall was a centre for messages and a safe meeting house for the Dublin battalions of the IRA. She narrowly escaped arrest several times as there were constant raids on Liberty Hall by the police and British military. Unlike so many of her comrades, Hackett took the pro-Treaty side during the Treaty debates and was an ardent supporter of Michael Collins.

Hackett continued to work in Liberty Hall for the rest of her career, running the ITGWU's newspaper and tobacconist shop at 33 Eden Quay. May O'Brien, who worked as a clerk in Liberty Hall, remembered Hackett's warm and engaging personality, describing her as 'a little wispy woman… the image of the little spinster teacher in the cowboy films: small, slight, grey hair in a bun with stray bits falling to her face, wire-rimmed glasses… and a rather prim expression'.[153] O'Brien also witnessed Hackett defending strenuously the sacrifices the women and men of 1916 had made when anyone disparaged them; in particular she described Hackett taking on a 'big brawny man' and challenging him to 'Just say again what you said about 1916. About the men and women of the Irish Citizen Army. Just mention again Connolly, a man who died to let scum like you live, you slimy slithery toad… was the pain and anguish and the blood that was shed, all the sacrifices, was it for nothing after all', she asked him, with tears in her eyes.[154] There were also happier days. In 1970, Hackett was presented with a gold badge by the ITGWU in recognition of her long service. When interviewed after the ceremony Hackett remarked that if only 'Mr. Connolly were living, women would not be in the backward position we are in today'.[155] Roseanna 'Rosie' Hackett died on 4 July 1976 and was buried in Glasnevin Cemetery with full military honours. She was eighty-three years old.

Margaret 'Maggie' Joyce
BORN: Dublin, 1896
ORGANISATION: Irish Citizen Army
POSITION DURING EASTER RISING: St. Stephen's Green/Royal College of Surgeons

Margaret Joyce was a member of the women's section of the Irish Citizen Army. In 1913 she volunteered in the soup kitchen in Liberty Hall with Countess Markievicz and in 1914 she joined the Irish Citizen Army. She trained in first aid in the classes held in Liberty Hall. Immediately prior to the Rising she was involved in making munitions in Liberty Hall. On Easter Sunday she took part in the Citizen Army route march. On Easter Monday she was part of the contingent sent to St. Stephen's Green, where she and the others came under heavy fire. On Tuesday, Joyce and her comrades retreated to the Royal College of Surgeons. During the week her main duties were cooking and first aid. Arrested after the surrender, she was taken to Richmond Barracks, then Kilmainham Gaol. She was released on 9 May.[156] In the post-Rising period she rejoined the Irish Citizen Army and was involved in the reorganisation of the Irish Citizen Army.

Her husband James Joyce, who was also a member of the Citizen Army, participated in the Rising and fought at St. Stephen's Green and Jacob's Biscuit Factory. James Joyce was a barman in Davy's Pub (now the Portobello Pub) prior to the Rising. This pub was occupied by members of the Irish Citizen Army during Easter Week.

After the surrender, James Joyce was arrested and imprisoned in England. He was not released until June 1917. Margaret and James Joyce lived at Dominick Street, Dublin. They had one daughter, Elizabeth. They were both later granted pensions for their participation in the Irish Revolution. Margaret Joyce died in 1943 and is buried in Glasnevin Cemetery. Her coffin was draped in the Tricolour.

Catherine 'Katie' Kelly

BORN: Lehenagh, Cashel, Co. Galway, 1885
ORGANISATION: Cumann na mBan
POSITION DURING EASTER RISING: St. Stephen's Green/Royal College of Surgeons

Katie Kelly was born in 1885 in Lehenagh, Cashel, Co. Galway. Her parents were Joseph D. Kelly and Mary Anne Galvin. In the 1911 census the twenty-three year old Katie was living with her parents, both of whom were national school teachers at Cashel National School, and two of her seven siblings, Ellie and Lizzie. Katie's mother, Mary Anne, was born in America. Her brother Patrick was living in Dublin by 1916, on the North Circular Road. Patrick Kelly was well connected within advanced nationalist circles and was particularly friendly with the Gifford sisters. Kelly had visited her brother many times in Dublin and had met the Giffords and other nationalist activists. She apparently met and was very impressed by Countess Markievicz.

On Easter Monday 1916, while visiting her brother in Dublin, Kelly heard that the Rising had begun. She made her way into the city, looking for the Countess with the intention of offering her services. She found the Countess at St. Stephen's Green and spent the rest of the week with the garrison at St. Stephen's Green and the Royal College of Surgeons. During the week she spent her time carrying dispatches, feeding the men and other duties and was arrested after the surrender. She said that Markievicz tried to intervene on her behalf at Richmond Barracks, and explained that Kelly was only a volunteer and not (yet) a member of Cumann na mBan. However, this did not work and Kelly was taken to Kilmainham Gaol with the rest of the women where she remained until the mass release of the female prisoners on 8/9 May.[157]

In the years following the Rising, Kelly was active with the Clifden branch of Cumann na mBan, and saw service in Cashel, Co. Galway and West Connemara. She worked closely with Alice Cashel. Cashel was a nationalist, a member of the

Gaelic League, Sinn Féin and an early member of Cumann na mBan. Cashel worked as a full time organiser for Cumann na mBan in the north and west of the country. During the War of Independence she was elected a Sinn Féin Councillor for Galway Co. Council and became Vice-Chairman of the Council. She also acted as a judge in the Sinn Féin courts throughout this time. Because of her activities her home in Cashel, Cashel House, was often raided by British forces. She relied on the help of her near neighbours and fellow Cumann na mBan member Katie Kelly for assistance in her republican work.

In 1919, working with Alice Cashel, Kelly set up a branch of the Volunteers in Cashel, Co. Galway. Members of this company of Volunteers often got the orders from HQ in Galway through Cashel and Kelly. Kelly and Cashel also tried to control the poitín traffic in Connemara. They visited fairs and markets and went on patrols seizing and destroying poitín and stills.[158] Kelly continued her service through the war, organising, carrying dispatches and providing a safe house. When Cashel House, where Alice Cashel was staying, was raided, Kelly found her and took her to her own house for safety. After that episode Cashel returned to Dublin. Kelly went to America for some years after the Civil War. On her return she set up a grocery and 'fancy goods' shop in her native Cashel. She lived her final years with her brother Joseph in Newcastle in Galway. Katie Kelly never married and died aged eighty-five in 1971.

Constance Markievicz (*née Gore-Booth*)
BORN: Sligo, 1868
ORGANISATION: Irish Citizen Army (later President of Cumann na mBan)
POSITION DURING EASTER RISING: St. Stephen's Green/Royal College of Surgeons

Constance Georgina Gore-Booth (later Markievicz) was born in 1868 to Sir Henry Gore-Booth of Lissadell, Co. Sligo and his wife Georgina Mary (*née* Hill). Although born in London she grew up at Lissadell with her four siblings. The Gore-Booths were a land-owning family who had been in Sligo since the seventeenth century. Markievicz was particularly close to her sister, Eva. In his poem *In memory of Eva Gore-Booth and Con Markievicz* (October 1927), recalling the sisters, W.B. Yeats wrote, 'Two girls in silk kimonos, both / Beautiful, one a gazelle'. The siblings were educated at home where they were taught the gentle arts of music, poetry and art, and in 1887 they were taken on a grand tour of Europe by their governess. Their lives were destined to be like those of countless aristocratic young women, with presentation at court, a good marriage, and life as a socialite, wife and mother.

While the sisters were debutantes, as expected of girls of their class, neither continued along their expected route in life. Initially Markievicz made her formal debut into society in 1887, when she was presented to Queen Victoria at Buckingham Palace. However, she did not make the expected proper marriage and instead, in 1893 she began her studies at the Slade Art School in London, despite family objections. By 1896 her life as an activist was beginning to take shape and, in that year, she presided over a meeting of the Sligo Women's Suffrage Society.

However, art was still her first love, and 1898 she went to Paris to further her artistic studies. In Paris she met Count Casimir Dunin-Markievicz, a Polish national, whose family held land in the Ukraine. They married in 1900 and had one daughter, Maeve, in 1901. The family returned to Dublin in 1902. Markievicz and her husband soon became involved in the cultural and political circuit in Dublin. She was involved in producing and acting in Abbey plays, in helping to establish the United Arts Club and in exhibiting her art. In 1908 she was introduced to Inghinidhe na hÉireann by Helena Molony and she also joined Sinn Féin. She was also a founder member of Inghinidhe's newspaper, *Bean na hÉireann*, and regularly contributed to its gardening column. In 1909 she played a major role in the formation of Na Fianna Éireann (the Irish Boy Scouts Movement) with Bulmer Hobson. The aim of Na Fianna was to train boys in drill and rifle firing, to aid in the establishment of an independent Ireland and to engage with Irish language and culture. By 1911 she was on the executive of Sinn Féin and was arrested that year whilst protesting against the visit of King George V to Dublin.

After 1911 Markievicz' politics moved to the left and she became more interested in socialism and in the burgeoning trade union movement, where she worked closely with James Connolly. In that year she spoke at the meeting to establish the IWWU.[159] By 1912 she had moved into Surrey House in Rathmines, and her home was to become a hot bed of advanced nationalist and trade union activities. During the 1913 Lockout she organised the soup kitchens in Liberty Hall and joined the Irish Citizen Army at its foundation. By 1914, Markievicz was aware of the coming revolution; she was supportive of the nationalist women's organisation Cumann na mBan and was instrumental in the merging of Inghinidhe na hÉireann with Cumann na mBan. She was against any Irish involvement in the First World War, co-founding the Irish Neutrality League in 1914 and opposed Redmond's call to the Irish Volunteers to join the war effort. By 1915 she was engaged in the training and mobilisation of the Irish Citizen Army and Na Fianna. Markievicz had always advocated military action to break the link with Britain and by 1916 she was more than ready to participate in the Easter Rising.

As members of the Citizen Army marched off on Easter Monday Markievicz loaded up Dr. Kathleen Lynn's car with first aid kits; as she later recalled, 'we carried a large store of first aid necessities and drove off through quiet dusty streets and across the river, reaching the City Hall'.[160] She then reported to Michael Mallin at St. Stephen's Green, where the occupation was well under way. She remained at the Green for the week and became Mallin's second-in-command. She was involved in organising the defence of the park. By early Tuesday the situation of the insurgents in St. Stephen's Green was deteriorating, the British had taken control of the buildings surrounding the park including the Shelbourne Hotel. Coming under increasing fire the garrison retreated to the Royal College of Surgeons where they would spend the rest of the week. On Sunday morning Elizabeth O'Farrell walked from Grafton Street towards the college, under a white flag. O'Farrell saw Markievicz first and handed the surrender note to her. She read the document and called Mallin; he read it and handed it back to O'Farrell who continued to the other Volunteer outposts in the city. Mallin ordered the white flag be hoisted over the college, Major DeCourcy-Wheeler arrived to accept the surrender. He met Mallin and Markievicz at the college door, she kissed her Mauser pistol and handed it over to the Major. Along with the other members of the garrison she was marched to Richmond Barracks.[161]

Markievicz was the only woman tried by court-martial in the aftermath of the Rising. Her defence was that '[I] went out to fight for Ireland's freedom, and it doesn't matter what happens to me. I did what I thought was right and I stand by it'.[162] She was sentenced to death but this was commuted to life imprisonment. She was transferred from Kilmainham Gaol, firstly to Mountjoy Gaol and then to Aylesbury Prison in England. She was eventually released under the general amnesty in June 1917, having served fourteen months. While in jail Markievicz took instruction in Catholicism and was baptised. On her release she quickly resumed her activities. She was elected to the executive of Sinn Féin and became President of Cumann na mBan. She was re-arrested in 1918 for her alleged involvement in the 'German Plot'. During this jail time she stood for election as a Sinn Féin candidate for Dublin's St. Patrick's division in the 1918 general election. She was successful and became the first women elected to the British Parliament. As a Sinn Féin MP, she followed the party's policy of abstention and did not take her seat. She was released again in March 1919 and was appointed Minister of Labour in the first Dáil Éireann. She continued her opposition to British rule in Ireland and was arrested in 1919 for making a seditious speech and was sentenced to four months hard labour. In September 1920 she was again arrested and sentenced to two years hard labour. She was finally released in July 1921 during the Truce.

After the Anglo-Irish Treaty was signed Markievicz was vehemently opposed to it. Always known for her theatricality and performance Markievicz, dressed in her full Cumann na mBan uniform, addressed the Dáil, where she condemned the Treaty and reiterated her advocacy of an Irish workers' Republic. She was re-elected president of Cumann na mBan and took the side of the anti-Treaty IRA during the Civil War. Elected to the Dáil again in 1923, she refused to take the Oath of Allegiance and therefore did not take her seat. She was arrested for the fourth and last time in November 1923 while attempting to collect signatures for a petition for the release of republican prisoners. While in prison she went on hunger strike until she and her fellow prisoners were released just before Christmas 1923. When de Valera formed Fianna Fáil in 1926 Markievicz became a member, finally breaking her ties with her old organisation, Cumann na mBan, who opposed Fianna Fáil. The winter of 1926 brought a coal strike and Markievicz spent a lot of time trudging around Dublin bringing food, fuel and necessities to the impoverished people of Dublin. During the general election of 1927 she conducted her own campaign and was re-elected to the Dáil. However years of hard work, a life on the run, five imprisonments, a hunger strike and the loss in 1926 of her beloved sister Eva, all took their toll and her health began to fail. She was admitted to Sir Patrick Dun's hospital, and declaring she was a pauper she was placed in the public ward. She died on 15 July, 1927. She was fifty-nine years old. She lay in state in the Pillar Room of the Rotunda Rink, where thousands of people came to pay their last respects to their 'Countess'. She is buried at Glasnevin Cemetery, Dublin. Éamon de Valera, the Fianna Fáil leader, gave the funeral oration.

Bridget Murtagh (*later O'Daly*)
BORN: Dublin, 1899
ORGANISATION: Cumann na mBan (Fairview branch)
POSITION DURING EASTER RISING: St. Stephen's Green/Royal
College of Surgeons

Bridget Murtagh was born in Dublin in 1889 to John Murtagh and his wife Mary. John Murtagh was a general labourer and in 1911 he and his wife and their children Elizabeth, John, Peter, Joseph and Bridget were living in a two-roomed house in Byrne's Lane in Dollymount, Dublin. Murtagh joined the Fairview branch of Cumann na mBan in 1914 and was involved in training in first aid, signalling and drill. When the Rising broke out Nora O'Daly called for May Moore and Bridget Murtagh, and the three women made their way to St. Stephen's Green.

Along with O'Daly, Murtagh was assigned to the first aid station there. On Tuesday the garrison was forced to evacuate to the College of Surgeons and Murtagh was again assigned to work as a first aid attendant with Rosie Hackett and O'Daly. Nora O'Daly later described how they set themselves up at one end of the lecture theatre: 'The large blind upon which lantern slides were shown (to illustrate lectures in the College) was drawn down and that end of the lecture room was sectioned off for Red Cross work only, no one but First Aid assistants being allowed past the barrier. These consisted of Miss Rosie Hackett, Miss B. Murtagh, and myself'.[163] In addition to her participation in the Rising, her brother Joseph, a member of Na Fianna, fought in the GPO.

Paddy O'Daly, widower of Nora O'Daly's sister Daisy, married Bridget Murtagh in 1921. Bridget O'Daly did not play any role in the Civil War. By 1930 her husband was a widower, when she died in childbirth. She was thirty-one years old. Interestingly Paddy O'Daly then married Norah Gillies, niece of his first wife Daisy Gillies. Bridget O'Daly is buried in Kilbarrack Cemetery, Dublin.

Nora O'Daly (*née Gillies*)
BORN: Dublin, 1883
ORGANISATION: Cumann na mBan
POSITION DURING EASTER RISING: St. Stephen's Green/Royal
College of Surgeons

Nora Margaret Mary Gillies was born in 1883 in Terenure, Dublin. Her father, John
Malcolm Gillies, was a Scot who had moved to Dublin in 1878 to become general
manager of the *The Freeman's Journal* newspaper. She was the fifth of eight children
of John and his wife Alice Maud. Interestingly John and Alice Gillies were Scots
Presbyterian but Nora and six of her siblings converted to Catholicism in their teenage
years. She was interested in Irish nationalism from an early age and, with several of
her siblings, she joined the Gaelic League. It was through their involvement in the
Gaelic League that Nora and her sister Daisy met their future husbands, brothers
Thomas and Paddy O'Daly, whom they married in a double wedding in 1910. Gillies'
husband Thomas O'Daly was an engineer. In 1911 Nora and Thomas were living with
her family in Clontarf.

In 1914 Nora O'Daly was a founder member of the Fairview branch of
Cumann na mBan and her husband was also active in advanced nationalism, joining
the Irish Volunteers.[164] The Fairview branch women undertook first aid classes and also
learned rifle cleaning and sighting, drill and others things which 'might prove useful
in assisting the men of the 2nd Battalion (Irish Volunteers)' to which the Fairview
Cumann was attached.[165] O'Daly was involved in hiding some of the arms brought in
during the Howth gun running and also gave out anti-recruitment leaflets, especially
those targeted at young women 'telling them not to walk out with soldiers'.[166]

By 1916 O'Daly had three young children (aged five, four and two) but, as
she later recalled, her house had become 'a regular arsenal of bombs which had been
made on the premises, dynamite, gelignite, rifles, bayonets, ammunition and what
not'.[167] In the weeks preceding the Rising she helped move arms and ammunition
around various safe houses. On Easter Sunday she was instructed by her brother-
in-law, Paddy O'Daly, to go to the Magazine Fort in the Phoenix Park with another
Cumann na mBan woman, Bridget Murtagh, and quietly scout around. While they
were there they fell into conversation with a friendly Irish Guard Lance Corporal. In
the course of their conversation with the soldier, O'Daly and Murtagh collected a

great deal of valuable information on the numbers of soldiers in the Fort, changes of guard, visits of officers, and the layout of the Fort; intelligence, she said, which was of value in the planned attack on the Fort.[168] The attack on the Fort had two objectives. Firstly a successful raid on the Magazine Fort would provide much needed weaponry for the Volunteers and secondly the attack was to signal the start of the Rising.

While O'Daly was dismayed to hear of the countermanding order on Easter Sunday, on Easter Monday she received word from some of her comrades that the Rising had begun. Leaving her three children in the care of her sister, she, with Bridget Murtagh and May Moore and a few others members of the Fairview branch, made their way by tram to St. Stephen's Green, where they found the Irish Citizen Army garrison commanded by Michael Mallin and Countess Markievicz. O'Daly spent the week of the Rising in St. Stephen's Green and the Royal College of Surgeons.[169] She said all her doubts and fears about the fight disappeared once she caught sight of Madeleine ffrench-Mullen, 'a plucky lady' who welcomed O'Daly and her group 'with joy and relief'. She was put working at first aid by ffrench-Mullen and treated the wounded, assisted by Rosie Hackett. Hackett she said was a 'tonic in herself, always cheerful and always willing'.[170] She attended to Margaret Skinnider when she was wounded and said that Skinnider 'showed wonderful bravery during the whole week and bore her frightful wounds with the greatest of bravery'.[171] O'Daly had a narrow escape herself when a shotgun was accidentally discharged near her.

On Sunday came the news that the garrison was to surrender, and, as good soldiers, they 'obeyed, bitter and hard though it was'.[172] They were marched to Richmond Barracks, where they were given some tea and biscuits. After dusk the women were marched to Kilmainham Gaol. O'Daly left a vivid account of her time in Kilmainham. She wrote about how she shared her cell with three other women; they were each given one blanket and one very tough biscuit. The women were all given numbers (hers was 202) and the sergeant in charge would bring their food which consisted of cocoa, stew, potatoes and dry bread. Efforts to break the bread, she said, were fruitless. Nora also mentions the shots heard by the women at 'the grey of dawn', as the executions began. She was released on 8 May.

After the Rising O'Daly transferred to the Central branch of Cumann na mBan and was involved in the reorganisation of that branch, anti-conscription activities and campaigning in Clontarf for Sinn Féin in the general election of 1918. Tragedy struck, in 1919, when her sister Daisy, wife of Paddy O'Daly, who was captain of 'B'

Company, 2nd Battalion, Dublin Brigade, Irish Volunteers, died.

During the War of Independence she was a judge in the Republican Courts in Dublin serving in the Fairview/Ballybough District. This was considered a very risky job as the courts were often raided and its members attacked and arrested. Despite periodic raids on her home, O'Daly also ran a safe house and sheltered Volunteer Joe Leonard after his involvement in the assassinations of British agents on the morning of 21 November 1920. This day has since come to be known as 'Bloody Sunday' and was orchestrated by Michael Collins, then Director of Intelligence, in an effort to destroy the British Intelligence service. Members of the Squad supported by the Active Service Unit of the Dublin Brigade IRA and Cumann na mBan, assassinated fourteen men across Dublin city at 9a.m. that morning.[173] O'Daly's brother-in-law Paddy was a member of the Squad, so her reliability would have been known to Collins and the other men. The Black and Tans described her as a dangerous woman.

Her husband Thomas opposed the Anglo-Irish Treaty and was a member of the anti-Treaty IRA during the Civil War. Despite this, O'Daly seems to have been neutral and was not involved in activities during the conflict. As well as her revolutionary activism she was also a member of the IWWU and worked for the rights of women workers. After the foundation of the State she worked as a secretary to the Dáil Courts winding up committee. She wrote poetry and prose as well as her memoirs of the Rising. In 1926 she published 'The Women of Easter Week; Cumann na mBan in Stephen's Green and in the College of Surgeons' in *An tÓglach* magazine, the magazine of the Irish Free State army. Nora O'Daly died in May 1943. She was sixty years old.

May O'Moore (*later Wisely*)
BORN: Dublin, 1896
ORGANISATION: Cumann na mBan (Fairview branch)
POSITION DURING EASTER RISING: St. Stephen's Green/Royal College of Surgeons

May O'Moore was born in 1896 and joined the Fairview branch, Cumann na mBan in 1914. She participated in route marches, first aid training, drilling and signalling.[174] She was involved in preparations for the Rising, making field dressings and other items for first aid kits in Thomas Clarke's house. On Easter Monday she, along with her friends

Nora O'Daly and Bridget Murtagh, took a tram into the city and arrived at St. Stephen's Green and joined the garrison there. On arrival, O'Moore was assigned to the first aid station and also distributed arms and hand grenades to the men stationed around the Green. She retreated with the insurgents to the College of Surgeons on Tuesday and remained there until the surrender. She was arrested and taken to Richmond Barracks and later Kilmainham Gaol. She was released on 8 May. (Her brother Seán also took part in the Rising, serving at the Four Courts garrison. In 1922 Seán married Esther Wisely, a member of Cumann na mBan and a 1916 veteran who had served in the GPO. She was distantly related to May O'Moore's future husband William Wisely.)

After her release May continued her involvement by helping to reorganise the Fairview branch of Cumann na mBan and was captain of the branch for two years from 1917 – 1919. She was involved in collecting for the Irish National Aid and Volunteer Dependents' Fund and was in charge of the anti-conscription campaign in the Fairview area. She also campaigned for Sinn Féin in the 1918 general election.[175] During the War of Independence she obtained the use of her future mother-in-law's (Mrs. Wisely) house to use as a safe house for men on the run and also to store arms and ammunition She was considered one of the most active members of Fairview Cumann na mBan. Máire (Cooley) McDonald in supporting O'Moore's pension application said that she 'never spared herself during that time' (1919 – 1921).

O'Moore married William Wisely and had seven children. William Wisely's sister who was a friend of O'Moore's, had also been a member of Fairview branch and had participated in the Easter Rising. In 1938 May Wisely was awarded an 'E' grade pension (the lowest grade) which disturbed her greatly. She wrote in her letter of protest, 'In all the years we worked for the cause and went into action, willing and ready to give our all, and went to jail [sic]and came out to carry on the good work, during all that time the thought of a possible award never entered our minds. But now that the country is in a position to give awards, I certainly think they aught [sic]to be given in a fairer and more generous spirit'.[176] Like so many of the women who got the lowest grade of pension, Wisely was not pleased that all of her work for 'the cause' was not recognised fully and fairly. May and William Wisely moved to live and bring up their family in Swansea, Wales. She died in 1946 and was brought home for burial in Clontarf Cemetery. She was fifty years old.

Kathleen 'Catherine' Seery (*later Redmond*)
BORN: Dublin, 1896
ORGANISATION: Irish Citizen Army
POSITION DURING EASTER RISING: St. Stephen's Green/Royal
College of Surgeons

Kathleen Seery was born in 1896 in Dublin to John Seery and Catherine Moore who were both originally from Wicklow. In the 1901 census the family was living in a tenement house in Henrietta Street and in 1911 Kathleen and her family were living in Luke Street. John Seery was a general labourer. He and his children Kathleen, James and Patrick, were members of the Irish Citizen Army and James, Kathleen and John took part in the Easter Rising.

Kathleen Seery joined the Citizen Army in 1915 and participated in route marches, learning drill and first aid. In the week before the Rising she was often in Liberty Hall helping out with all operations. She delivered messages and brought material which had been hidden under her mother's floorboards to Liberty Hall. As she lived near Liberty Hall, at Beresford Place, she went home on Easter Sunday but reported for duty at 8am the next morning. She was then ordered to go with the contingent led by Michael Mallin and Countess Markievicz to St. Stephen's Green. Her father John and brother Patrick were also with this group, while her other brother James went with the Citizen Army to Dublin Castle. She spent Easter Monday in the Green and then retreated with the garrison to the Royal College of Surgeons on Tuesday 25 April. During the rest of the week she was involved in procuring food and cooking for the garrison. She made several sorties out to Cuffe Street and Camden Street to get food, oil, matches and other necessities. After the surrender she was taken with the garrison to Richmond Barracks and then to Kilmainham Gaol. She was released on 8 May. Seery said in her pension application that she was doing the usual activities after the Rising. This would have included continuing her training in first aid, drills, carrying messages and collecting funds for the Irish Citizen Army.[177]

On 25 May 1921 the Dublin Brigade IRA attacked the Custom House. The attack was carried out primarily by the 2nd Battalion IRA, but was supported by the members of the remaining battalions of the Dublin Brigade who surrounded the vicinity to provide cover against enemy attack, and also took control of the city's fire brigade stations. That day Seery was ordered to carry two revolvers, a pliers and fifteen rounds of ammunition from her father's house at Beresford Place to the Custom House, where she handed it over to 'some chap' who was involved in the attack.[178]

Seery married Francis Redmond in 1922 and continued her activities. She opposed the Anglo-Irish Treaty and assisted the anti-Treaty IRA during the Civil War. During this time her house was raided by Free State troops. She was arrested and taken to Oriel House and interrogated there. Seery was released after a few hours. Oriel House was located on Westland Row, Dublin 2. The Intelligence Division of the Free State army was based there during the Civil War. For her work she was later awarded the 1916 Medal, the Service (1917–1921) Medal (for her active service with the Irish Citizen Army, Dublin), the 1916 Survivors Medal in 1966 and the Truce Commemoration Medal in 1971. Kathleen Redmond died in 1977 aged eighty-one.

OTHER WOMEN ARRESTED

Kathleen Browne
BORN: Wexford, 1876
EASTER RISING: Wexford
ORGANISATION: Cumann na mBan

Kathleen Browne was born in 1876 in Wexford. Her father Michael Browne of Bridge-town and Rathronan was a member of the Land League and involved in the Land War in Wexford. He was also an ardent supporter of Home Rule. Her mother Mary's family, the Saffords of Baldwinstown Castle, were also well connected in local and national politics. In the 1911 census Browne signed herself as 'Caitlín de Brún' and she often used this Irish version of her name in her publications. She described herself in the census as a farmer and throughout her life referred to herself as a 'practical farmer'. In 1911, inspired by the work of Sir Horace Plunkett's cooperative endeavours, Anita Lett of Bree, Co. Wexford, founded United Irishwomen (UI) which saw its mission to improve the lives of rural people, especially rural women and farmers' wives. United Irishwomen became the Irish Countrywomen's Association in 1935.

Kathleen Browne was an early and enthusiastic member of UI, and much of her later political career was spent defending the rights of farmers' wives. She also joined the Wexford Agricultural Society (and later, in 1919, the Loch Garman Co-op) and was a great admirer of Sir Horace Plunkett. Browne was involved in the cultural revival and had joined the Gaelic League in the early 1900s. She immersed herself in the language revival as well as educating herself in the dialect of south Wexford, Yola.[179] She liked to be photographed in Celtic costume and became the county secretary of the Gaelic League in Wexford. She knew Arthur Griffith, and by 1909 was a member of Sinn Féin and a member of the Ard Chomhairle for several years. Among the members of Sinn Féin whom she became associated with were W.T. Cosgrave and Seán T. O'Kelly. Her brother John was also a member of Sinn Féin. From 1913 Browne was involved in the setting up of the south Wexford branches of the Irish Volunteers and helped establish Cumann na mBan in Wexford from 1914.

When the Rising broke out in 1916, Browne was at her home, Rathronan Castle in south Wexford. She had been involved in the local Cumann na mBan with her close friend Nell Ryan of Tomcoole, Wexford. On Thursday of Easter Week local

Volunteers accompanied by members of Cumann na mBan had taken the Athenaeum in Enniscorthy, with orders from James Connolly to shut down the railway line from Rosslare. Enniscorthy was the nearest big town to Browne's home at Rathronan and, hearing of the activities of the Irish Volunteers and Cumann na mBan in the town, and perhaps intending to join them, she raised the Tricolour over Rathronan Castle. She was immediately arrested and imprisoned in Waterford Gaol. *The Wexford People* of 13 May 1916 described the arrests: 'the work of lining up the insurgents in Co Wexford is still proceeding... nearly 300 insurgents and their sympathisers have been captured, including six women; prominent amongst them are Miss Browne, Rathronan Castle (whose brother [James] is a lieutenant in the army) and Miss Neillie Ryan, secretary of the Co Wexford Insurance Committee'.[180] The report further states that 'Miss Browne and Miss Ryan... were removed from Waterford to Dublin last Monday'.[181] This was Monday 8 May, when Browne and Nell Ryan were taken to Richmond Barracks and then to Kilmainham Gaol. Browne was not among those released from Kilmainham, but was transferred to Mountjoy Gaol with twelve women.

Letters survive in the Browne family archive written from Kathleen in Mountjoy Gaol to her fretting mother and family in Rathronan. On 11 May she wrote to her mother to reassure her that all was well in Mountjoy, stating that, 'I am not the least bit nervous myself as I hope to get out soon. Tell John [her brother] there is no need to go to any trouble on my case at all. I want a clean blouse and bodice rather badly but nothing else at present'. She was also very concerned for her friends the Ryans, writing that, 'Kit [Mary Kate] is very delicate and is feeling prison life very much. It is very unjust and cruel to keep her here as whatever charges may be against the rest of us there is nothing against her'.[182] Her brother John managed to get in to visit her and brought her much needed supplies.[183] On 27 May she wrote to her sister Maisie that all the women had been praying to Pearse as, 'he did more than a man's part all his life. His death was a fit ending'. He was, she later said, 'in the long line of Ireland's martyrs... the noblest. He is our greatest loss'.[184] Browne had been in Kilmainham during the executions and like many of the imprisoned women had heard the sound of gunfire as the leaders of the Rising were shot. Browne had feared she would be among those deported to England, but on 4 June she was released. As soon as she was released Browne went to pay her respects to Mrs. Margaret Pearse, mother of Patrick and Willie Pearse.

After the Rising she remained active in Cumann na mBan with Nell Ryan.

She was particularly involved in the anti-conscription campaign of 1918, and she was a prominent campaigner and canvasser for Sinn Féin in Wexford during the 1918 general election. During the War of Independence Rathronan was a safe house, and Browne worked tirelessly to fund raise and provide support for the families of men on the run. She wrote that she worked to keep 'the Volunteers together and the Gaelic League going. I had to take terrible risks and go to much expense, even giving them a house in the village (Bridgetown) free of rent… from 1916 I had to keep the families of the men who were arrested'.[185]

Browne supported the Anglo-Irish Treaty, and joined the pro-Treaty female organisation, Cumann na Saoirse. This caused a lifelong rift with her good friend, Nell Ryan, who opposed the Treaty. She later wrote that she 'considered the Treaty the best possible settlement… [and] independence was embodied in the Treaty'.[186] The anti-Treaty forces threatened to burn her out during the Civil War and Rathronan was guarded by Free State troops for the duration of the conflict. A letter in the Browne family archive shows the bitterness that the Civil War caused between old friends and comrades. 'We were saved from being burnt out [only] by a military guard [of the National Army] and threats from the officers to burn Miss Ryan's place in Tomcoole to the ground if mine were meddled with'.[187] In an article on the Browne families of Co. Wexford, Kathleen Browne is described as a 'hard uncompromising, dogged individual… self-opinionated, self-righteous [who] alienated many of her neighbours and erstwhile friends especially after the Civil War'.[188] In 1924 she received a special grant of £200 from the Dáil Special Fund to compensate her for the 'suffering' endured during the Civil War and its aftermath.[189]

Browne joined Cumann na nGaedhael in 1922 and was branch secretary of the party in Wexford. In 1925 she ran, unsuccessfully, for the Senate on a women's platform, along with Mrs. Mary (Min) Mulcahy (formerly Min Ryan of Tomcoole) and feminist activist and nationalist Patricia Hoey. Although Browne and the other women campaigned countrywide, none of them were elected. In 1929 she was appointed to the Senate and served as Senator until 1936. She was a stalwart defender of the rights of farmers and farmers' wives and was active on women's issues. As Rosemary Cullen Owens wrote, 'women members of the 1922 – 1936 Senate, in particular Jennie Wyse Power, Kathleen Clarke, Eileen Costello and Kathleen Browne… across party lines… consistently opposed legislation which sought to restrict the role of women in Irish society'.[190]

One of Browne's great fears was the rise of communism and she regarded Fianna Fáil to be in league with Russia. When Fianna Fáil took power in 1932, she joined the Army Comrades Association (ACA), which she felt was committed to eradicating communism. She was also an avid supporter of Eoin O'Duffy's Blueshirts. In 1934 she claimed to have recruited hundreds of young men and women into the organisation, and in February of that year she challenged the government by wearing the 'blue-blouse' uniform of the women into the Senate. This caused a debate on the wearing of political emblems in the Houses of the Oireachtas, and the passage of the Wearing of Uniform (Restriction) Bill in 1934. She left national politics in 1936 although she continued to have active public roles. In 1938 she was a key organiser of the 140th anniversary of the 1798 Rebellion.

As well as a politician, she was a keen historian and linguist. She was an active member of many historical and antiquarian organisations, including the Royal Society of Antiquaries of Ireland, the Society for the Preservation of the Memorials of the Dead and the Ui Cinnsealaigh Historical Society. She published widely on the history and antiquities of Co. Wexford and her short history of Co. Wexford was approved as a textbook for schools by the Department of Education in 1927. She was an authority on Yola, a dialect spoken by the Welsh and Flemish followers of the early Norman invaders, which persisted in the Wexford baronies of Forth and Bargy until the mid-nineteenth century. A keen naturalist, she was instrumental in having the Great Saltee Island conserved as a bird sanctuary (1938). She lived at Rathronan with her sister Maisie. Neither woman married but the house was full of children as they raised the five children of their sister Margaret (Hassett) who had died aged thirty-seven in 1927. Kathleen Browne died in 1943. She was sixty-seven years old.

Ellen 'Nell' Humphreys (*née O'Rahilly*)
BORN: Co. Kerry, 1871
ORGANISATION: Cumann na mBan
POSITION DURING EASTER RISING:
54 Northumberland Road (residence)

Ellen 'Nell' Humphreys was born Mary Ellen O'Rahilly in 1871 in Ballylongford, Co. Kerry. Nell, as she was better known, was the sister of Michael The O'Rahilly. She married David Humphreys, an eye surgeon, in 1895 and they lived in Limerick city. They had three children before her husband died prematurely in 1903. Soon after Humphreys and her sister Áine 'Anno', moved to 54 Northumberland Road, Dublin. Áine O'Rahilly was a founder member of Cumann na mBan with her sister-in-law, Nancy 'Nannie' O'Rahilly. The Humphreys were a nationalist family and were all Gaelic speakers. Humphreys' son Richard 'Dick' fought with his uncle, The O'Rahilly, in the GPO during the Rising but was made to leave on Nell's orders. He did however return to the GPO and was arrested after the Rising.

During the first days of the Rising, Humphreys was unconvinced of the rightness of what was taking place. As her sister Anno mentioned in her witness statement, Humphreys went to the GPO on Easter Monday to see The O'Rahilly and her son Dick. She brought a number of medals of Our Lady of Perpetual Succour and distributed them among the Volunteers. According to her sister, 'She went again on Tuesday. She was very brave because the bullets were flying all round, but she always had great courage'.[191] Her daughter Sighle wrote in her memoirs of that week that on Monday evening her mother went to the GPO to persuade Pearse, The O'Rahilly and others to give up. As Sighle explained, 'in all fairness to my mother at that stage of the fight, we did not know that any building except the GPO had been taken over by the Volunteers. My mother had no way of knowing how many volunteers had ignored McNeill's order and turned up on Easter Monday morning'.[192]

During the Rising the Humphreys and O'Rahilly women were very aware of the violent turn of events. They could see British reinforcements marching towards the city, while close to home two Volunteers, Lieutenant Michael Malone and Seamus Grace, members of the 3rd Battalion, had taken over No. 25 Northumberland Road. Sighle described the aftermath of an attack by young British soldiers on No. 25. She wrote that on 'Wednesday, we heard the tramp of marching men and looking out the window saw lines and lines of soldiers with full military kit marching towards the city. Suddenly a volley rang out from No. 25 and all threw themselves on the ground. Many never rose again. Michael Malone and Jim Grace, the two volunteers who had taken over No. 25 Northumberland Road, did not open fire until the soldiers had arrived at the Haddington Road junction. The soldiers had no idea from whence the firing was coming'.[193]

Her mother wrote that Sighle and Anno saw many soldiers killed on the assaults on No. 25. Humphreys also wrote to her sister, a nun in Australia, mentioning the role of women in the Rising. She was concerned about the effect that women taking part in the Rising had on her young daughter: 'Did you hear at all of the part women took in the Rising? I used to feel ashamed of Sighle, as being unwomanly when Anna told me that at times it was difficult to keep her from taking a shot herself, that the way she gloried when the enemy fell was actually inhuman, and her nerve during the whole thing was wonderful'.[194] During the Rising Humphreys was arrested at her home, which was known to the authorities as a place freely used by the Volunteers. She was taken to the RDS, Ballsbridge where she was held in a horsebox. After the surrender she was taken to Richmond Barracks, and then transferred to Kilmainham Gaol where she was held prisoner until 9 May.

After her release, she, her family and her home were at the centre of republican activities. During the War of Independence her family home on Ailesbury Road, Dublin was used as a safe house by the IRA. As Anno wrote in her statement, they were raided frequently and valuables often taken by the soldiers. They sheltered many men on the run; and when their new home on Ailesbury Road was built they had one of the rooms 'camouflaged after construction by Batt. O'Connor, principally to harbour Cathal Brugha, who was on the run too. The camouflage had to be added after the house was built because the military kept watching it during construction'.[195]

When the Anglo-Irish Treaty was signed in December 1921 all of the Humphreys family opposed the Treaty and during the Civil War Nell opened her home to the anti-Treaty IRA. Ernie O'Malley was arrested at her home by pro-Treaty forces in November 1922. A gunfight broke out between the troops, O'Malley and Humphreys' daughter Sighle. Her sister Áine was wounded. Both Humphreys and Sighle were arrested and imprisoned in Mountjoy Gaol and later Kilmainham Gaol. Áine was taken to hospital and was imprisoned on her recovery. Humphreys was released in July 1923.

Nell Humphreys was a member of the O'Rahilly Sinn Féin Club in Donny-brook, but resigned in 1924. Like many of these republican women, such as Nora Connolly, Helena Molony, Máire Comerford, Eithne Coyle, and Margaret Buckley, the O'Rahilly/Humphreys women were prominent political activists in the following decades. Many of these women were involved as leaders of left-wing initiatives in the 1930s. Like Humphreys, their social radicalism helps explain why most of the politically active women in the movement were strongly opposed to the establishment of the new state, a state which didn't seem to guarantee any of the promises of equality mentioned in the Proclamation, political or social. All the women remained involved in Republican politics until their deaths. Nell Humphreys died in 1939 and is buried in Glasnevin Cemetery. She was sixty-eight years old.

Elizabeth 'Lizzie' Mulhall
BORN: Dublin, 1865/1866
ORGANISATION: Cumann na mBan

Lizzie Mulhall was born in either 1865 or 1866 in Dublin city. At the time of the 1911 census she was living in No. 137 Emmet Road, New Kilmainham. The Mulhalls were a family of drapers in Kilmainham and by 1901, Mulhall and her sisters Catherine, Teresa and Josephine, were all working in the drapery business. In 1911 she was still a draper and at the time of the Rising, she had her own drapery business opposite Richmond Barracks. She was also a Poor Law Guardian, a member of Sinn Féin and a founder member of Cumann na mBan. Mulhall did not take an active part in the Rising. She was, however, arrested. Not all Dublin citizens were opposed to the Volunteers and their attempts to free Ireland. While being marched to Richmond Barracks, many locals from the James' Street area up to Inchicore did not throw food and spit at them as has been widely supposed. Instead several of the crowd cheered on the men and women. Lizzie Mulhall was one such person. As a member of Cumann na mBan she was cheering her comrades as they marched to imprisonment in Richmond Barracks. It seems that her cheers drew the attention of the British military and she was promptly arrested. She was taken prisoner and held in Richmond Barracks and Kilmainham Gaol. There is no other information about Mulhall after her release from Kilmainham on 9 May 1916.

Mary Partridge (*née Hamilton*)
BORN: Dublin, 1886
ORGANISATION: N/A

In 1909, William Partridge married Mary Hamilton, daughter of a Kilmainham locksmith, Francis Hamilton in Dublin. Through her husband Mary Partridge was connected with much of the labour history of the period 1909–1916. William Partridge was an active leader in the ITGWU and played a leading role in the 1913 Lockout. Elected to Dublin City Council in 1912, he brought attention to issues such as public health and housing, a very pertinent issue given the tenements of Dublin. He travelled extensively throughout Ireland in 1913 on behalf of the ITGWU and was sent to England twice during the Lockout, where he spoke about and fundraised for the strikers in Dublin. Instrumental in the formation of the Irish Citizen Army, William Partridge fought with the ICA in the College of Surgeons during Easter Week. Already ill before the Rising, after the surrender he was imprisoned in Dartmoor and Lewes prisons in England where his health deteriorated. He was released on health grounds in April 1917. He went to stay with his family in Ballaghaderreen, Co. Roscommon where he died three months after his release. Constance Markievicz delivered his funeral oration in Ballaghaderreen, in which she described Partridge as 'the purest-souled and noblest patriot Ireland ever had'.

While her husband was conducting his union activities Mary Partridge was raising their children (three daughters and one son) at Patriotic Terrace, Kilmainham. Mary Partridge was friends with many in the nationalist and trade union movements. She and her husband were especially close to Markievicz, and William Partridge served as Markievicz' sponsor for her baptism into the Catholic Church. The authorities would have known of her associations with the leaders of the Rising and despite taking no active part in the events of Easter Week, Mary Partridge was arrested, taken to Richmond Barracks and later Kilmainham Gaol. She was detained in Kilmainham for several weeks after the Rising. Within a year she was a widow. Mary Partridge never remarried. She lived at 589 South Circular Road, Kilmainham and died in March 1959. She was seventy-three years old.

Marie 'Mary'/ 'May' Perolz (*later Flanagan*)
BORN: Limerick, 1874
ORGANISATION: Irish Citizen Army and Cumann na mBan
EASTER RISING POSITION: Courier and GPO

Mary 'May' Perolz was born in Limerick in 1874, the daughter of Richard Perolz and Bridget Carter. The Perolz family was of Huguenot descent. In 1901 the family, widower Richard and daughters May, Anna and Delia, was living at 54 Mountjoy Square, Dublin. May was working as a fruit shop assistant. She joined the Gaelic League and took part in the 1898 procession to commemorate the 1798 Rebellion. Perolz later joined Inghinidhe na hÉireann and participated in their many theatrical and cultural activities.[196] She appeared in several of their *tableaux vivants* which illustrated episodes from ancient Irish sagas. She was in one of the first Irish language plays produced in Dublin, *Eilís agus an Bhean Deirce* (1902). She also taught Irish language classes and Irish history to children.

She was a member of the Irish Citizen Army and the IWWU from 1913.[197] She worked closely with her good friends Countess Markievicz and James Connolly on nationalist and trade union issues, and was the registered owner of *The Spark*, a trade union paper printed by Connolly in Liberty Hall, where she worked as an intelligence officer. Perolz was also involved in procuring arms prior to the Rising; she mentioned buying a machine gun from a soldier stationed in Dublin Castle.[198] In March 1916, Markievicz was excluded under the Defence of the Realm Act from addressing the Fianna Éireann festival in Tralee, Co. Kerry. With the Easter Rising so close, she was ordered by Connolly not to defy the ban and risk arrest. Perolz, who physically resembled Markievicz, stood in as her replacement. Posing as Markievicz up to the moment of her address, she was shadowed by detectives all the way to Tralee. She conveyed regrets to the gathering from Markievicz for not appearing, and delivered the latter's lecture on the 1867 Fenian Rising.[199]

In the week preceding the Rising, Perolz was sent to Waterford, Dungarvan and Cloughjordan with messages for local Volunteers telling them that the Rising was imminent. On Easter Monday she was sent to Cork city bringing the remobilisation order issued by Pearse for Tomás MacCurtain, rescinding the Eoin MacNeill countermand. Perolz failed to make direct contact with MacCurtain so she returned to Dublin. She also brought dispatches to Mallow, Tralee, Dungarvan and Waterford. She got back to Dublin on Friday 28 April 1916.[200] She was arrested on 2 May, interned in Richmond Barracks, Kilmainham Gaol and Mountjoy Gaol and was one of five women internees deported to England in June 1916. Released the next month on appeal, Perolz was for a time the most prominent republican woman free to circulate actively in Dublin. In her witness statement she wrote about being 'depressed' in Kilmainham as she knew the men, her comrades, were being executed. Only for Bridget Foley who, 'kept up my courage and tried to force me to eat', she felt she would have died.[201] Her incarceration so scandalised some members of her family that they changed their surname to 'Prole' to avoid association with her.

After her release, Perolz stated that she was 'interested in everything that was going on, as usual'.[202] She was active in reviving the IWWU with activists like Helena Molony and Rosie Hackett. She became acting president of the IWWU in 1917 and represented the union at the first post-Rising convocation of the Irish Trade Union Congress and Labour Party held in Sligo in August 1916. At the convocation she moved amendments to resolutions, to ensure the phrasing included reference to 'working women' as well as to 'working men'. One of her proposed amendments to the draft national labour programme advocated strategies to improve the health of working class women and children. In 1917 she travelled to England with Helena Molony and Kathleen Lynn to greet the men being released from internment, and while there they heard that Markievicz was also being released – they accompanied her on the journey back to Dublin. Perolz was active in the 1918 general election on behalf of Sinn Féin.

In 1919 she married James M. Flanagan, although, unusually for the time, she continued to use her maiden name. The couple lived in Glasnevin and Sutton in Dublin. Perolz remained a champion of the rights of the woman worker. For over twenty years she acted as inspector under the 'Children's Act of the Dublin Board of Assistance'. She died in December 1950, aged sixty-six years old. She is buried at Mount Jerome Cemetery, Dublin. Senator Margaret Pearse unveiled a memorial over her grave in August 1955. Senator Pearse said of Perolz, 'she was a great woman, a great Catholic, and a great patriot', and was 'one of a very small band of Irish-women who accomplished unpleasant and dangerous work which many men would have failed to perform'.[203]

Countess Mary Josephine Plunkett (*née Cranny*)
BORN: Co. Dublin, 1858
ORGANISATION: None

Countess Josephine Plunkett was born in Co. Dublin in 1858. She was the daughter of Patrick and Maria Cranny (*née* Keane) of Muckross Park, Donnybrook. Patrick Cranny was originally from Borris in Co. Carlow but moved to Tralee, Co. Kerry, where he met and married Maria Keane, daughter of a wealthy Tralee family. Patrick and Maria Cranny came to Dublin in 1842. By 1856, with the help of his wife's money, Patrick Cranny had started building houses on Wellington Road, Ballsbridge, part of the Pembroke Estate. He was also involved in building houses in Donnybrook. Maria Cranny's cousin Elizabeth 'Bess' Noble married Patrick Plunkett. The Crannys and Plunketts continued to be very close through their lives. The Plunketts were Catholic and nationalist, claiming a descent from St. Oliver Plunkett. In 1884 George Noble Plunkett, son of Patrick and Bess Plunkett, married his cousin Mary Josephine Cranny, uniting the two families.[204]

Count Plunkett was very involved in nationalist politics. In the 1892 election he was a Parnellite candidate for mid-Tyrone, but in a three-way fight, he withdrew in case of a unionist win. He stood again as a nationalist candidate in Dublin in 1895 and 1898. He was a writer and editor, part-editing Charles O'Kelly's memoir *The Jacobite War in Ireland* in 1894. In 1911 he published his revised edition of Margaret McNair Stokes *Early Christian Art in Ireland*. In 1907 he became Director of the National Museum of Ireland. His wife kept home and supported him in his work. She worked tirelessly in the cause for the beatification of Oliver Plunkett. In 1914 she toured the United States in this cause and was present at the beatification ceremony in Rome with her husband. Interested in the arts, her obituary notes that Countess Plunkett 'founded Hardwicke Hall as a theatre, where Joseph Plunkett produced his play, "*Dance or Osirus,*" [*sic*] under the guidance of Edward Martyn, Thomas MacDonagh and John MacDonagh.'[205]

George and Josephine Plunkett had seven children. Their three sons, Joseph, George and Jack, all fought in the Easter Rising. Joseph Plunkett had planned the strategy of the Rising and was a signatory of the Proclamation. He was executed in Kilmainham Gaol on 4 May, having married Grace Gifford in the prison chapel a few hours before his execution. Countess Plunkett and her husband were themselves arrested at their home in the immediate aftermath of the Rising and both were held in Richmond Barracks and then Kilmainham Gaol. They arrived in Kilmainham the night before the execution of their son, Joseph, and neither were allowed see him before his death. They would have heard the gunshots which killed Joseph early the next morning. On her release a short time later the Countess and her husband were sent by the authorities to live in Oxford, England. They returned to Ireland following the general amnesty in 1917 and lived in Elgin Road, Ballsbridge.

In January 1917, Count Plunkett stood as a candidate in a by-election in North Roscommon and won the seat. Although elderly, Countess Plunkett was also active in post-Rising politics. In the reorganisation of Sinn Féin, the Countess was the only women representative on the 'Council of Nine', although many political women 'were unhappy at this situation, doubtful whether the elderly Countess was suitable for the task and angry that their sex should have been given only one representative.'[206] These women, including Áine Ceannt, Madeleine ffrench-Mullen, Kathleen Lynn and Helena Molony, met at the home of Countess Plunkett and formed the League of Women Delegates. They wanted more representation in Sinn Féin and as the Countess was unwell, Dr. Lynn was chosen to replace her as representative on the 'Council of Nine'. Despite her illness, Countess Plunkett hosted a meeting of the League at her home the weekend before the 1917 Sinn Féin convention. At the convention the resolution proposed by the women that, 'the equality of men and women in this organisation be emphasised in all speeches and leaflets' was passed.

The family continued to be involved in republican politics throughout the War of Independence. As a result of her sons' activities, Countess Plunkett's home was constantly raided by the authorities, even though she was not an active participant in the War of Independence or the Civil War that followed. The Plunketts were vehemently anti-Treaty. During the Civil War, Count Plunkett was interned and not released until December 1923. The Countess continued to earn money from the many family properties in Donnybrook and Ballsbridge which she managed. In the 1940s she bought Ballymascanlon House near Dundalk where she lived until her death in 1944. She was eighty-six years old and is interred in Glasnevin Cemetery.

Barbara Retz/Reitz
BORN: Germany, 1885
ORGANISATION: Unknown

Barbara Retz has the most unusual surname among the seventy-seven women.[207] There is only one family in the 1911 census which is probably hers. In 1911 George and Babette Retz lived at Dufferin Avenue off the South Circular Road in Dublin. In the late nineteenth century, pork butchers from around Stuttgart had migrated to Britain and then on to Ireland. In Dublin, quite a number including Haffner, Olhausen, Speidel and Mogerley, ran very successful pork businesses, many in the South Circular Road area. According to the 1911 census, George and Babette Retz were both born in Germany and were originally Protestants. George was a pork butcher with his own shop. During this period there were over 1,000 Germans in Ireland, mostly living in Dublin. Interestingly the Retz family became members of the Church of the Latter Day Saints or Mormons. On a single night in 1914, several businesses were attacked by an anti-German mob. On 17 August 1914, the *Irish Independent* reported that the German Pork Butchers of Reitz/Retz and Lang 'had a rough time on Saturday night.'[208] A mob of 'youths' attacked the shops, breaking the windows and leaving the shops wrecked. In addition over £20 was taken from the till. In seeking compensation for the damage George Retz said that he had lived in Britain for twenty six years and was not eligible for military service in the German Army. In the *Irish Independent* the writer Padraic Colum condemned the attack, writing that he hoped 'there are a few Irish men or women who have read without deep indignation the account of unprovoked attacks upon German shops in our capital and in other towns in Ireland. What have these defenceless trader done to the citizens of Dublin… I remember when the Anglo-Irish and the English universities mocked Irish civilisation… it was from the German universities that the word went forth that made our culture respected'.[209]

Interestingly *The Irish Worker,* the labour newspaper (edited by James Connolly), also condemned the outrage. On 22 August 1914, the newspaper reported that the mob were indulging 'German baiting' and that the authorities had turned a blind eye, noting that the Dublin Metropolitan Police had actually arrested George Retz and allowed the destruction of his shop. The paper made it clear that if the homes and businesses of Germans were attacked again, 'an appeal to the men of the Transport

Union and the Citizen Army to act as a guard for their houses would not fail to produce good results'.[210] This connection between the protection offered by the ITGWU and the Citizen Army to German businesses may be the reason Barbara/Babette Retz was arrested and held in Richmond Barracks and Kilmainham Gaol after the Easter Rising 1916. Barbara Retz was released on 8 May.

How Barbara Retz came to be arrested or what her involvement was in either Cumann an mBan or the Citizen Army is not clear from the records. She may simply have been in the wrong place at the wrong time and swept up in the chaos and arrests post-Rising. There is also no evidence that any of the family were involved in republican activities after the Rising. Retz and her family remained in Ireland until 1948 when they travelled to New York. She died on 25 May 1948 in New York.

Mary Kate 'Kit' Ryan (*later O'Kelly/Ó Ceallaigh*)
BORN: Wexford, 1878
ORGANISATION: Cumann na mBan

Mary Kate 'Kit' Ryan was born in 1878, one of the Ryans of Tomcoole, Co. Wexford, a well-known constitutional nationalist family in south Wexford. John and Eliza Ryan (*née* Sutton) had a 150 acre farm at Tomcoole and were supporters of John Redmond and Home Rule. They had twelve children, eight girls and four boys. Many of the Ryan siblings, especially the girls, played an active role in Irish cultural and revolutionary politics. Education was very important to the family. Of the twelve siblings, nine got university degrees. Kit was educated at the local national school, then the Loreto School in Gorey, Wexford, and then the Loreto College on St. Stephen's Green, Dublin, where her older sister Johanna (Jo) was already a student. Like many of the girls there, she was prepared for the Royal University's degree exams and she graduated in 1902 with a first class degree in Modern Languages. She then went to Cambridge to take a teaching qualification. During her years in England her emerging nationalism became obvious as she became involved in the Gaelic League.

In 1910 Ryan returned to Ireland and was hired as a teaching assistant to Édouard Cadic, Professor of French at the National University. At this time, several of her sisters were in Dublin attending UCD and were part of the youthful and exciting intellectual, cultural, nationalist and feminist circles in Dublin. Ryan was becoming close to her sister Nell's friend, Seán T. Ó Ceallaigh (O'Kelly). Ó Ceallaigh was a member of the IRB, a founder member of Sinn Féin and the Irish Volunteers in 1913. They all became part of the Gaelic League circle, and were often invited to the nationalist parties held by Alice Stopford Green at her home on St. Stephen's Green. Her sisters Nell and Min (Josephine Mary) were particularly involved in these circles, with Min becoming closely acquainted with Seán MacDiarmada.

For some time before the Easter Rising, Ryan had established her home at 19 Ranelagh Road as a nationalist salon which became a meeting place for many of those who would fight in the Rising. Frequent visitors included Seán MacDiarmada, Liam O'Briain, Sean Forde and Seán T. Ó Ceallaigh. By 1913 she was moving further away from the Redmondite politics of her upbringing. In a letter to her sister Min in 1913, she spoke about attending the funeral of one of the victims of the 1914 Bachelor's Walk massacre.[211] The Volunteers and members of the Irish Citizen Army had led the funeral. By 1914 when John Redmond called on the Irish Volunteers to answer the call to arms on the Western Front, her nationalism was advanced enough for her to view this as the worst thing he could have done for the country. As well as engaging in the exciting world of nationalist politics, she was determined to take advantage of the new opportunities opening up for educated young women of the time. With her sisters Min and Nell, she became a member of Cumann na mBan, joining the Central branch in Dublin. She resisted marriage and continued to work in UCD. When Professor Cadic died in 1914 she took over his responsibilities as temporary professor of French for the next five years, as the war prevented the appointment of a professor to the position. Despite the attentions of Ó Ceallaigh, she wrote that she 'preferred the Bohemian life by far'.[212]

Ryan was not at any garrison during the Rising, although her younger brother James, a medical student and member of the Irish Volunteers, was chief medical officer to the garrison in the GPO, and her sister Min was active as a dispatch carrier there. Despite the fact that she was not involved, she was arrested after the surrender and taken to Richmond Barracks and then imprisoned in Kilmainham Gaol along with her sister Nell. She was subsequently moved to Mountjoy Gaol along with Nell and ten other women and was released on 5 June without charge. As Kit had not been an active participant in the Rising, her arrest was most likely due to her address and the knowledge the authorities had of the people who attended parties there, rather than any activity on her part. Many of her friends had participated in the Rising and many, including Seán T. Ó Ceallaigh, were imprisoned. Ó Ceallaigh was interred in Frongoch, Wales and was released in December 1916. He had been aide-de-camp to Patrick Pearse in the GPO during the Rising and after his release resumed his revolutionary activities.

In 1918, after many years of courtship, Ryan married Ó Ceallaigh. However, the early years of their marriage were marked by long separations as she remained teaching in UCD and Ó Ceallaigh was sent as an envoy from the Dáil to Paris (and the peace conferences) from 1919–1922, and then as envoy to the United States for Éamon de Valera from 1924–1927. She put her house, resources and energies at the disposal of the Republican Government in Dublin, 1919–1921.

Ryan and her husband opposed the Anglo-Irish Treaty. She was so opposed to it that she wrote to her sister Min advising her to leave her husband Richard Mulcahy who was pro-Treaty. The Treaty split the Ryan family. Nell, Kit, Phyllis and their brother James took the anti-Treaty side while Min and Agnes supported the Treaty. Their other siblings chose to remain neutral. The Civil War separated Ryan and her husband again. He returned to Ireland in April 1922 and began supervising republican propaganda but was arrested at the outbreak of the Civil War and detained in Kilmainham Gaol and Gormanston internment camp until December 1923. Soon after he was released, he was sent as De Valera's envoy to America. They were reunited in 1926 when Ó Ceallaigh returned to Ireland, but by 1928 she was in very poor health.

By 1925 she had been promoted to the position of lecturer in French and she also used her training in modern languages to help Ó Ceallaigh become proficient in French. While Ó Ceallaigh continued his work and travels on behalf of Fianna Fáil, Kit shared their home on St. Stephen's Green with her sister Phyllis. She remained lecturing in UCD until ill health prevented her from continuing. In early 1934 her doctor sent her to Bad Nauheim in Germany, noted for its salt springs. She died there in July 1934 from advanced rheumatic heart disease aged fifty-five. Her remains were returned to Ireland and brought for requiem Mass to the University Church at St Stephen's Green. The coffin, draped in the Tricolour, was taken to Glasnevin Cemetery where Kit Ryan Ó Ceallaigh was interred. In the *Irish Independent* of 19 July 1934 it was noted that she had 'a quiet, placid disposition, [and] her keen sense of humour and imperturbable good temper rendered the late Mrs. O'Kelly [sic] exceedingly popular with all who knew her. Her wide tolerance and unfailing good sense enabled her to keep all her friends throughout the storm and stress of recent politics, and she will he sincerely mourned in both political camps, for she was a lady of many friends and no enemies'.[213] In 1936 Seán T. Ó Ceallaigh married Phyllis Ryan, sister of Kit.

Ellen Mary 'Nell' Ryan
BORN: Wexford, 1881
ORGANISATION: Cumann na mBan

Ellen Mary 'Nell' Ryan was born in Tomcoole in 1881 to John and Eliza Ryan. Like her sisters, she was educated locally at national school and then attended the Loreto School in St. Stephen's Green in Dublin. She joined the Loreto Nuns in Rathfarnham (as did her older sister Johanna), but left after a short time. She spent the next few years travelling and teaching. She taught in San Sebastián, Spain and in Fulda, Germany for some years. After her return to Ireland, she became involved in the revolutionary movement and was the most devotedly nationalist of the sisters. Indeed, in their letters home, they often gently mocked her ardent commitment, but were in turn influenced by her. Nell joined Cumann na mBan in 1914 and was an organiser in Wexford. One of her close friends was Kathleen Browne of Rathronan who was also involved in revolutionary activities. In 1916 she was living at home in Tomcoole and working as secretary of the Co. Wexford Insurance Company.

Ryan was in Wexford when the Rising began and was arrested along with Kathleen Browne and imprisoned in Waterford Gaol. On Monday 8 May 1916 she, along with others detained after the Rising in Enniscorthy, was transported by train to Dublin, interned in Richmond Barracks and later moved to Kilmainham Gaol. She was one of the twelve women transferred to Mountjoy Gaol after the rest of the women were released. An *Irish Press* profile stated, 'her character with Dublin Castle even then, must not have been good, because she was one of the few women deported after the Rising'.[214] In June 1916, along with Countess Markievicz, Marie Perolz, Helena Molony, Bridget Foley and Winifred Carney, she was deported to Aylesbury Prison in England, where she was one of the longest serving female prisoners. She was eventually released on 13 October 1916. On her return to Ireland she resumed her revolutionary activities with Cumann na mBan, reorganising and expanding branches in Wexford. During the War of Independence she lived at Tomcoole, which became a headquarters for the local Volunteers.

During the Treaty debates Ryan emphatically supported the anti-Treaty side. In Wexford she worked as a dispatch carrier for the anti-Treaty forces. Like hundreds of anti-Treaty Cumann na mBan women she was arrested during the Civil War and was again imprisoned in Kilmainham Gaol. In March 1923 over ninety of the imprisoned women went on hunger strike in Kilmainham over withdrawal of postal services, and

Ryan was one of them. The strike ended successfully but by then she had started another hunger strike for her release and was joined by others. She said March 1923 was 'a poor Easter, but it has often been an anxious time of year in this unhappy land'.[215] Her sister, Min Mulcahy had received a number of appeals from her family for her husband, Free State General Richard Mulcahy, to agree to her release, but he refused to be influenced. After over thirty days on hunger strike she was released, after concerns about the hunger strikers' health were expressed, and after de Valera had signed his 'dump arms' order ending the Civil War. Ryan returned to live at Tomcoole, where the farm was managed by her brother Jack.

She continued to be active in politics. She became a supporter of Fianna Fáil after it was established in 1926, serving on the national executive as the representative of south Wexford. She was a member of many boards and committees including Wexford Harbour Board, Wexford Vocational Educational Committee and the Wexford Board of Health. She was elected as a Wexford Co. councillor and remained in local politics until she retired in 1954. As chairman of the Co. Board of Health she had 'the responsibility for the management of all social services, hospitals, including the Mental Hospital and the Co. Home, medical examination of schools, outdoor relief, boarded-out children and, in fact, practically every public humanitarian service for the benefit of the sick, the afflicted, the poor, and the helpless'.[216] She tackled all these responsibilities with 'plenty of ability, with an enthusiasm and energy that are boundless and also with ready wit'.[217]

The family home at Tomcoole remained a welcoming place for all the family and the next generation of nieces and nephews recall many wonderful holidays there. Whenever the Ryan family gathered at Tomcoole, political discussion was suspended thus helping to heal the deep rifts caused by the Civil War and the next generation grew up without that bitterness dividing them. Nell Ryan died in a nursing home in Wexford in 1959. She was seventy-eight years old and is buried in Glynn Cemetery. At her funeral her coffin was draped in the Tricolour and members of Cumann na mBan formed a guard of honour. [218] Her brother-in-law, Seán T. Ó Ceallaigh, called her a friend and confidant of practically every leader in the republican movement.

Martha Browne
Eileen Byrne
Julia McCauley

These three women appear on the list of women released from Kilmainham Gaol on 8/9 May 1916. However, despite extensive searches there are no extant records available for them at the time of writing. There are no records to indicate if they belonged to either Cumann na mBan or the Irish Citizen Army.

Notes

1   These short biographies are based on sources such as the 1901/1911 census returns, the Bureau of Military History Witness Statements, Military Service Pension Applications, Cumann na mBan and Irish Citizen Army membership lists, newspaper archives, political, family and personal papers held in the National Library of Ireland, UCD Archives, Kilmainham Gaol, RTE Archives, Irish Labour History Society Archives, Allen Library, National Archives of Ireland, Linen Hall Archives, the Sinn Féin Rebellion Handbook, as well as memoirs, diaries, oral histories and private family papers. Information has also been gleaned from the many publications on women and 1916 which have appeared in the last four decades – see the select bibliography for details of these.

2   In the summer of 1916 the Irish Volunteer Dependents' Fund was founded by Sorcha McMahon, Áine Ceannt and Kathleen Clarke to raise funds for the families of the 2,500 imprisoned or dead Volunteers. At the same time the Irish National Aid association was founded by a broad coalition of influential women and men. This was much more widespread than the IVDF and had the support of the clergy. In September 1916 the above organisations were amalgamated to form the Irish National Aid and Volunteer Dependents' Fund (INAAVDF).

3   IE/MA MSP34REF20583 (Bridget Davis/O'Duffy)
4   BMH WS 546 (Roseanna 'Rosie' Hackett), p. 10
5   IE/MA MSP34REF20583 (Bridget Davis/O'Duffy)
6   Ibid.
7   IE/MA MSP34REF1670 (Elizabeth Lynch/Kelly)
8   BMH WS 357 (Kathleen Lynn), p. 1
9   Ibid., p. 2
10   hÓgartaigh, *Kathleen Lynn*, p. 25
11   BMH WS 357 (Kathleen Lynn), p. 2
12   Ibid.
13   BMH WS 357 (Kathleen Lynn), p. 11
14   Ó hÓgartaigh, *Kathleen Lynn*, p. 40
15   http://eastwallforall.ie/?p=3085 accessed 13/10/15
16   R.M. Fox *Rebel Irishwomen* (Dublin 1935), 119–32 (interview) p. 120
17   Ward, *Unmanageable Revolutionaries*, p. 86
18   BMH WS 391, (Helena Molony), p. 2
19   Mary Cullen 'Women, Emancipation and Politics' p. 847
20   BMH WS 391, (Helena Molony), p. 10
21   Nell Ryan, 'Helena Molony', in Cullen and Luddy, p. 142
22   Ibid.
23   Ferghal McGarry, 'Helena Molony: a revolutionary life' in History Ireland, Issue 4 (July – August 2013), Volume 21
24   Ibid., p. 145
25   NAI, Dublin Metropolitan Police Chief Commissioner to the Chief Secretary, 8 December, 1916
26   McGarry, 'Helena Molony: a revolutionary life'
27   Helena Molony, 'James Connolly and Women' in *James Connolly Souvenir Book*, Dublin 1930
28   Mary Jones, *Those Obstreperous Lassies* p. 185
29   *Irish Independent*, 30 January, 1967
30   Matthews, *Renegades*, p.
31   IE/MA MSP34REF6982 (Annie Norgrove/Grange)
32   Matthews, *The Irish Citizen Army*, p. 144
33   IE/MA MSP34REF10154 (Jinny Shanahan)

34   Taillon, *When History was Made*, p. 55

35   IWWU Twentieth Annual Report, 1936 – 37 (Irish Labour History Society Archives)

36   IE/MA MSP34REF20238 (Máire Carron)

37   IE/MA MSP34REF16216 (Nellie Ennis/Costigan)

38   Kenneth Griffith and Timothy E. O'Grady, *Curious Journey: An Oral History of Ireland's Unfinished Revolution* (Boulder: Roberts Rinehart, 1999 reprint edition), p. 75

39   IE/MA MSP34REF48830 (Carrie Mitchell/McLoughlin)

40   IE/MA MSP34REF2462 (Mary Pauline Mokan/Keating)

41   Like the Cooneys, as the O'Sullivan sisters were active together in 1916, they have a joint biography.

42   IE/MA MSP34REF14759 (Louisa O'Sullivan/Pollard) and MSP34REF20236 (Mary O'Sullivan/O'Carroll)

43   Helga Woggan, *Silent Radical: Winifred Carney, 1887 – 1943: A Reconstruction of Her Biography* (Dublin: SIPTU, 2000)

44   BMH WS 398 (Bridget Foley/Martin)

45   BMH WS 398 (Bridget Foley/Martin), pp. 14 – 18

46   Ibid., p. 15

47   Ibid., p. 16

48   Ibid., p. 18

49   Ibid., p. 20

50   Ibid., p. 22

51   Ibid., pp. 25 – 26

52   Ibid., p. 26

53   IE/MA MSP34REF64289 (Bridget Foley/Martin)

54   Foy and Barton, *The Easter Rising*, p. 210

55   Ferghal McGarry, '"Too many histories" The Bureau of Military History and Easter 1916' in *History Ireland*, Issue 6 (Nov/Dec 2011), Revolutionary Period 1912 – 23, Volume 19

56   *Irish Times*, 1934

57   BMH WS 568 (Eilís Bean Uí Chonaill/Ní Riain), p. 38

58   *Irish Press*, 24 August 1935

59   MSP34REF11828 (Martha Kelly/Murphy)

60   Ibid.

61   Ibid.

62   BMH WS 359 (Aoife de Burca), p. 26

63   BMH WS 357 (Ó hOgartaigh, *Kathleen Lynn*, p. 27)

64   IE/MA MSP34REF849 (May Doyle/Byrne)

65   Ibid.

66   As the Cooney sisters were active together throughout the revolutionary decade their biographies have been combined.

67   Ibid.

68   All information on the Cooney sisters is based on their pensions applications, IE/MA MSP34REF8936 (Eileen Cooney/Harbourne), IE/MA MSP34REF8809 (Annie Cooney/O'Brien) and their Bureau of Military History witness statements , BMH WS 805 (Annie O'Brien/Cooney) and Lily Curran /Cooney), as well as oral histories from their descendants.

69   BMH WS 482 (Rose McNamara), Appendix B

70   McCoole, *No Ordinary Women*, p. 155

71   IE/MA MSP34REF1970 (Bridget Hegarty/Harmon)

72   IE/MA MSP34REF8912 (Josephine Kelly/Greene)

73   Ibid.

74   BMH WS 185 (Margaret Kennedy), p. 1
75   IE/MA MSP34REF596 (Margaret 'Loo' Kennedy)
76   Ibid.
77   Ibid.
78   Ibid.
79   *Irish Press,* 1 June, 1953
80   As the Liston sister were active together in 1916, their biographies are included together.
81   BMH WS 482 (Rose McNamara), pp. 6–8
82   IE/MA MSP34REF1426 (Michael Liston)
83   IE/MA MSP34REF751 (Priscilla Quigley/Kavanagh)
84   BMH WS 482 (Rose McNamara), pp. 6–8
85   IE/MA MSP34REF967 (Rose McNamara)
86   IE/MA MSP34REF1729 (Rose Mullally/Farrelly)
87   IE/MA MSP34REF376 (Kathleen Murphy)
88   Ibid.
89   Ibid.
90   The growing violence against Catholics in Belfast led the Dáil in Dublin to impose the 'Belfast Boycott' against Belfast banks and businesses in 1921.
91   Ibid.
92   IE/MA MSP34REF2229 (Lily O'Brennan)
93   Margaret Buckley, *Jangle of Keys* (Dublin, 1938), p. 68
94   The Irish White Cross was a reputable, non-political, non-sectarian organisation which was established to help disperse funds collected by the American Committee for Relief in Ireland to those in need.
95   *Cambridge Dictionary of Irish Biography*; Lily O'Brennan
96   IE/MA MSP34REF1235 (Margaret O'Flaherty/Timmons)
97   IE/MA MSP34REF2399 (Sheila O'Hanlon/Lynch)
98   Ibid.
99   Ibid.
100 Ibid.
101 IE/MA MSP34REF4302 (Josephine O'Keefe/McNamara)
102 Ibid.
103 Ibid.
104 Ibid.
105 Ibid.
106 *Irish Press,* 24 May, 1966
107 IE/MA MSP34REF1041 (Emily O'Keefe/Hendley)
108 Ibid.
109 Ibid.
110 Ibid.
111 IE/MA MSP34REF59908 (James Kevin MacNamee)
112 BMH WS 0805, (Annie O'Brien/Cooney and Lily Curran /Cooney), p. 12
113 IE/MA DP25144 (Agnes MacNamee)
114 Ibid.
115 Ibid.
116 IE/MA MSP34REF4997 (Marie Quigley/Clince)
117 Ibid.
118 IE/MA MSP34REF751 (Priscilla Quigley/Kavanagh)
119 Ibid.
120 Ibid.

121   Ibid.

122   Ibid.

123   Ibid.

124   Ibid.

125   BMH WS 482 (Rose McNamara), Appendix A, Names of members of Inghinidhe branch members of Cumann na mBan prior to 1916.

126   Ibid.

127   IE/MA CMB/126 – Cumann na mBan membership of Dublin City Council. The District was comprised of the following branches which were attached to the following Irish Volunteer Battalions: Ard Craobh (or 'Central branch', 1st Battalion, Dublin Brigade), Ranelagh (2nd Battalion, Dublin Brigade, not in existence in 1916), Fairview (2nd Battalion, Dublin Brigade), Columcille (1st Battalion, Dublin Brigade), Drumcondra (2nd Battalion), University (3rd Battalion, Dublin Brigade), Éamonn Ceannt (4th Battalion, Dublin Brigade), Ringsend (3rd Battalion, Dublin Brigade), Inighinidhe (3rd and 4th Battalion, Dublin Brigade).

128   BMH WS 482 (Rose McNamara), Appendix A, Names of members of Inghinidhe branch members of Cumann na mBan prior to 1916

129   Lane, *Rosamond Jacob*, p. 50

130   O'Daly 'The Women of Easter Week', *An tÓglach*, 1926 p. 3

131   BMH WS 585 (Frank Robbins), p. 76

132   *Cambridge Dictionary of Irish Biography*; Madeleine ffrench-Mullen

133   Ó hÓgartaigh, *Kathleen Lynn*, pp. 68–69

134   *Irish Press*, 27 May, 1944

135   http://www.labour.ie/download/pdf/seven_women_of_the_labour_movement1916.pdf

136   IE/MA MSP34REF10326 (Mary Gahan/O'Carroll)

137   Ibid.

138   BMH WS 1693 (John Kenny), pp. 17–18

139   IE/MA MSP34REF10326 (Mary Gahan / O'Carroll)

140   *Cambridge Dictionary of Irish Biography*; Helen Ruth ('Nellie') Gifford Donnelly

141   Ibid.

142   BMH WS 256 (Nellie Donnolly), pp. 2–3

143   Taillon, *When History was Made*, p. 69

144   Ibid., p. 98

145   *Cambridge Dictionary of Irish Biography*; Helen Ruth ('Nellie') Gifford Donnolly

146   IE/MA MSP34REF8920 (Bridget Goff)

147   BMH WS 546 (Roseanna Hackett), p. 1

148   Ibid., p. 2

149   Ibid., p. 3

150   Ibid., p. 5

151   BMH WS 546

152   Ibid., p. 8

153   May O'Brien, *Clouds on my windows: a Dublin memoir* (Dingle: Brandon Press, 2004), pp. 50–51

154   Ibid.

155   *Irish Press*, 1 September, 1970

156   IE/MA MSP34REF1861 (Margaret Joyce)

157   IE/MA MSP34REF63780 (Katie Kelly)

158   http://www.irishmedals.org/saint-stephen-s-green.html accessed 10/07/15

159   McAuliffe 'Rosie 'Roseanna' Hackett', p. 54

160   Constance Markievicz, 'Some Women of Easter Week (1926)', in Dennis L. Dworkin (ed.) *Ireland and Britain, 1798–1922 An Anthology of Sources* (London: Hackett Publishing

Company, 2012), p. 211

161   J. Shannon, 'Remembering RCSI and the 1916 Rising' in *Irish Journal of Medical Science*, Vol. 175, No. 2, p. 8

162   Margaret Skinnider on Countess Markievicz, 'The Green Jacket: A Portrait of Constance Markievicz' (1960); http://www.rte.ie/archives/category/war-and-con flict/2015/0515/701266-the-woman-they-called-madame/

163   O'Daly, 'The Women of Easter Week', *An t'Óglach*, p. 4

164   Brian Crowley, *A History of Fairview Cumann na mBan* (Dublin, 1998), p. 1

165   O'Daly, 'The Women of Easter Week', *An t'Óglach*, 1926, p. 3

166   Ibid

167   Ibid.

168   Ibid.

169   IE/MA MSP34REF13563 (Nora Mary Margaret O'Daly)

170   O'Daly, 'The Women of Easter Week', *An t'Óglach*, 1926 pp. 3–6

171   Ibid.

172   Ibid.

173   IE/MA MSP34REF13563 (Nora Mary Margaret O'Daly)

174   IE/MA MSP34REF47647 (May O'Moore/Wisely)

175   Ibid.

176   Ibid.

177   IE/MA MSP34REF33364 (Cathleen Seery/Redmond)

178   Ibid.

179   McAuliffe, *Senator Kathleen A. Browne* pp. 67-75

180   *The Wexford People*, 13 May, 1916

181   Ibid.,

182   McAuliffe *Senator Kathleen A. Browne,* pp. 14-18

183   Ibid.

184   Ibid.

185   Ibid., pp. 81–83

186   Ibid.

187   Ibid.

188   Ibid.

189   Ibid.

190   Cullen Owens, *A Social History of Women in Ireland* p. 322

191   BMH W.S. 333 witness Statement of Aine O'Rahilly

192   Sighle Humphreys Papers, UCD, P106/976 (UCDA)

193   Sighle Humphreys Papers, UCD P106/384 (UCDA)

194   Sighle Humphreys Papers, UCD P106/384 (UCDA)

195   BMH W.S. 333

196   BMH WS 246 (Marie Perolz/Flannagan), p. 1

197   Ibid., p. 2

198   Ibid., p.2

199   Ibid., p. 2

200   Ibid., p. 11

201   Ibid., pp. 11–12

202   Ibid., p. 12

203   *Irish Press,* 29 August 1955, p. 5

204   *Cambridge Dictionary of Irish Biography;* Plunkett, Count George Noble, *History Ireland,* Issue 3, 1996

205   *Irish Press*, 7 March, 1944

206   Ward, 'The League of Women Delegates & Sinn Féin' *History Ireland* Issue 3 1996

207   Many thanks to Manus O'Riordain whose research steered the authors in the direction of the Reitz family butchers and the connection with the Irish Citizen Army.

208   *Irish Independent*, 17 August 1914, p. 2

209   *Irish Independent,* 18 August 1914

210   http://comeheretome.com/2014/03/18/when-dublin-mobs-attacked-german-pork-butchers-august-1914/ accessed 20/10/2015

211   As British soldiers were marching along the quays back to their barracks on 26 July 1914, having confronted Volunteers bringing guns from Howth earlier in the day, they were jeered by members of the public. A large crowd had gathered and was hurling stones and rotten fruit at the soldiers. At Bachelors Walk, the Major in charge ordered the crowd to disperse, when they didn't the soldiers opened fire into the crowd. When the firing stopped three civilians were dead and thirty-two were wounded.

212   Roy Foster *Vivid Faces,* p. 121

213   *Irish Independent*, 19 July Thursday 1934, p. 4

214   *Irish Press*, Monday, 22 March 1937, p. 5

215   Judith Harford, and Claire Rush (eds) *Have Women Made a Difference?: Women in Irish Universities, 1850-2010* (Oxford: Peter Lang, 2010), p. 117

216   *Irish Press*, Monday 22 March 1937, 1937, p. 5

217   *Irish Press*, Monday 22 March 1937, p. 5

218   *Irish Examiner*, Friday 11 December, 1959

CONCLUSION

—

Forgetting & Remembering:
The 77 Women of 1916

The revolutionary men and women must insist that men and women in Ireland have equal rights and duties and a surrender of any of those rights or duties is treason to Ireland.

— NORA CONNOLLY O' BRIEN

OUNTESS MARKIEVICZ was the woman with whom the authorities and the media were most concerned immediately after the Rising. Her self-created military dress, her class and her perceived militancy provided the public with one way to view female participation in the Rising. In particular, it was a way a society not used to or accepting of women taking a role in 'male affairs' could understand and speak about why so many women had been combatants. Almost immediately the language used by reporters was highly gendered and demeaning of the women. *The Irish Times* of 28 April 1916 refers to the arrest of the 'prominent' Countess Marckieviesz [*sic*] while 'fantastically dressed in male attire'.[2] On 6 May 1916 *The Irish Examiner* included a report from the *Daily Telegraph* which, somewhat breathlessly, reported that:

> amongst the prisoners taken away… were women in male clothing. One or two of the captives has a distinctly feminine appearance. However, young women in male attire were bearing arms in the streets against British soldiers and it is believed carried on fairly successful sniping.[3]

The report went on to say that Countess Markievicz 'was seen on several occasions conducting and directing men in their operations'.[4] The *Anglo-Celt* of the same day remarked on the 'conspicuous number of women fighting with the rebels'.[5] The newspaper quotes a 'gentleman' eyewitness who reported that he saw a:

> number of women marching into Dublin on Sunday. Some of them had naval revolvers strapped round their waists. They were wearing the dark green uniform similar to that of the male insurgents and slouch hats. They consist largely of young women….[and] I believe they have had training with the men for they do not lack a certain discipline and organisation.[6]

This witness also stated that 'there have been cases of British military officers shot from behind by women'.[7] The headline in the New York newspaper, *The Evening World*, reported that 'she [Markievicz] had shot six rebels who refused to follow orders' and "in man's clothing and flashing a brace of revolvers" she had led an attack on the Shelbourne Hotel'.[8] On 6 May the headline in the *Kerryman* was 'A Garrison of Women', and the article went on to describe the rebel garrison at the Royal College of Surgeons as 'under the command of the Countess Markievitz [sic]'.[9] It described how 'many of the garrison were women. They had been fighters and carried rifles. They wore no skirts, but had men's uniform, including trousers and puttees'.[10] The report also speaks of the other women rebels, 'who were nurses and displayed the Red Cross'. A further report in the *Kerryman* refers to 'The Amazon', a woman or women among the rebels, using a revolver and acting in some leading capacity.[11]

The *Irish Times* described Markievicz at the surrender at the College of Surgeons as 'dressed in top boots, breeches, service tunic and a hat with feathers', she took out her revolver 'kissed it affectionately' and handed it to the British officer.[12] The paper reported that she had been in charge of rebels at the College of Surgeons. On 29 April it also reported that several women rebels were armed with naval revolvers.[13] In New York Sidney Gifford (sister of insurgent Nellie Gifford) described how reports from England described Countess Markievicz as a 'sinister figure who had a room in her house entirely filled with human skulls'.[14] Headlines such as 'Countess shot Six' and 'Woman Rebel leader' indicate the discomfort generally felt about combatant women.

These reports[15] helped reinforce the idea that the women who participated in the Rising were different. They were accused of aping male behaviour; they wore male clothing and fought as men in the Rising. The underlying disgust at these gender transgressions, sartorial, political and societal committed by the women of 1916, comes through almost immediately in these news reports. The women were not only threatening as rebels in the traditional sense, they were also threatening to society as a whole. Violence as used by men, however traumatic, was a known quality, but the image of a woman in trousers, holding a gun, was unthinkable. It produced, as Weihman has argued, 'an even more disturbing challenge to Irish society, an anarchic reverberation that similarly but more transgressively underlined the seriousness of national upheaval'.[16] A country where the women were out of control was a country in serious trouble. Even the female rebels who dressed in 'normal' clothing, in long dresses and coats, were transgressing as they used their ability to move more or less unhindered through the city, carrying dispatches, arms and supplies to and from the various rebel outposts. The women in trousers and the women in dresses subverted the roles allowed to women by society.

It was not only the newspapers who found the participation of the women in the Rising problematic. The authorities and a good portion of wider society also found this activity by women hard to accept. Their male comrades had, for the most part, appreciated the participation of the women. But their praise was couched in very traditional gendered terms. Irish Volunteer Fintan Murphy, who was stationed in the GPO during Easter Week, sang the praises of the 'gallantry and goodness to us of that brave band of women, some only in their teens, who tended and cared for us during the week', however he was also willing to admit that 'some of them risking their lives in crossing the street to our outposts there and all ready and willing to undertake dangerous missions to other commands and elsewhere'.[17] The attitude of many of their male comrades was similar to this. Leslie Price said of the Volunteers, when told to go home at the GPO, 'the kind of men they were: they thought that we should be away from all that danger'.[18] They were grateful for the aid the women gave, either as nurses or cooks and accepted that they did some dangerous work of dispatch carrying. As John J. Doyle stationed in the GPO later reported 'I had about twelve Cumann na mBan for the nursing inside. A number of them were looking after the cooking arrangements under Miss Gavan Duffy'. In his witness statement he praised Cumann na mBan 'at G.H.Q. during Easter Week for their courage and devotion and work; it was magnificent'.[19]

The real work of revolution however, the fighting and dying, was understood to be the preserve of the men. The women had overcome serious obstacles to be part of the Rising, as Bridie O'Mullane wrote:

> I had a good deal of prejudice to overcome on the part of the parents, who did not mind their boys taking part in a military movement, but who had never heard of, and were reluctant to accept, the idea of a body of gun-women. It was, of course, a rather startling innovation and, in that way, Cumann na mBan can claim to have been the pioneers in establishing what was undoubtedly a women's auxiliary of an army. I fully understood this attitude and eventually, in most cases, succeeded in overcoming this prejudice.[20]

Women did regard themselves as combatants in a violent uprising, operating in a space in which they were in danger and faced the possibility of losing their lives. They expected that they would play their part and 'do their bit', as Margaret Skinnider titled her memoir of her role in the Rising.

Did your daughters run and hide from the sound of guns?'[21]

In 1963, Helena Molony was interviewed about her role and that of other women in the Rising. She said that:

> When people question me about the part the women played in Ireland's last fight for freedom I feel they might as well ask me what did the tall fair haired men do in the wars and what did the small dark men do? The answer in both cases has to be the same. They did whatever came to their hands to do, from day to day, and whatever they were capable of in aptitude or training.[21]

For Molony the participation of women in the Rising was not extraordinary. As a political woman, involved in radical politics for at least a decade prior to 1916, she believed her part was no more or less than that of her comrades, male and female. She stated that she 'was a member of the Irish Citizen Army, whose idea of freedom was of the widest and most comprehensive kind, the abolition of the domination of nation over nation, class over class and sex over sex'.[22] She complained to Seán O'Faoláin that many men 'seem to be unable to believe that any woman can embrace an ideal –accept it intellectually, feel it as a profound emotion and then calmly decide to make a vocation of working for its realisation'.[23] She despaired that men could not understand that women could embark on a journey of politicisation and come to believe in and fight for a cause (of nation, of gender, of class). Women, she said, were not necessarily involved in events like the Rising because they were 'in love with some man or looking for excitement, or limelight, or indulging their vanity'.[24] She believed it was self-evident that a woman could work 'as a man might work' for a cause, in this case, the cause of Ireland.[25] It was unthinkable that she, a political woman who had worked for Ireland from the early part of the twentieth century, needed the imprimatur of a man to motivate her.

Despite the traditional attitudes towards women in the public realm and the continuing battle for equality in the post-Rising period, especially within Sinn Féin, the period from 1916 – 1922 seemed to hold much promise for women and their claim to equal citizenship in any new Republic. This promise was further enhanced by the part played by women in the War of Independence (1919 – 1921). An enlarged and expanded Cumann na mBan provided safe houses and first aid services for men on the run, they protected arms dumps and transported arms, messages and dispatches for the IRA during the 1919 – 1921 war. The work women undertook evolved beyond the expected roles of caring and nurturing, as had happened during Easter Week. Women acted as couriers, kept lines of communication open between different IRA brigades and undertook surveillance and intelligence work. Lily O'Brennan, for example, as well as providing nursing services, was a District Judge in the Republican courts, while also working for the Dáil's Department of Labour with the Minister of Labour, Countess Markievicz. Sheila O'Hanlon, a member of the Inghinidhe branch, carried out surveillance work on suspected spies, while Brigid Foley befriended an Auxiliary, John Reynolds, at Michael Collins' request and received vital information about troop movements from him.

Josie O'Keeffe and her sister Emily stored bombs, arms and ammunition in their house and provided these at a moment's notice for IRA actions. The three Cooney sisters were part of the back-up for the men who assassinated suspected British Intelligence officers on Bloody Sunday, 21 November 1920. The sisters brought the weapons used in the assassinations to St. Stephen's Green, handed them to the members of the 'Squad', later took the guns back and sheltered men in their home, which was a safe house. Rose McNamara also undertook dangerous work during the War of Independence. She had oversight of first aid services provided by Cumann na mBan in Dublin. On receiving word of impending ambushes or actions she would prepare first aid stations to receive wounded IRA men, who could not use hospitals for fear of arrest.

Women were also involved in propaganda and training work. Priscilla Quigley was responsible for distributing republican propaganda leaflets, posters and post-cards. Many of the women were given responsibility for different parts of the country, with Quigley going to areas in the midlands to give lectures in special training in first aid, morse code, signalling and organisation. In Galway, Katie Kelly assisted Alice Cashel in the Republican Courts, while Nora O'Daly was a judge in the Fairview/Ballybough district Republican Courts. Nell Humphreys and Áine O'Rahilly had moved to a new home on Ailesbury Road where they had 'a room camouflaged' by their builder to harbour Cathal Brugha, who was on the run. The camouflage had to be added after the house was built because the military kept watching it during construction.[26] Other women such as Meg Carron befriended British soldiers and persuaded them to sell arms and ammunition, while May Gahan managed to buy a machine gun from a soldier stationed at Ship Street Barracks. But women did not escape untouched by the violence during the War of Independence. While IRA men could go on the run, women remained at home, exposed to raids that might be undertaken by the Black and Tans or Auxiliaries.[27] Lil Conlon, a member of the Cork City branch, Cumann na mBan said in her memoir that by the summer of 1921 attention was more focused on women as the authorities realised their importance to the IRA campaign. The 'going was tough' she wrote 'on the female sex' as they could not go on the run like their male comrades. They were there when their homes and communities were raided:

> To intensify the reign of terror, swoops were made at night, entries forced into their homes, and the women's hair cut off in a brutal fashion as well as suffering other indignities and insults. General Sir Nevil Macready recognised that the women co-operated in no small degree with the Volunteers, even though his tributes were not too complimentary.[28]

Despite these risks Cumann na mBan countrywide continued their activities and were more or less on a military footing. In 1921 several IRA commandants said in a letter that:

> there was no question of the girls only helping. In despatch carrying, scouting, and intelligence work, all of which are highly dangerous, they did far more than the soldiers. In addition to this the Flying Columns would have collapsed early this year were it not for the assistance of the women, organised and unorganised.[29]

The War of Independence ended when a truce was declared between Great Britain and Ireland on 11 July 1921. Tense negotiations between the British government and an Irish delegation took place over the next five months. Everyone in Ireland waited to see what the outcome of these negotiations would be and none more so than the women of Cumann na mBan. The Anglo-Irish Treaty, signed on 6 December 1921, fell far short of the Republic that so many men and women had fought for in the preceding years. The six women who had been elected to the Dáil in the 1921 general election – Countess Markievicz, Kathleen Clarke, Margaret Pearse, Kate O'Callaghan, Mary MacSwiney and Ada English – voted against the Treaty after delivering imp-assioned speeches at the Dáil debates in January 1922. Accused of speaking for the dead and not considering the living, the women were asked to remember that the 'earth belongs to those who are on it, and not to those who are under it, and to the living and not the dead we owe our votes'.[30] Dr. Ada English responded vehemently that the women did not only:

> have the opinions they have because they have a grievance against England, or because their men folk were killed and murdered by England's representatives in this country. It was a most unworthy thing for any man to say here. I

can say this more freely because, I thank my God, I have no dead men to
be thrown in my teeth as a reason for holding the opinions I hold.[31]

The arguments against the Treaty swayed the majority of Cumann na mBan, including
most of the seventy-seven women. Cumann na mBan was the first organisation to
debate and reject the Treaty at its specially convened convention in February 1922.
While a few such as Brigid Lyons Thornton and Kathleen Browne supported the Treaty,
the majority were opposed to it. The anti-Treaty women included both Cumann na
mBan and those who were previously in the Irish Citizen Army. The former members of
the Citizen Army who opposed the Treaty included Kathleen Barrett, Kathleen Lynn,
Helena Molony, the Norgrove sisters, Jinny Shanahan, Madeleine ffrench-Mullen and
Countess Markievicz. Members of Cumann na mBan who were anti-Treaty included
Meg Carron, Winifred Carney, Julia Grenan, Elizabeth O'Farrell, Annie Higgins,
Martha Kelly and many others. Like their comrades in the IRA, which had also split
as a result of the Treaty, these women opposed to the Treaty would do everything
in their power, both politically and militarily, to uphold the Republic proclaimed in
1916 and to which they gave their loyalty.

With the outbreak of the Civil War on 28 June 1922 it seemed like history
was repeating itself. Once again Dublin city was a battleground. The anti-Treaty
forces occupied buildings in the city centre, most notably and symbolically, the Four
Courts. Once again the citizens of Dublin awoke to hear gunfire and explosions and
once again the women of Cumann na mBan were in the thick of it, alongside their
anti-Treaty comrades, many serving in the garrisons they had been in during the
Rising. Martha Kelly served as a dispatch carrier for Cathal Brugha, the anti-Treaty
leader, while he was in the Four Courts prior to the outbreak of fighting. The Cooney
sisters served around Marrowbone Lane Distillery, as they had done during the
Rising. The sisters transported arms and ammunition for the anti-Treaty IRA. As a
result, their home and the homes of many of the women were raided by the pro-Treaty
forces. Margaret Kennedy, who was anti-Treaty, commanded over 300 Cumann na
mBan women to aid the Republican side in Dublin. She was also given the task of
organising the members of Cumann na mBan to act as stewards and march in the
funeral processions of Cathal Brugha and Harry Boland, both killed in the first few
weeks of the Civil War.

Many of the seventy-seven women were arrested during the Civil War and
returned to Kilmainham Gaol where they had spent ten days in May 1916. Among

them were Lily O'Brennan, May Gahan, Josie O'Keeffe, Countess Markievicz, Nell Humphreys (along with her daughter Sighle and sister Áine O'Rahilly), Sheila O'Hanlon, Maggie Timmons and Nell Ryan, who were all again imprisoned, this time by their former comrades. Most of them undertook hunger strikes while incarcerated and the medical officer charged with looking after them in Kilmainham Gaol was Brigid Lyons Thornton, who had fought with them in 1916.

The Civil War brought bitter divisions, not just brother against brother but sister against sister. Nell Ryan was vehemently anti-Treaty and was imprisoned during the Civil War. Her sister Min was married to Richard Mulcahy, Chief of Staff of the National Army after the death of Michael Collins in August 1922. Nell Ryan spent over thirty days on hunger strike in Kilmainham Gaol and despite the familial connection, Mulcahy refused to intervene on his sister-in-law's behalf. In Wexford, the friendship between Kathleen Browne and Nell Ryan was irrevocably broken by the Treaty – Browne having taken the pro-Treaty side. In fact, such was the enmity between them, Browne claimed that anti-Treaty forces threatened to destroy her home and that:

> we were saved from being burnt out [only] by a military guard [from the National Army] and threats from the officers to burn Miss Ryan's place [in Tomcoole] to the ground if mine were meddled with.[32]

The participation of women in large numbers on the anti-Treaty side lead to a growing anxiety, first expressed among sections of society and in the media in the post-Rising period, but now reiterated. These ungovernable women with guns, the shadow of the gun-women, had become a threat to the very fabric of society.

P.S. O'Hegarty, speaking to the Dail in 1922, claimed the 'hysterical' women of Cumann na mBan fermented conflict when men would end it, he stated that 'Woman's business in the world is with the things of life [...] but these women busied themselves with nothing but the things of death'.[33] Militant women, this 'army of women', whose activities once were necessary to fight and win a war, were now dangerous, evil, unmanageable subversives. Without re-imposing control these women had the potential to destroy society and the Irish nation. The growing concern about armed girls and women was reflected in a report issued by the Free State on 1 January 1923 which, as the *Irish Independent* reported, stated that 'neurotic girls are among the most active adherents to the irregular cause'.[34] W.T. Cosgrave, President of the Executive, said in a speech that, unhappily for Ireland, 'die-hards are women whose ecstasies at their extremest can find no outlet so satisfying as destruction'.[36] His successor, Éamon de Valera, regarded the women as 'at once the boldest and most unmanageable of revolutionaries'.[37] By 1925 women were being advised not to join Cumann na mBan as 'women who go around taking dispatches and arms from one place to another are furies… who would respect them or who would marry them?'.[38]

Forgetting and remembering

> For they sing the Men of the West
> And the Boys of Wexford too.
> Were there no women living round these parts:
> Tell me, what did they do…?[39]

The space that women had taken up in the public realm for the first two decades of the twentieth century was now closing to them. Their contribution to the new State was to be as respectable wives and mothers and their contributions to the Easter Rising and the revolutionary years began to enter the footnotes of history. Even when the women were included, the unease many had felt and continued to feel about the presence of women in violent revolution was now openly expressed. O'Hegarty was particularly vicious about Republican women in *The Victory of Sinn Féin* (1924) seeing them as 'unsexed' because of their experience of war. Helena Molony disliked Seán Ó'Faoláin's biography of *Countess Markievicz* (1934) because of its sneering, unsympathetic tone. Where women were remembered in the male centred histories of the revolutionary period it was the 'loyal and courageous' Cumann na mBan who cared for and looked after the men as they [the men] fought to free Ireland. For many women this indeed was their experience of Easter Week, 1916. They worked in the kitchens of the outposts, they set up the first aid stations and they 'kept house' as the fighting raged around them. In Boland's Mill garrison de Valera regretted not allowing women to join him as his men had to do the 'women's' work, which took them away from the 'real' work of combat. The work that women undertook did free men for military roles. But women also undertook more dangerous roles, that of dispatch carrier, transportation of food and weaponry around the city, intelligence gathering and scouting. This they did in a city under bombardment, using their ability to move as seemingly unthreatening women around the combat zones. Other women were front line combatants, leading attacks, using weapons, killing. However the memory of the supportive nurses and carers came to be the predominant memory of the women of 1916. In most histories, Markievicz (and to a lesser extent Skinnider 'the sniper'), the woman with the gun was an outlier; the 'nurse' ideal came to represent the true image of the woman of the Rising.

Memory is contested and subjective and often gendered. Can the women of 1916 be considered combatants? The image of the nurse, the carer and the cook who looked after the men in the Four Courts, the GPO, the Royal College of Surgeons resonates as the proper image of the women in the Rising. The combatant with the gun is male; the carer at the first aid station is female. This, of course, is also a subjective gendered memory as not all men held or used guns. Many were in charge of logistics, ran the commissariat at a number of outposts and provided first aid. However their status as combatants is unchallenged, they were men who were there and therefore, they were soldiers. The complexities of women's participation in the Rising and the reason for their participation in 1916, became victim to selective remembering; downplayed, overlooked or indeed simply forgotten. Women were there to be the emotional and caring support to the fighting men; courageous, loyal and brave but not combatants. In recent decades, however, historians have been revising the Rising, which has allowed a process of recovery of the women's histories, in all their complexities. Revising existing archival sources and using newly available material allows us to expand on the detail of which women were there, why they were there and what they did. Even within this sample of seventy-seven women who fought in 1916, the complexities of political ideology, class, age, and motivation are evident.

Among the seventy-seven there are radical, separatist feminists such as Helena Molony or trade unionists like Jinny Shanahan. There are women from Cumann na mBan who didn't question their auxiliary status and there were Cumann na mBan women who demanded a more equal role. Annie Cooney spent the week in the kitchen in Marrowbone Lane. Nora O'Daly spent the week working in a first aid station in the College of Surgeons. Brigid Foley spent the week delivering dispatches to and from the GPO. Marie Perolz spent the week delivering dispatches around the country and was disgusted she missed the fight when she arrived back in Dublin just after the surrender. Margaret Skinnider demanded she be allowed a combat role and was wounded three times. Countess Markievicz and Kathleen Lynn both served as commanding officers. Rose McNamara refused to escape before the surrender because she was a rebel just like the men and would surrender with them. Nell Humphreys, writing to her sister in Australia after the Rising, stated that she was very conflicted about the role of women; conflicted that women wanting to fight was somehow unwomanly but proud too that her daughter had such nerve:

> Did you hear at all of the part women took in the Rising? I used to feel ashamed
> of Sighle, as being unwomanly when Anna (sic) told me that at times
> it was difficult to keep her from taking a shot herself, that the way she gloried
> when the enemy fell was actually inhuman, and her nerve during the whole
> thing was wonderful.[40]

The roles the women managed to undertake in combat, even in such a gendered space, were many and varied. Among the seventy-seven women were nurses, cooks, dispatch carriers, spies, couriers, snipers and soldiers. They were motivated by nationalism, feminism, and socialism – they were radical feminists, militant nationalists, trade unionists and some were influenced by aspects of all three ideologies. They were from the middle and working classes and they were mainly unmarried and young – a youthful generation inspired by the ideas of a free Ireland in which women would take their place as equal citizens. No longer are they simply remembered as the loyal and courageous 'nurse' who nurtured and cared, or indeed as the dangerous woman who wore trousers and carried a gun. Their contributions and motivations are understood as being as complex and politically motivated at those of their male comrades. Their activities during the Rising and after, how their contributions was viewed by themselves, society and their comrades, as well at the 'selective amnesia' which dictated their place or lack of place, in the history books, form the central focus of this research and analysis. As Máire Nic Shiubhlaigh wrote of her participation in 1916, it was a 'great thing... that what you had always hoped for had happened at last. An insurrection had taken place and you were actually participating in it'.[41] They, these seventy-seven women, were there during Easter Week 1916: their lives, their activism, their contributions and those of the almost 200 other women who were there, are central to the history of the Rising. Their histories deserve to be known.

Notes

1   Nora Connolly O'Brien 'Women in Ireland, Their Part in the Revolutionary Struggle', *An Phoblacht*, 25 June 1932 in Ward *In Their Own Voice* p. 175

2   *The Irish Times*, 28 April 1916, p. 3

3   *The Irish Examiner*, 6 May 1916, p. 6

4   Ibid.

5   *The Anglo-Celt*, 6 May 1916, p.1

6   Ibid.

7   Ibid.

8   http://comeheretome.com/2014/01/21/peter-pearse-larkinites-and-the-german-submarines-american-coverage-of-the-1916-rising/ accessed 07/09/15

9   *The Kerryman*, 6 May 1916, p. 5

10   Ibid.

11   Ibid. p 3

12   *The Irish Times*, 12 May 1916, p.5

13   *The Irish Times*, 29 April 1916, p. 3

14   Alan Hayes (ed.), *The Years Flew By; Recollections of Madame Sidney Gifford Czira* (Dublin, Arlen House, 2000), p. 78

15   http://comeheretome.com/2014/01/21/peter-pearse-larkinites-and-the-german-submarines-american-coverage-of-the-1916-rising/ accessed 07/09/15 and The Kerryman, 6 May 1916, p. 5

16   Lisa Wiehman, 'Doing My Bit for Ireland: Transgressing Gender in the Easter Rising' in *Éire-Ireland* 39.3&4 (2004), p. 228

17   BMH WS 373 (Fintan Murphy), p. 4

18   BMH WS 1,754 (Leslie Price / Barry), p. 7

19   BMH WS 748 (John J. Doyle) p. 16

20   BMH WS 450 (Brighidh O'Mullane), p. 2–3

21   From a poem by Brian Moore, 'Invisible Women' in Taillon *Women of 1916*, p. vii

22   Helena Molony interviewed in *Women of the Rising* (RTE, 1963)

23   Ibid.

24   BMH WS 391 (Helena Molony), p. 62

25   Ibid. pp. 62–63

26   Ibid. p. 63

27   BMH WS 333 (Áine O'Rahilly), p.10

28   The Black and Tans, officially the Royal Irish Constabulary Reserve Force, was a force of temporary constables recruited to assist the Royal Irish Constabulary. They were nicknamed Black and Tans because of their mix and match uniforms of khaki and black. The Auxiliary Division of the Royal Irish Constabulary (ADRIC), generally known as the Auxiliaries or Auxies, was a paramilitary unit of the Royal Irish Constabulary. Both operated in Ireland during the War of Independence.

29   Lil Conlon, *Cumann na mBan and the Women of Ireland 1913–25* (Kilkenny People Ltd, Kilkenny, 1969), p. 224

30   Ibid. p. 240

31   Dáil Eireann, Official report: debate on the treaty between Great Britain and Ireland signed in London on the 6 December 1921 (Dublin Talbot Press, 1922) p.178b

32   Ibid., p. 250a

33   Department of the Taoiseach, NAI Cabinets 7691, letter from Kathleen Browne dated 23 November 1925

34   Gerry Kearns, 'Mother Ireland and the revolutionary sisters' in *Cultural Geographies* 2004, 11, p. 462

35   Louise Ryan, 'Furies' and 'Die-hards' Women and Irish Republicanism in the early Twentieth century in *Gender and History*, Vol 11, No. 2, July 1999, p. 266

36   Ibid.

37   Sikata Banerjee, *Muscular Nationalism: Gender, Violence, and Empire in India and Ireland, 1914–2004* (New York, NYU Press, 2012), p. 86

38   Advice from a Catholic Bishop in 1925. Banerjee Muscular Nationalism, p. 88

39   Ibid.

40   Sighle Humphreys Papers, UCDA P106/384 (UCDA)

41   Máire Nic Shiubhlaigh *The Splendid Years* (Dublin: Duffy, 1955), p. 182

Select Bibliography

PRIMARY SOURCES

Allen Library
    Madeleine ffrench-Mullen, memoir/diary
    Elizabeth O'Farrell, The Personal Account of the Surrender

Kilmainham Gaol Archives
    Helena Molony Papers
    Elizabeth O'Farrell Papers

National Library of Ireland
    Hanna and Francis Sheehy Skeffington papers
    Rosamond Jacobs Papers/Diary
    Grace Plunkett Papers
    Ryan Family Papers
    Louise Gavan Duffy Papers

National Archives of Ireland
    Bureau of Military History Witness Statements (www.bureauofmilitaryhistory.ie)
    The 1901 and 1911 Census of Ireland (http://www.census.nationalarchives.ie/)
    Chief Secretary's Office, Crime branch: Dublin Metropolitan Police (DMP)
    Movement of Extremists 29 May 1915 – 20 April 1916

The Military Archives of Ireland
    The Military Service Pensions Collection
    The Cumann na mBan Series
    The Irish Citizen Army Series
    An tÓglach magazine

The Irish Labour History Society Archives

Newspapers
    An Claidheamh Soluis
    Anglo-Celt
    Bean na hÉireann
    Catholic Bulletin
    Freeman's Journal
    Irish Citizen
    Irish Independent
    Irish Press
    Irish Worker
    Irish Times
    The Kerryman
    New York Times
    Sinn Féin

SECONDARY SOURCES

Barton, Brian, *The Secret Court Martial Records of the 1916 Easter Rising* (Dublin: The History Press, 2013)

Bourke, Angela, et al (eds), *The Field Day Anthology of Irish Writing, Vol. V: Irish Women's Writing and Tradition* (Cork: Cork University Press, 2002)

Buckley, Margaret, *Jangle of Keys* (Dublin: 1938)

Caulfield, Max, *The Easter Rebellion* (Dublin: Gill and Macmillan, 1995)

Cambridge Dictionary of Irish Biography

Clare, Anne, *Unlikely Rebels: The Gifford Girls and the Fight for Irish Freedom* (Cork: Mercier Press, 2011)

Coleman, Marie, *Co. Longford and the Irish Revolution, 1910-1923* (Dublin: Irish Academic Press, 2006)

Colum, Mary, *Life and the Dream* (New York: Doubleday and Company, 1947)

Conlon, Lil, *Cumann na mBan and the Women of Ireland 1913–25* (Kilkenny: Kilkenny People Ltd., 1969)

Connell, Joseph E. A., *Who's Who in the Dublin Rising, 1916* (Dublin: Wordwell, 2015)
— *Dublin Rising, 1916* (Dublin: Wordwell, 2015)

Connolly, Linda, *The Irish Women's Movement: from Revolution to Devolution* (Dublin: Lilliput Press, 2003)

Coulter, Carol, *The Hidden Tradition: feminism, women and nationalism in Ireland* (Cork: Cork University Press, 1993)

Cowell, John, *A Noontide Blazing: Brigid Lyons Thornton:Rebel, Soldier, Doctor* (Dublin: Currach Press, 2005)

Crowley, Brian, *A History of Fairview Cumann na mBan* (1998)

Cullen, Mary and Luddy, Maria (eds), *Female Activists: Irish Women and Change 1900–1960* (Dublin: The Woodfield Press, 2001)

Cullen, Mary, *Telling It Our Way: Essays in Gender History* (Dublin: Arlen House, 2013)

Cullen Owens, Rosemary, *A Social History of Women in Ireland, 1870–1970* (Dublin: Gill and Macmillan, 2005)
— *Smashing Times: A History of the Women's Suffrage Movement, 1889-1922* (Dublin: Attic Press, 1984)

Daly, Mary and O'Callaghan, Margaret (eds), *1916 in 1966: Commemorating the Easter Rising* (Dublin: Royal Irish Academy, 2007)

Devine, Francis (ed.), *1913: A Capital in Conflict: Dublin City and the 1913 Lockout* (Dublin: Dublin City Public Libraries, 2013)

Dworkin, Dennis L. (ed.), *Ireland and Britain, 1798–1922; An Anthology of Sources* (London: Hackett Publishing Company, 2012)

Enright, Seán, *Easter Rising 1916: The Trials* (Dublin: Merrion Press, 2014)

Ferriter, Diarmaid, *A Nation and not a Rabble: The Irish Revolution, 1913–1923* (London: Profile Books, 2015)
— *The Transformation of Ireland, 1900–2000 (London: Profile Books, 2004)*

Foster, Roy, *Vivid Faces: The Revolutionary Generation in Ireland, 1890-1923* (London: Allen Lane, 2014)

Fox, R.M., *The History of the Irish Citizen Army* (Dublin: James Duffy and Co. Ltd., 1944)
— *Rebel Irishwomen* (Dublin: Progress House, 1967)

Foy, Michael and Barton, Brian, *The Easter Rising* (The History Press, 2011, reprint ed.)

Foy, Michael T., *Michael Collins and the Intelligence War* (Stroud: Sutton Publishing, 2006)

Gillis, Liz, *The Fall of Dublin* (Cork: Mercier Press, 2011)
— *Revolution in Dublin: A Photographic History 1913–23* (Cork: Mercier Press, 2013)
— *Women of the Irish Revolution 1913–1923: A Photographic History* (Cork: Mercier Press, 2014)

Good, Joe, *Inside the GPO 1916: A First-hand Account* (Dublin: O'Brien Press, 2015)

Goff, Henry, *Wexford has Risen: A Short Account of the 1916 Easter Week Rebellion in Wexford* (Wexford: 1916 Trust Ltd., 2007)

Griffith, Kenneth and O'Grady, Timothy E., *Curious Journey: An Oral History of Ireland's Unfinished Revolution* (Boulder: Robert Rinehart, 1999 reprint edition)

Harford, Judith and Rush, Claire (eds), *Have Women Made a Difference?: Women in Irish Universities, 1850 – 2010* (Oxford: Peter Lang, 2010)

Haverty, Anne, *Constance Markievicz: An Independent Life* (London: Pandora, 1988)

Hill, J. R. (ed.), *A new History of Ireland VII, Ireland 1921 – 1984* (Oxford: Oxford University Press, 2003)

Hopkinson, Michael, *Green Against Green: The Irish Civil War* (Dublin: Gill and Macmillan, 1998)
— *The Irish War of Independence* (Dublin: Gill and Macmillan, 2004)

Hughes, Brian, *16 Lives: Michael Mallin* (Dublin: O'Brien Press, 2012)

Jeffery, Keith, *The GPO and the Easter Rising* (Dublin: Irish Academic Press, 2006)

Jones, Mary, *Those Obstreperous Lassies: A History of the IWWU* (Dublin: Gill and Macmillan, 1988)

Kiberd, Declan, *1916 Rebellion Handbook* (Dublin: Mourne River Press, 1998)

Laffan, Michael, *The Resurrection of Ireland: The Sinn Féin Party,1916 – 1923* (Cambridge: Cambridge University Press, 1999)

Lane, Leeann, *Rosamond Jacob: Third Person Singular* (Dublin: UCD Press, 2010)

Lee, J.J., *Ireland 1912–85: Politics and Society* (Cambridge: Cambridge University Press, 1989)

Litton, Helen, *Kathleen Clarke: Revolutionary Woman* (Dublin: O'Brien Press, 2008)

Luddy, Maria, *Women in Ireland: A Documentary History 1800-1918* (Cork: Cork University Press, 1995)

McAuliffe, Mary (ed.), *Rosie: Essays in Honour of Roseanna 'Rosie' Hackett (1893 – 1976); Revolutionary and Trade Unionist* (Dublin: Arlen House, 2015)
— with Clara Fischer (ed.) *Irish Feminisms: Past, Present and Future* (Dublin: Arlen House, 2014)
— *Senator Kathleen A. Browne (1876 – 1943): Patriot, Politician and Practical Farmer* (Roscrea: Walsh Publications, 2008)

McCarthy, Cal, *Cumann na mBan and the Irish Revolution* (Cork: The Collins Press, revised ed. 2014)

McCoole, Sineád, *Guns and Chiffon* (Dublin: Stationary Office, 1997)
— *No Ordinary Women: Irish Female Activists in the Revolutionary Years, 1900–1923* (Dublin: O'Brien Press, 2003)

McDiarmid, Lucy, *At Home in the Revolution: What Women Said and Did in 1916* (Dublin: Royal Irish Academy, 2015)

Macardle, Dorothy, *The Irish Republic* (Dublin: Irish Press Ltd., 1951)

MacCurtain, Margaret, *Ariadne's Thread: Writing Women into Irish History* (Dublin: Arlen House, 2008)

MacEoin, Uinseann, *Survivors* (Dublin: Argenta Publications, 1987, 2nd ed.)

MacPherson, D.A.J., *Women and the Irish Nation: Gender, Culture and Irish Identity, 1890 – 1914* (London: Palgrave Macmillan, 2012)

McGarry, Ferghal, *The Easter Rising, Ireland: Easter 1916* (Oxford: Oxford University Press, 2010)
— *Rebels: Voices from the Easter Rising* (London: Penguin Books, 2011)
— *The Abbey Rebels of 1916: A Lost Revolution* (Dublin: Gill and Macmillan, 2015)

McIntosh, Gillian and Urquhart, Diane (eds), *Irish women at War: the twentieth century* (Dublin: Irish Academic Press, 2010)

Matthews, Ann, *Renegades: Women in Irish Republican Politics 1900 – 1922* (Cork: Mercier Press, 2010)
— *Dissidents: Irish Republican Women 1923 – 1941* (Cork: Mercier Press, 2012)
— *The Irish Citizen Army* (Cork: Mercier Press, 2014)

Marreco, Anne, *The Rebel Countess: The Life and Times of Constance Markievicz* (London: Phoenix Press, 1967)

Molyneux, Derek and Kelly, Darren, *When the Clock Struck in 1916: Close Quarter Combat in the Easter Rising* (Cork: Collins Press, 2015)

Mooney Eichacker, Joanne, *Irish Republican Women in America: Lecture Tour, 1916 – 1925* (Dublin, Irish Academic Press, 2003)

Mulcahy, Ristéard, *Richard Mulcahy (1886-1971): A Family Memoir* (Dublin: Aurelian Press, 1999)

North Inner City Folklore Project, *The Forgotten Women 1916 – 1923: Honouring All Women in the Struggle for Irish Freedom* (Dublin, 2008)

O'Brien, May, *Clouds on my Windows: a Dublin memoir* (Dingle: Brandon Press, 2004)

O'Brien, Paul, *Uncommon Valour: 1916 and the Battle for the South Dublin Union* (Cork: Mercier Press, 2010)
— *Crossfire: The Battle for the Four Courts 1916* (Dublin: New Island Press, 2012)

O'Farrell, Mick, *A Walk Through Rebel Dublin* (Cork: Mercier Press, 1999)

O'Farrell, Padraic, *Who's Who in the Irish War of Independence and Civil War 1916–1923* (Dublin: Lilliput Press, 1997)

Ó hÓgartaigh, Margaret, *Kathleen Lynn: Irishwoman, Patriot, Doctor* (Dublin: Irish Academic Press, 2006)

O'Meara, Liam, *From Richmond Barracks to Keogh Square* (Dublin: Reprint Books, 2015)

O'Rahilly, Aodogan, *Winding the Clock: O'Rahilly and the 1916 Rising* (Dublin: Lilliput Press 1991)

Pašeta, Senia, *Irish Nationalist Women: 1900–1918* (Cambridge: Cambridge University Press, 2013)

Pyle, Hilary (ed.), *Cesca's Diary 1913–1916: Where Art and Nationalism Meet* (Dublin: Woodfield Press, 2005)

Ryan, Annie, *Witnesses inside the Easter Rising* (Dublin: Liberties Press, 2005)

Ryan, Meda, *Michael Collins and the Women in his Life* (Cork: Mercier Press, 1996)

Skinnider, Margaret, *Doing My Bit For Ireland* (New York: Century, 1917)

Steele, Karen, *Women, The Press and Politics during the Irish Revival* (New York: Syracuse University Press, 2007)

Taillon, Ruth, *When History was Made: The Women of 1916* (Belfast: Beyond the Pale Publications, 1996)

The Irish Citizen Army (Dublin: Stoneybatter and Smithfield People's History Project, 2015)

Valiulis, Maryann Gialanella, (ed.) *Gender and Power in Irish History* (Dublin: Irish Academic Press, 2009)

Walsh, Maurice, *Bitter Freedom: Ireland in a Revolutionary World 1918–1923* (London: Faber and Faber, 2015)

Ward, Margaret, *Unmanageable Revolutionaries: Women and Irish Nationalism* (London: Pluto Press, 1983)
— *In Their Own Voice* (Cork: Attic Press, 2001)
— *Hanna Sheehy Skeffington: a life* (Dublin: Attic Press, 1997)

Wills, Claire, *Dublin 1916: The Siege of the GPO* (London: Profile Books, 2009)

Woggan, Helga, *Silent Radical: Winifred Carney 1887–1943: a Reconstruction of her Biography* (Dublin: SIPTU, 2000)

Wren, Jimmy, *The GPO Garrison Easter Week 1916: A Biographical Dictionary* (Dublin: Geography Publications, 2015)

Picture Acknowledgements (Biographies)

The majority of the biography photos are taken from the photograph of the Irish National Aid Association and Volunteer Dependents' Fund fundraising event in the home of Mr. and Mrs. Ely O'Carroll in Peter's Place, Dublin in the summer of 1916. (*Courtesy of Kilmainham Gaol Museum, 18PO-1B53-02*)

Kathleen Browne courtesy of Bernard Browne and the Browne family

Brigid Davis courtesy of Maureen Dawson

Winifred Carney courtesy of Kilmainham Gaol Museum

Elizabeth Cooney courtesy of Orla McKeown and family

Nell Humphreys courtesy of UCD Archives

Katie Kelly courtesy of Ian Kelly

Brigid Lyons courtesy of the McGuinness Collection

Florence Meade courtesy of Mick Walsh

Annie and Emily Norgrove courtesy of Peter Grange and family

Acknowledgements

In the course of writing this book we have been overwhelmed with the support of so many people.

Firstly we would like to thank the members of the Richmond Barracks Advisory Committee, Dublin City Council, Tara Doyle and Dublin City Public Libraries, Four Courts Press, Commandant Padraic Kennedy and the staff at the Military Archives, the Capuchin Archives, Kilmainham Gaol Archives, National Library of Ireland, The Allen Library and The National Archives of Ireland.

Special thanks to the members of the 'Seventy-Seven Women of Richmond Barracks Committee' including Rita Fagan, Jo Kennedy, Melanie Hoewer and Roseanna Farrell who have encouraged us throughout.

Thanks also to Marja Almqvist, her artistic team and the seventy-seven participants engaged in the 77 Women Commemoration Quilt project as well as all the relatives and descendants of the seventy-seven women who have shared their stories with us, both writing this book and on the quilt project. We would like to especially thank Éadaoin Ní Chléirigh who has gone above and beyond to make this book a reality. Our thanks to Eibhlín Ní Chléirigh, who volunteered her time and talent to creating our outstanding book cover.

We would also like to thank our families, friends and colleagues who have supported us in our determination to write this book and who understand our passion in our quest to tell these stories and more.

Lastly we would like to thank the seventy-seven women interned in Richmond Barracks in the aftermath of the Easter Rising. Although you have been overlooked for the last century, you told your stories, you wrote them down and one hundred years later we were able to discover them and hear your voices. Just like in the Easter Rising you are not in the shadows. You were there in 1916 and you are here in 2016. Thank you for your bravery, your commitment and your dedication. You have shown us that no matter where you come from or what your background, you can always make a difference.

Index of the 77 Women

n.12, 62 n.14, 62 n.16. 62 n.17, 62 n.21, 62
n.25, 62 n.27, 75, 88, 91 n.86, 94, 95, 97,
98, 99, 100, 103, 105 n.14, 107, 108, 111,
112, 113, 114–6, 121, 128, 160, 163, 167,
203, 204, 205, 210, 211, 217, 235, 237, 245
n.8, 245 n.10–14, 246 n.63, 248 n.133, 257,
260, 268

Lyons, Brigid, 4, 13 n.13, 48, 29, 50, 52, 62 n.35,
62 n.38, 62 n.41, 62 n.45, 142–3, 149, 257,
258, 265

M

MacNamee/McNamee, Agnes, 73, 167, 198–9,
247 n.113

Maher, Kathleen 'Katie', 73, 202

Markievicz, Constance, 4, 11. 13 n.23, 16, 19,
20, 21, 24, 25, 27, 30, 31, 33, 34, 35 n.16, 36
n.43, 38, 39, 41, 60, 75, 76, 79, 80, 81, 82,
83, 86, 89 n.33, 89 n.36, 90 n.49, 90 n.53,
91 n.79, 94, 98, 99, 100, 102, 103. 104, 105
n.1, 105 n.31, 107, 108, 110, 113, 114, 115,
117, 119, 120, 127, 130, 136, 152, 155, 157,
160, 182, 187, 204, 207, 209, 211, 213, 214,
215–8, 221, 224, 233, 234, 235, 242, 248
n.160, 249 n.162, 251, 252, 255, 256, 257,
258, 259, 260, 266, 267, 247 n.81, 247 n.84,

Martin, Bríd S., 10, 48, 52, 144

Martin, Brigid 'Bríd'/'Bridget' *see* Foley,
Brigid 'Bríd/'Bridget'

Martin, Kathleen 'Kate', 10, 48, 144

McBride, Winifred 'Winnie' *see* Carney,
Winifred 'Winnie'

McCauley, Julia 244

McGowan, Josephine 'Josie', 8, 33, 70, 73, 102,
181–2,

McLoughlin, Caroline 'Carrie', *see* Mitchell,
Caroline 'Carrie'

McLoughlin, Margaret 'Maggie', 53, 150

McNamara, Josephine 'Josie' *see*
O'Keeffe/O'Keefe, Josephine 'Josie'

McNamara, Rose, 2, 3, 10, 13 n.4, 15, 28, 29, 32,
33, 34, 35 n.2, 66, 68, 71, 72, 73, 74, 89 n.4,
89 n.11, 89 n.18, 89 n.24, 89 n.28, 95, 100,
101, 164, 167, 177, 180, 182–4, 198, 202,
246 n.69, 247 n.84–5, 247 n.101?, 248
n.125, 248 n.128, 255, 260

Meade, Florence 'Flossie', 7, 17, 52, 145–6, 147,
148, 149, 270

Miller, Mrs Cathleen *see* Murphy, Kathleen

Mitchell, Caroline 'Carrie', 4, 32, 52, 146,
246 n.38

Molony, Helena, 4, 8, 11, 13 n.1, 13 n.23, 16, 18,
19, 20, 21, 24, 27, 28, 30, 31, 35 n.15, 36
n.49, 40, 41, 42, 43, 44, 45, 46, 61, 62 n.1, 62
n.8, 62 n.19, 62 n.22, 62 n.26, 86, 96, 97, 99,
101, 102, 103, 107, 111, 113, 114, 115,
117–20, 121, 123, 125, 182, 210, 211, 212,
216, 232, 235, 237, 242, 245 n.18, 245
n.20–24, 245 n.26–7, 254, 257, 259, 260,
262 n.22–6, 264

Morkan, Pauline, 3, 4, 13 n.8, 13 n.16, 47, 48,
53, 147, 148, 149

Mulhall, Elizabeth 'Lizzie', 19, 88, 98, 232

Mullally, Roseanna 'Rose' *see* Hackett, 25, 28,
73, 184–5, 196, 247 n.86

Murphy, Bridget 'Brigid' *see* Brady, Bridget
'Brigid'

Murphy, Martha *see* Kelly, Martha

Murphy, Kathleen, 33, 69, 69–70, 73, 95,
185–6, 247 n.87,

Murtagh, Bridget 'Brigid', 11, 34, 39, 76, 78, 82,
103, 211, 219, 220, 221, 223,

S

Seery, Kathleen 'Catherine', 34, 82,

Shanahan, Jane 'Jinny', 8, 12, 22, 27, 28, 31, 36
n.51, 40, 41, 42, 44, 45, 95, 96, 100, 101, 111,
113, 123 – 5, 212, 246 n.33, 257, 260

(Spicer) Spencer, Josephine, 10, 28, 73, 202

T

Thornton, Lyons, Brigid *see* Lyons, Brigid

Timmons, Margaret 'Cissie' *see* O'Flaherty,
Margaret 'Cissie'

Treston, Catherine 'Kathleen' *see* Ryan,
Catherine 'Kathleen'

W

Wisely, May *see* O'Moore, May